Close-up

STUDENT'S BOOK A1+

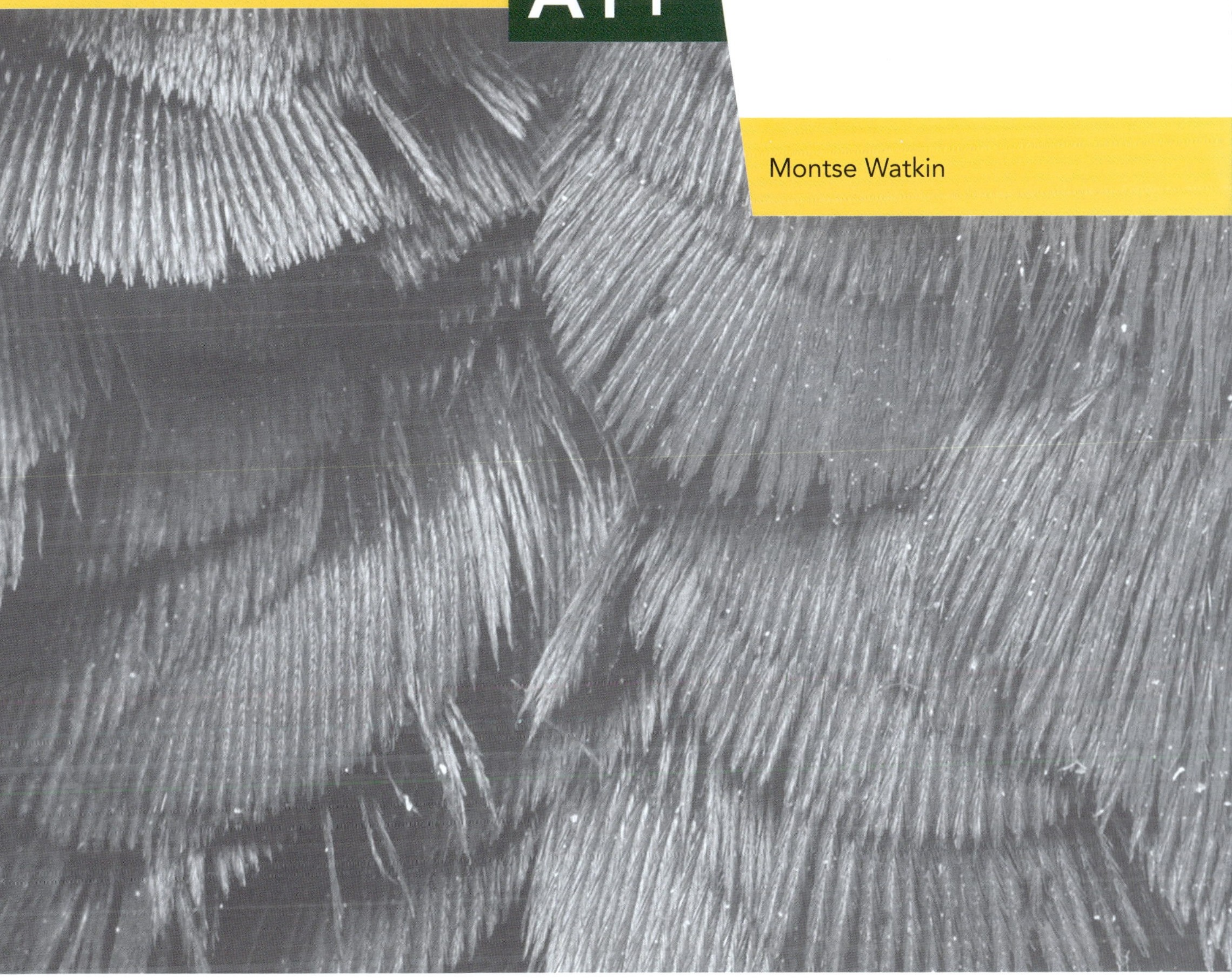

Montse Watkin

NATIONAL GEOGRAPHIC LEARNING

Australia • Brazil • Canada • Mexico • Singapore • United Kingdom • United States

Contents

Listening	Speaking	Writing	Video
matching, choosing the correct option	asking & answering questions, talking about yourself, giving personal information	a personal description, writing about yourself, giving information about yourself, writing tips for the exam	Super Dogs
multiple-choice, listening to instructions	asking & answering about hobbies, asking to hear something again, understanding the questions	responding to an advert, identifying who to write to for more information, showing interest, writing beginnings & endings in emails	Yoro, the Fulani Boy
gap-fill, reading & listening to instructions	asking & answering about travel, practising saying numbers	an email, recognising verb patterns, writing a postcard, using clues	Town Rescue
gap-fill, listening for specific & detailed information	asking & answering about a celebration, describing a celebration, giving dates, practising pronunciation	a recipe, using sequencers, reading carefully	The Magic of Diwali
multiple-choice (pictures), noticing differences	asking & answering about the perfect day, talking about activities with *to go*, showing interest, extending your answers	a diary, adding details, expressing positive feelings, giving reasons, planning a draft	Laughter Yoga!
matching, listening for false information	asking & answering about pets, talking about pets, giving reasons	a fact file, writing facts, expressing animal facts, asking about animals, checking your spelling	Tip of my Tongue!
gap-fill, spelling correctly	asking & answering about a science fair, giving directions, listening for the question word	captions, adding information in captions, expressing purpose, completing forms with more detailed information	An Exciting Invention
multiple-choice, listening for the answer	asking & answering about a game, asking questions about games, forming questions	instructions, sequencing, making suggestions & responding, making suggestions	Testing!
multiple-choice, focusing on specific information	asking & answering about an extreme sports class, asking for & giving details	a blog, thinking about your readers, using adjectives, looking back & checking	Extremely Spectacular
multiple-choice (pictures), listening for specific information	describing photos, asking how someone is feeling, talking about your health, responding to advice, giving advice	a note, apologising & making excuses, expanding your answers	Tasty Snacks!
gap-fill, listening for times & dates	asking & answering about preferences, expressing preferences	a short narrative, using a writing formula, connecting events in a story, writing a draft	Creative Recycling
multiple-choice, reviewing your answers	prompt-card activity, asking about holidays	an invitation, writing & responding to an invitation, understanding language functions	Best Summer Job

1 This Is Me!

Reading:	right or wrong, reading for main ideas
Vocabulary:	numbers, family, personal information, favourite things
Grammar:	*be*, *have got*, questions with *be* & *have got*, *this*, *that*, *these*, *those*, possession
Listening:	matching, choosing the correct option
Speaking:	asking & answering questions, talking about yourself, giving personal information
Writing:	a personal description, writing about yourself, giving information about yourself, writing tips for the exam

A young girl, dressed in traditional clothing, blows a pink bubble. Garoka, Papua New Guinea

Reading

A What are your favourite things and activities? Tell your partner.

My favourite thing is my ... because ...
My favourite activity is swimming.

B Look at the noticeboards. What do you find out about about Rosa and Marco?

C Write the correct topic headings next to the lists below. Which things in the lists tell you about Rosa? Which tell you about Marco?

Age Animals Countries Food Sport

1 ____________ : swimming basketball mountain biking karate
2 ____________ : watermelon pizza ice cream cheese
3 ____________ : rabbit horse goldfish tortoise
4 ____________ : Argentina Mexico Germany Italy
5 ____________ : twelve thirteen fourteen fifteen

D Circle the correct information about Marco. Look at his noticeboard to help you.

1 My name's Marco and I'm 13 / 14 years old. I live in Italy / Mexico.
2 I love doing sport. I like riding / doing karate but my favourite sport is riding my horse / my mountain bike. It's so much fun!
3 I like reptiles / cats so that's why I have a tortoise / kitten. I wanted a snake but my mum doesn't like snakes!
4 My favourite food is ice-cream / pizza, of course! The best pizza is the one my dad makes!

E Read the two texts quickly. What topics from C do they talk about?

This is me!

1 **Yessica**

My name's Yessica and I'm 12 years old.

I live on a small farm in Peru with my brother and two younger sisters.

We have a lot of animals and I enjoy helping my dad on the farm. My favourite animals are the chickens. They're very funny to watch and I also love collecting their eggs every morning with my two sisters.

My favourite thing is my handloom. I really like making clothes.

2 **Akash**

I'm Akash and I'm 13 years old. I'm a teenager!

I live in India with my parents and grandmother. I'm an only child but I have lots of really good friends.

My favourite thing is my kite. I love flying my kite! It's a very popular activity and great fun.

Cows are very special in my country and they're my favourite animals. Insects are interesting, but I hate hearing mosquitoes!

Word Focus

farm: a house with land for growing plants and keeping animals

handloom: a simple machine used to make material for clothes

only child: a child with no brothers or sisters

popular: liked by many people

special: better or more important

F Read the *Exam Close-up*. Underline key words in each text in E.

G Now complete the *Exam Task*. Use your underlined words to help you answer the questions.

Exam Close-up

Reading for main ideas

- Read the heading first to find out about the topic. Then read the text quickly to find out more.
- Read the text again and underline the main pieces of information.

Exam Task

Read the two texts. Are sentences **1 – 8** '**Right**' (**A**) or '**Wrong**' (**B**)?

1 Yessica is older than her sisters. ☐
2 Yessica and Akash are from the same country. ☐
3 Yessica and Akash are both teenagers. ☐
4 Akash has two brothers. ☐
5 Yessica and Akash both like farm animals. ☐
6 Akash's favourite animal is big. ☐
7 Yessica makes clothes. ☐
8 Akash loves flying. ☐

H Underline the following words in the two texts: *like, love, enjoy, hate*. What do you notice about the words that come after them?

I Complete the sentences with the correct form of the verbs in brackets.

1 I really like ____________ (swim) in competitions.
2 I love ____________ (ride) my mountain bike at the weekend.
3 I don't like ____________ (eat) broccoli or spinach.
4 I enjoy ____________ (write) in my diary.
5 I hate ____________ (hear) my alarm clock on Monday morning.

Ideas Focus

- What things or activities do you like that your friends don't?
- 'My family is more important than friends.' Do you agree? Why? / Why not?

Vocabulary

A **Write the numbers as words.**

1 18 ___eighteen___ cousins
2 80 ________ years old
3 12 ________ o'clock
4 50 ________ pounds
5 36 ________ Belleview Street
6 96 ________ Ash Road
7 365 ________ days
8 420 ________ schoolchildren
9 500 ________ kilometres
10 1,000 ________ metres

B **Look at Joe's family tree. Complete each sentence using the words from below.**

dad   brother   grandma   ~~mum~~   aunt   granddad   sister   uncle

1 Zoe is Joe's ___mum___ .
2 Dylan is Joe's ________.
3 Helen is Joe's ________.
4 Andrea is Joe's ________.
5 Robert is Joe's ________.
6 Kevin is Joe's ________.
7 Julia is Joe's ________.
8 Tom is Joe's ________.

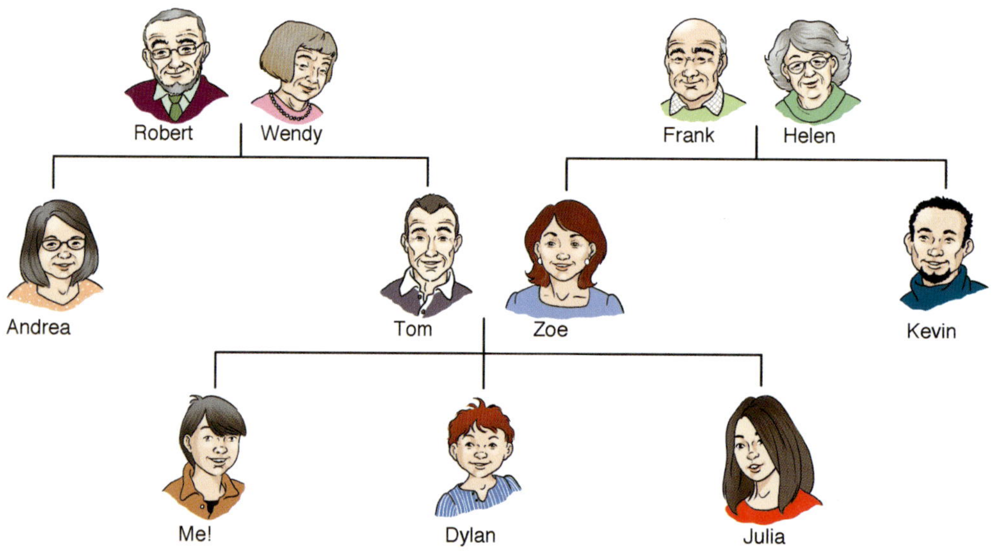

C **Look at Veronica's family photo below. Veronica is in the middle in the pink and white T-shirt. Who do you think the other people are? How old are they?**

"I think this is Veronica's sister. I think she's about 18 years old."

D Complete the text with the correct words.

first   Mrs   surname   Rio de Janeiro   parents   married   husband   teenager

Me and my family

Hi, this is a photo of a younger me! My (**1**) ______________ name is Rafael and my (**2**) ______________ is Ribeiro. I'm Brazilian and live in (**3**) ______________. I'm 13 years old so now I'm a (**4**) ______________. I have two older sisters. Isabelle is 24 and lives at home with me and my (**5**) ______________ but she has a boyfriend. Gabriela is 27. She is (**6**) ______________. Her (**7**) ______________, Jason Williams, is American, so now she is (**8**) ______________ Williams!

Young Brazilian boy flying a kite in Rio de Janeiro, Brazil

E Write the words under the correct picture.

diary   football boots   kitten   necklace   photograph   poster   smartphone   watch

1 

____

2 

____

3 

____

4 

____

5 

____

6 

____

7 

____

8 

____

F Complete each sentence with a word from E.

1 I really like my new ______________. Now I can play football again!
2 This ______________ is my favourite present. It's made of gold.
3 I don't like my brother's ______________ on our bedroom wall!
4 I love my ______________. She's so soft and cute.
5 I hate that baby ______________ of me. I have no hair!
6 I don't like my ______________. It's too big and often falls off.
7 My ______________ is the best thing ever! I chat with my friends and play games.
8 I enjoy writing in my ______________ every day.

G What things from E do you have? Which do you like best and why? Tell a partner.

Ideas Focus

- How many people are in your family?
- Would you like a bigger or smaller family? Why?

Grammar

Be

A **Read the sentences and underline the parts of the verb *be*. The first ones are done for you.**

1 Hi. I'm Anabel and he's my brother, Jack.
2 Are you from Italy?
3 My favourite colours are green and orange.
4 We're not sisters. We're best friends.
5 Isabelle and Gabriela are Brazilian.
6 'Is she an only child?' 'No, she isn't.'

B **Complete the table with the correct parts of *be*. Use your answers in A to help you.**

	+	–	?
I	I am / I'm	I am not / I'm not	Am I ...?
you	______ / you're	______ / ______ / ______	______ ...?
he / she / it	______ / ______	______ / ______ / ______	Is he / she / it... ?
we	are / ______	______ / ______ / ______	______ ...?
they	______ / ______	______ / ______ / 're not	______ ...?

Have got

C **We can use *have got* to talk about possessions and relationships. Read the questions carefully. Then complete the answers with the correct form of *have got*.**

1 A Have you got any brothers and sisters?
B Yes, I have. I ____________ one brother.
2 A Have your grandparents got a pet?
B Yes, they have. They ____________ a rabbit.
3 A Has Akash got a new kite?
B No, he hasn't. He ____________ a new bike.

D **Complete the rules with *have, has, haven't, hasn't* or *got*.**

1 With *he/she/it* we use ____________ in affirmative sentences.
2 In negative sentences we use *have not got / has not got* or ____________ *got* / ____________ *got*.
3 In questions, we put ____________ or ____________ before the subject (*I, you, he*, etc.).
4 We don't use ____________ in short answers.

Questions with *Be* & *Have got*

E **Underline the subject in each question. The first one is done for you. Then tick the correct rules.**

1 What is your teacher's name?
2 Where are you from?
3 What are your favourite colours?
4 How many brothers and sisters have you got?
5 What pets has your partner got?

Question forms =

a question word + *is/are* + subject ☐
b question word + *have/has* + got + subject ☐
c question word + *have/has* + subject + *got* ☐

Grammar Focus p. 161 (1.1 to 1.2)

F **Choose the correct answers.**

1 ______ got any watermelons, please?
a Are you b Have you
2 Why ______ mountain biking your favourite sport?
a is b has got
3 My mum ______ six brothers and sisters.
a is b has got
4 ______ new football boots?
a Are you b Have you got
5 How old ______ your granddad?
a is b has got
6 I ______ a smartphone.
a 'm not b haven't got
7 Our tortoise ______ 100 years old!
a is b has got

G **Circle the correct words.**

1 We 're / 's French, but we not / aren't from Paris.
2 My dog's name Buster / is Buster.
3 'Are / is you in this class?' 'Yes, I'm. / I am.'
4 Sasha's noticeboard aren't / isn't very big, but it are / is interesting.
5 'Is / Are Marco and Yessica best friends?' 'No, they 's not / 're not.'
6 Vanilla and chocolate am / are my favourite flavours of ice cream.

H **Read the answers. Write the questions.**

1 Where ____________? He's from Argentina.
2 Who ____________? They're my best friends from Greece.
3 How many ____________? I've got four uncles.
4 What ____________? My favourite fruit is pineapple.
5 What ____________? She's got a diary in her bag.

Grammar

This, That, These, Those

I **Look at the photos. Complete the table with *this*, *that*, *these* and *those*. Then choose the correct words to complete the rule.**

	Here	There
Singular		
Plural		

You can use *this/that/these/those* in front of / after a noun, e.g. *these football boots*, or on its own before / after a verb e.g. *This is a great pizza; This is Henry.*

1

This is a great pizza.

2

These photographs are special.

3

That's the Eiffel Tower!

4

Those hills are really far away.

Possession

J **These words are used to show possession. Read the two examples then complete the sentences.**

~~my~~ ~~your~~ its her their his our

Examples: I'm Max, and this is **my** brother.
Here's a photograph of **you** and **your** parents.

1 **He** and ________ family are from Italy.
2 **It**'s a cat, and ________ babies are called kittens.
3 **She** hasn't got ________ basketball boots on.
4 **We** have got ________ English exam now.
5 **They** love ________ new baby sister.

K **Circle *'s* or *s'*. Then complete the rules.**

1 Jamie s' / 's brother is my best friend.
2 Those are my dad 's / s' football boots.
3 My grandparent s' / 's dog is called Woody.
4 The children 's / s' kite is in up in the tree.

- We can add *'s* to a name to show possession or a relationship. For example: "Jamie's brother is my best friend."
- When the noun/person is singular we add ______. For example: dad's
- When the noun/person is plural we add ______. For example: grandparents'
- When the plural noun/person is irregular (e.g. *children* NOT *childs*, *women* NOT *womans*) we add ______. For example: children's

Grammar Focus pp. 161 & 162 (1.3 to 1.5)

L **Read the sentences. Is the person/thing in each sentence here/near (H) or there/far (T)?**

1 Excuse me, is that your dog? ______
2 I like these football boots. Have you got them in red? ______
3 I think that's my grandma at the door. ______
4 Mum, this is my karate teacher, Miss Márquez. ______
5 I hate that poster! ______
6 These goldfish are really beautiful. ______

M **Rewrite the sentences using *'s*.**

1 That kitten belongs to Penny. "That's Penny's kitten."
2 This necklace belongs to my Aunt Georgina. This is ________________.
3 That poster belongs to my sister. That is ________________.
4 Jeni is my cousin. I am ________________.
5 Helen is the wife of Matt. Helen is ________________.
6 Those books belong to my teacher. Those are ________________.
7 Is Fraser your brother? Are you ________________?

N **Circle the correct words.**

Look at my (**1**) grandfather's / grandfathers' photographs. The girls (**2**) is /are my sisters. My (**3**) sister's / sisters' names are Polly and Daisy. In one photo, my sisters (**4**) are / has got on the sofa. (**5**) Her / Their kitten, Mono, is between them. My grandfather (**6**) have / has got a cat too, but (**7**) my / his cat is old. (**8**) It's / Its name is Sunny and look, it (**9**) doesn't got /hasn't got a tail!

1 This Is Me!

Listening

A **Work with a partner. Look at the photos. What are the people all doing?**

B 1.1 **Listen to Paul and Alisha. Choose the correct answer.**

1 Alisha's sister's name is ______
   a Karen   b Ciara
2 Alisha's cousin lives in ______
   a Mexico   b Malaysia
3 Rachel is ______
   a Alisha's sister   b John's sister
4 Joanne and Richard are ______
   a John's friends   b John's parents
5 Alisha's grandparents' wedding was ______
   a 52 years ago   b 53 years ago

C **Read the *Exam Close-up*. Then read the questions in D carefully.**

Exam Close-up

Choosing the correct option

- In this task, you listen to a long conversation and match five pieces of information.
- The answer options are all very similar, but only one is correct for each question number.
- Listen for words and phrases like *no, but, actually* and *in fact*. They mean one speaker is going to correct what the other speaker said. This will help you choose the correct answer.

D 1.2 **Listen and tick the correct answer. Notice the use of *but, actually* and *in fact*.**

1 a It's his sister's wedding day. ☐
   b It's his cousin's wedding day. ☐
2 a His sister's favourite colour is yellow. ☐
   b His sister's favourite colour is red. ☐
3 a The wedding was small. ☐
   b The wedding was big. ☐

E 1.3 **Now listen and complete the *Exam Task*.**

F 1.4 **Listen again and check your answers.**

Exam Task

Listen to a woman talking about her wedding. Who is each item from?
For questions **1 – 5**, write a letter **A – G** next to each item.

You will hear the conversation twice.

1	Uncle Fred	☐	A	Painting
2	Mum	☐	B	Watch
3	Dad	☐	C	Photo album
4	Grandparents	☐	D	Tree
5	Husband	☐	E	Flowers
			F	Camera
			G	Towels

Speaking

A **Look at the photos. What are they saying to each other? Match each statement to a photo.**

1 They don't know each other. ______

2 They know each other. ______

B **Write these conversations in the correct order.**

Conversation A	Conversation A
~~Hi Angie!~~	A: Hi. Angie.
Great!	B: ______
How are you?	A: ______
I'm good thanks. What about you?	B: ______
Hi Charlie!	A: ______

Conversation B	Conversation B
Nice to meet you. I'm Carl.	A: ______
Pleased to meet you.	B: ______
Hi. I'm Tom Oakes and this is my sister, Anne.	A: ______

C 1.5 **Listen to the conversations in B. Check your answers. Then have similar conversations with your classmates.**

D **Read the personal information below. Write the questions. The first one is done for you.**

1 *How old are you?* ______ ?
I'm 13.

2 ______ ?
My birthday's in April.

3 ______ ?
I'm from Chile.

4 ______ ?
I live in Quebec.

5 ______ ?
I've got one brother.

E **Read the *Exam Close-up*. Ask and answer the questions you wrote in D with a partner.**

F **Now work in pairs and complete the *Exam Task*. Use the *Useful Expressions* to help you.**

Exam Close-up

Giving personal information

- Talk to your classmates as much as possible in English.
- Practise giving and asking for personal information.
- Listen to your partner's answers and show interest.
- Give as much information as possible.

Exam Task

Student A: Using the prompts, ask the questions in Quiz 1.
Student B: Answer the questions.

Quiz 1

Brothers or sisters? How many? ______
What / brother's/sister's name? ______
What / favourite colour? ______
What / favourite food? ______
What / your hobbies? ______

Student B: Using the prompts, ask the questions in Quiz 2.
Student A: Answer the questions.

Quiz 2

Any pets? What pets? ______
What / pet's name? ______
What / favourite animals? ______
What / favourite sport? ______
What / your hobbies? ______

Useful Expressions

Talking about yourself

I've got one brother/two sisters/a cat.
I haven't got any brothers/sisters/pets.
My brother's/sister's/pet's name is …
My favourite colour/food/animal/sport is …
In my free time I usually …
My hobby is swimming.
My hobbies are swimming and football.

Ideas Focus

- 'It's easy to make new friends.' Do you agree?
- Is it a good idea to have a pet? Why? / Why not?

1 This Is Me!

Writing: a personal description

Learning Focus

Writing about yourself

Using different verbs can make your descriptions more interesting to read.

- Always check that your verb ending agrees with your subject.
- Use *and/also/too* to add information.
- Use *but/however* to show contrast.

A **Look at the photos on the page. Work with a partner. What would you like to know about these teenagers? Write three questions for each photo.**

B **Read their personal descriptions. Do they answer your questions?**

Hi. My name's Britta and I'm from Sweden. I live in the capital city, Stockholm, with my mother and my twin sister, Erika. We're 13 years old, but Erika is 12 minutes older than me. She's also my best friend. My father lives in Norway. He's got a small hotel there.

My favourite colour is yellow, like the sun, and I like playing the guitar. However, my favourite thing isn't my guitar; it's my snowboard. I love snowboarding with my sister and our friends. It's the best sport in the world!

I'm Rasmus and I'm from Stockholm, in Sweden. I'm an only child but I've got two dogs: Thor and Frida. Thor is black but Frida is brown and white. I've got a lot of friends at school but my dogs are actually my best friends.

I love rap music and hip hop, but I like classical music, too. Strange! ☺ My favourite sport is swimming and my favourite thing is swimming in the lake with my friends. It's great!

C **Read these questions. Which questions do Britta and Rasmus answer? Tick ✓ the boxes.**

	Britta	Rasmus
1 What's your name and where are you from?	☐	☐
2 How old are you?	☐	☐
3 Can you tell me about your family?	☐	☐
4 Who is your best friend?	☐	☐
5 What kind of music do you like?	☐	☐
6 What are your favourite things?	☐	☐

D **Underline all the verbs in the descriptions in B. How many of the verbs can you find in each description? Write a number.**

	be	have got	like	love
Britta				
Rasmus				

E **Underline the subjects in each sentence. The first one is done for you.**

1. We're 13 years old, but Erika is 12 minutes older than me.
2. My father lives in Norway.
3. Thor is black but Frida is brown and white.
4. I love rap music and hip hop, but I like classical music, too.
5. It's great!

F **Find and circle *and*, *also*, *too*, *but* and *however* in Britta and Rasmus's descriptions.**

G **Complete these sentences with *and* or *but*.**

1. Erika loves pizza ____________ I don't like it.
2. My favourite music is guitar music ____________ I also love playing the guitar.
3. Our mother lives with us in Sweden ____________ our father lives in Norway.
4. We've got two dogs ____________ we haven't got any cats or other pets.
5. I live in Stockholm ____________ I love my city!

The town of Gamla Stan in Stockholm, Sweden

H **Write a personal description of yourself. Think about the following things. Write between 60 and 70 words.**

- age
- name
- where from?
- family
- animals
- music
- best friend

Useful Expressions

Giving information about yourself
My name is …
I live in … with
I love …
My favourite thing is …

Being positive
It's the best … in the world!
It's great!
They're fantastic!
I love my …

I **Check that you have done the following in your personal description:**

- answered at least three questions from C Yes? ☐
- used different verbs Yes? ☐
- used a subject with all your verbs Yes? ☐
- included sentences with *and* Yes? ☐
- included sentences with *but* Yes? ☐
- checked your spelling Yes? ☐

J **Read the *Exam Close-up*. Then read the *Exam Task* and underline the three questions and circle who you are writing to.**

Exam Close-up

Writing tips for the exam

- You must write 25–35 words and answer three questions.
- Underline the three questions in the task.
- Remember you are writing to someone. Circle who you are writing to.

K **Now complete the *Exam Task*.**

Exam Task

Read the email from your new class tutor.

Email Message

From: Ms Adams
To: Class 7A

Dear All,

I am your new tutor, Ms Adams. I want to learn all about you! Who do you live with? What are your favourite things? What are your hobbies? I want to make a big poster for the classroom, so please send me your descriptions and a photo!

Best wishes,
Ms Adams

Write an email to Ms Adams and answer the questions.
Write **25 – 35** words.

Video 1 Super Dogs

Before you watch

A **Dogs are great pets but they also help humans in many ways. Match photos A–F with 1–6.**

A

B
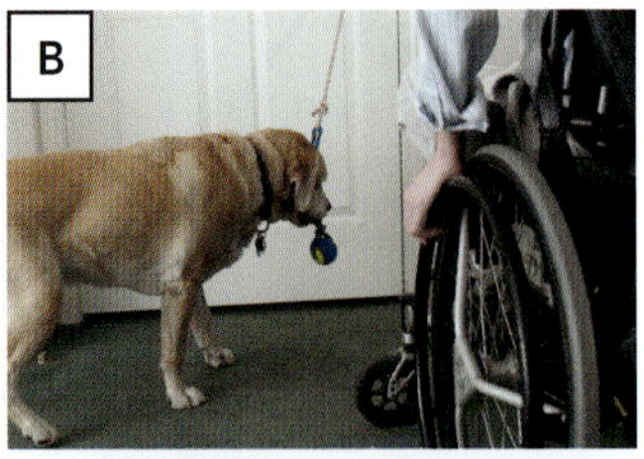

C

D

E

F

1 a pet ☐
2 a police dog ☐
3 a carer dog ☐
4 a guide dog ☐
5 a guard dog ☐
6 a mountain rescue dog ☐

While you watch

B **Watch the video. Circle the type of dog in A you see in the video. Decide if these statements are T (True) or F (False).**

The special school for dogs teaches dogs to …

1 open doors. ☐
2 read signs. ☐
3 switch on lights. ☐
4 press an emergency button. ☐
5 carry their owner on their back. ☐
6 pick up objects. ☐

After you watch

C **Complete the summary of the video below using these words.**

airport body camp home sixteen super supermarket trainer

Jennifer Arnold is a **(1)** ___________ at a special dog **(2)** ___________. She is training dogs to be **(3)** ___________ dogs so they can look after people with disabilities. Dogs learn best before they are **(4)** ___________ weeks old. They do training for their brain and their **(5)** ___________. First, they learn about their home and then, when they are eight weeks old, they learn about life outside the **(6)** ___________. This includes visits to the **(7)** ___________, rides on buses and a trip by train to the **(8)** ___________. With training, these amazing dogs become super dogs and can save lives.

Ideas Focus

- Do you think dogs are the best pets? Why? / Why not?
- 'Robots will one day replace dogs as carers.' Do you agree?

2 Friends & Fun

Reading:	matching, predicting language
Vocabulary:	clothes, activities, personality adjectives, verbs & verb phrases
Grammar:	present simple for routines & habits, negatives, *yes/no* questions & short answers, question words, adverbs of frequency, time expressions
Listening:	multiple-choice, listening to instructions
Speaking:	asking & answering about hobbies, asking to hear something again, understanding the questions
Writing:	responding to an advert, identifying who to write to for more information, showing interest, writing beginnings & endings in emails

A group of people taking part in a native blanket toss. Kotzebue, Alaska

2 Friends & Fun

Reading

A **Work with a partner. Match each sentence with a picture.**

A

B

C

D

E

F

1 I go **swimming** every Wednesday. ☐
2 We do **drama** at Theatre Club on Tuesdays and Fridays. ☐
3 My mum goes **running** every evening. ☐
4 My brother plays **chess** at the school chess club every Monday. ☐
5 I play **basketball** at the weekend. I like doing sport. ☐
6 He does **bhangra** on Thursdays and **street dance** on Saturdays. ☐

B **Read the sentences again. Which day of the week is missing?**

C **Look at the photos of Aysha and Sanjay. What do you think their hobbies are?**

D **Now read the texts and check your ideas.**

Word Focus

homework: work given by teachers for students to do at home

hungry: feeling that you want to eat something

laugh: what you do when something is very funny

play: a drama you can see at the theatre, with actors

show: something you see at the theatre, often with singing and dancing

stage: the place in a theatre where the actors, dancers or singers do their shows

What we do for FUN

Aysha

My name's Aysha. I go to a drama club twice a week and I love it. We do plays and musical theatre. It's great because our families and friends come to our shows two or three times a year. We need to be patient because we always learn a lot of words and we have to repeat them again and again. Drama and singing is ok if you are usually a shy person because it's different when you're on stage. Mr Redgrave is our drama teacher and he's very creative. He always has fantastic ideas. I see my friends at drama club and we laugh a lot. I love it – it's never boring.

Sanjay

My name's Sanjay. My friend Namit and I go to bhangra classes. Bhangra is a dance style; it's fun and the classes are very sociable. You need to be friendly – we always smile when we dance – and energetic or sporty. Namit and I usually go once a week on Thursdays, but we sometimes have extra classes or shows at weekends. Thursday is my favourite day because Namit always comes to my house for pizza after bhangra class – we're always very hungry – and we sometimes play video games for an hour after our homework.

E **Read the texts again and circle the correct name.**

1 Aysha / Sanjay goes to classes with a friend.
2 Aysha / Sanjay always has a lot of words to learn.
3 Aysha / Sanjay sometimes does their hobby more than one day a week.
4 Aysha / Sanjay always does their hobby two days a week.
5 Aysha / Sanjay has a fun time with friends.
6 Aysha / Sanjay eats pizza at a friend's house once a week.

Exam Close-up

Predicting language

- Read the whole conversation first to understand the situation.
- Think about the kind of answers or information that is missing (e.g. a person, a place, a time, a thing).
- Look for question words (e.g. *What*, *When*, *Who*, etc.) to help you choose the correct answers.

F **Read the *Exam Close-up*. Then match each question word in 1–4 with an answer from the box.**

guitar classes   my uncle Alan   on Friday   Paris

1 When …? ______________________
2 Who …? ______________________
3 Where …? ______________________
4 What …? ______________________

G **Now read the conversation in the *Exam Task*. Complete the sentences below. Do NOT complete the *Exam Task* yet.**

1 In **(1)** you need a sentence with hobbies / days of the week / names.
2 In **(2)**, the answer probably begins with Yes or No / a date / Because.
3 In **(3)**, the answer probably begins with Yes or No / a name / a hobby.
4 In **(4)**, you need a sentence similar to Never! / That's great! / Who?
5 In **(5)**, you need a sentence with hobbies / days of the week / names.

H **Now complete the *Exam Task*.**

Exam Task

Complete the conversation. What does Sanjay say to Aysha? Choose the correct answer **A – G**. There are two letters you do not need to use.

Aysha: What activities do you do after school?
Sanjay: **(1)** ______
Aysha: Why do you go to chess club?
Sanjay: **(2)** ______
Aysha: Does Namit go to chess club with you?
Sanjay: **(3)** ______
Aysha: I'd like to come to chess club with you.
Sanjay: **(4)** ______
Aysha: When is it?
Sanjay: **(5)**

A I go because it's difficult, but I like it a lot.
B Yes, he does. He's very good.
C I do bhangra and chess club.
D We usually eat pizza and cheesecake.
E It's on Mondays, after school.
F Ruth doesn't come to chess club.
G Great! It's good fun.

I **Find the words in red below in the texts on page 18 and underline them. Choose the correct words for sentences 1–6. Then tell your partner which sentences are true for you.**

1 I find it difficult to talk to new people. friendly / shy
2 I love tennis and football. sporty / patient
3 I don't get tired - I love being active. creative / energetic
4 I can wait for a long time. sporty / patient
5 I am good at art and making clothes. creative / sociable
6 I like meeting new people and I like parties. shy / friendly and sociable / patient

Ideas Focus

- Would you like to do drama, singing or dancing? Why? / Why not?
- 'If you have a hobby, you have no time for family, friends and homework.' Do you agree? Why? / Why not?

2 Friends & Fun

Vocabulary

A Unjumble the clothes vocabulary.

1 cosks s____________
2 horsts s____________
3 t-thirs t-____________
4 irtks s____________
5 outrsers t____________
6 nejas j____________
7 obost b____________
8 yhood h____________
9 rtihs s____________
10 aitrerns t____________

B Look at the photo of the two teenagers. Write Felix or Emily.

1 __________ is wearing a sweatshirt.
2 __________ is wearing a shirt.
3 __________ is wearing a T-shirt.
4 __________ is wearing shorts.
5 __________ is wearing jeans.

C What are you wearing? Complete the description.

Today I'm wearing ____________________ and ____________________.
I'm also ______________________________.

D Tick the correct verb that goes with each of these activities.

	go	play	do
chess			
drama			
basketball			
judo			
street dance			
skateboarding			
swimming			
running			
tennis			

E Add one more activity to the last row of the table and tick the correct verb. Compare with a partner.

F Match the person with an adjective to describe them.

1 Petra doesn't like meeting new people.
2 Tim does bhangra classes every day.
3 Naomi always wears sweatshirts and tracksuit bottoms.
4 Eva goes out with friends every weekend.
5 We say our lines for our show again and again.
6 Benji loves drawing and doing origami.
7 Zoe writes all her activities in a notebook.

a organised
b sociable
c patient
d shy
e creative
f energetic
g sporty

G Circle the correct word or phrase.

My best friend

My best friend's name is Julia. She's very (**1**) energetic / comfortable and she's sociable but she isn't very (**2**) patient / shy. She always wears colourful, (**3**) shy / sporty clothes like trainers, (**4**) T-shirts / dresses and tracksuit bottoms. We see (**5**) each other / us every afternoon because we (**6**) do / play drama club together. Sometimes we go for (**7**) swimming / pizza or ice cream. We both love (**8**) going /playing football and listening (**9**) music videos / to music. We have a lot of fun together.

H Read and choose the best suggestion. What other activities can you recommend for each person?

art chess dance drama instrument tennis

Angie I'm energetic.
Ben Why don't you do ________________ classes?

Jay I'm creative.
Ben Why don't you start ________________ classes?

Dan I'm shy.
Ben Why don't you do ________________?

Ellie I love sport.
Ben Why don't you play ________________?

Finn I enjoy board games.
Ben Why don't you join a ________________ club?

Laura I like music.
Ben Why don't you learn to play an ________________?

I Complete the dialogue using the correct words.

chat to hang out with have fun get on go for go out meet up

Freddie: Do you (**1**) ________________ with your twin sister?
Becky: Yes! She's my best friend!
Freddie: What do you do together in your free time?
Becky: We (**2**) ________________ each other and we sometimes (**3**) ________________ to the cinema.
Freddie: Do you have the same friends?
Becky: Yes, we (**4**) ________________ with friends at the weekend and often (**5**) ________________ a pizza in town.
Freddie: That's great!
Becky: We always (**6**) ________________.
Freddie: You're lucky. I never (**7**) ________________ my sister!

- Which hobbies and activities do you think are boring and which do you think are fun? Why?
- Is what you wear important? Why? / Why not?

Ideas Focus

Grammar

Present Simple for routines & habits

A **Read the sentences and underline the verbs in the present simple.**

1 My best friend goes to my chess club.
2 I cycle to the park every weekend.
3 My dog takes me for a walk in the morning.
4 We meet every Sunday.

B **Read and tick the correct rule.**

1 After *he/she/it* the verb ends in *-s*. ☐
2 After *he/she/it* the verb stays the same. ☐

Negatives

C **Underline the negative form of the verb. The first one is done for you. Complete the rules.**

1 I like drawing but I don't like painting.
2 Ed doesn't play an instrument but I play the flute.
3 My classmates don't go to the cinema very much.

- We use don't or __________ + verb in present simple negatives.
- __________ = do not, __________ = does not

Yes / No Questions & Short Answers

D **Underline the forms of *do* in the dialogue.**

A Do you play a sport?
B No, I don't. Do you play a sport?
A Yes, I do. I play basketball.
B Does your best friend have the same hobby as you?
A No, she doesn't.
B Do your brother and sister know your best friend?
A Yes, they do.

E **Tick the correct rules for forming *yes/no* questions and short answers.**

1 We use *Do* or *Does* to form *yes/no* questions. ☐
2 We use *What* for *yes/no* questions. ☐
3 In a short answer we repeat the main verb. ☐
4 In a short answer we use the auxiliary verb *do/does/don't/doesn't* and we don't repeat the main verb. ☐

Question Words

F **Complete the questions with the correct question word.**

1 __________ does your best friend live?
2 __________ do you chat to on your phone?
3 __________ do your classes start?
4 __________ does he wear in the play?
5 __________ do they get to the sports centre?
6 __________ do you like painting?

G **Look at your answers in F and write the words in the correct order below.**

verb	subject	question word	*do /does*	?

__________ + __________ + __________ + __________ + __________

Grammar Focus p. 162 (2.1 to 2.2)

H **Match the answers to the questions in F.**

a On Saturday afternoon. ______
b Their mum takes them. ______
c Near the centre of town. ______
d Because it's relaxing. ______
e A big coat and boots. ______
f My best friend, Charlie. ______

I **Write the questions in the correct order.**

1 drama club / do / you / When / go to ?
____
2 do / your friend / after school / does / What ?
____
3 people / have / Why / hobbies / do ?
____

J **Circle the correct answers.**

1 They don't / doesn't play tennis in the rain.
2 The course finish / finishes at five o'clock.
3 Do / Does you speak Portuguese? No, I don't / doesn't.
4 Anita don't / doesn't go out during the week.
5 We visit /visits my grandparents every Sunday.
6 Do /Does Tim do judo? Yes, he do / does.

Adverbs of Frequency

K **Adverbs of frequency are used to say how often we do something. Underline the adverbs of frequency in these sentences. The first one is done for you.**

1 I often go for pizza after my dance class.
2 My brother is hardly ever at home because he's with his girlfriend.
3 Isabelle's parents sometimes invite me to the cinema.
4 I never go to bed after 10 p.m. on a school day.
5 John and Marc are always late for football training.
6 We usually like the same kind of music.

L **Circle the correct words to complete the rules. Write the adverbs from K in the correct place on the line.**

Adverbs of frequency go *before / after* the verb *be*.
Adverbs of frequency go *before / after* main verbs.

0% ——|——|——|—— 100%

________ ________ ________ ________ always

Time expressions

M **Underline the time expressions in these Present Simple sentences. The first one is done for you.**

1 Greg has chess club on Wednesday afternoons.
2 We see a film at the cinema once a month.
3 On Saturdays I go to a street dance class.
4 I visit my cousins twice a year.
5 My mum and dad have tennis classes every summer.
6 My granddad chats to my mum in the afternoons.

N **Complete 1–5 with a word from the box.**

on every at in once

1 ________ week, month, year
2 ________ a day, twice a month, three times a year.
3 ________ Mondays, Wednesdays, Friday afternoons
4 ________ the morning(s), the afternoon(s), the evening(s)
5 ________ the weekend(s)

Grammar Focus p. 162 (2.3)

O **Complete the sentences with the adverb and correct form of the verb in brackets.**

1 Ivan and Joseph ____________ a football match at the weekend. (sometimes / watch)
2 My classmate ____________ energetic. (always / be)
3 We ____________ shells on the beach. (often / look for)
4 My art teacher ____________ outside. (usually / paint)
5 Monica ____________ messages when she is on holiday. (never / read)
6 I ____________ at home on Saturday night. (hardly ever / be)

P **Choose the correct answers.**

1 Sam and I go swimming ______ the mornings.
a in b at
2 My friends watch videos ______ Thursday.
a every b in
3 The judo club meets ______ a week.
a on b once
4 My family goes shopping ______ a month.
a twice b two
5 I only go cycling ______ the weekends.
a at b in
6 We play volleyball ______ Tuesday afternoons.
a in b on

2 Friends & Fun

Listening

A **Look at the photos and circle the hobbies you can see. Then number them from 1 (the best) to 8 (the worst) for you. Explain your choices to a partner.**

1 horse riding	☐	5 cycling	☐
2 flying a kite	☐	6 making models	☐
3 climbing	☐	7 photography	☐
4 scrapbooking	☐	8 dancing	☐

A

D

B

C

B 2.1 **Listen and complete the sentences using these names and choosing the correct words.**

Phil Carla Amanda Jacob

1 Listen to ____________ talking about the climbing wall at her school / at the climbing centre.

2 Listen to Amanda asking ____________ about street dance / Zumba dance classes.

3 Listen to ____________ describing her photos / camera to a friend.

4 Listen to ____________ arranging to meet his best friend in the park / at the beach to fly their kites.

C **Read the *Exam Close-up*. Then read the *Exam Task* and underline the speakers and the topic.**

Exam Close-up

Listening to instructions

- Always listen carefully to the instructions. They will tell you about the speaker and the topic.
- There are five questions with three possible answers. Use the time at the beginning to quickly read the questions before the listening starts.

D 2.2 **Now listen and complete the *Exam Task*.**

E 2.3 **Listen again and check your answers.**

Exam Task

You will listen to a teenager talking to a friend about his hobby. For each question choose the right answer (**A**, **B** or **C**).

You will hear the conversation twice.

1 What does Phil love doing?
A meeting his friends
B flying his kite
C going to kite-making classes

2 Who does he share his hobby with?
A his elder brother
B two cousins
C a friend

3 When do they meet?
A every Sunday
B once a month
C every day after school

4 Where do they go?
A to a beach
B to a park
C to a farm

5 When will Phil and Paolo see each other again?
A at the beach at ten o'clock
B on the bus at nine o'clock
C on Sunday at ten o'clock

Speaking

A Yarn bombing

B Singing

C Camping

A Look at the photos. Why do some people enjoy these hobbies? Would you like to do any of them? Discuss with a partner.

"I think people enjoy yarn bombing because..."

B Match the hobbies in A with the personality adjectives below. Write (A) for yarn bombing, (B) for singing and (C) for camping. Discuss your ideas with a partner.

1 adventurous	______	5 kind	______
2 confident	______	6 patient	______
3 creative	______	7 shy	______
4 friendly	______	8 sociable	______

"I think adventurous people like / don't enjoy... "

C Read a student's answers to questions about her favourite hobby. Write the correct question word next to each answer.

Why? Where? Who ... with? How often? What?(x2)

1 ____________ In my free time, I like going camping.
2 ____________ I go with my cousins.
3 ____________ We usually go once a month.
4 ____________ We often camp in Snowdonia National Park.
5 ____________ I like camping because I enjoy being outside.
6 ____________ We do lots of things. We build a fire, we cook and we play games.

D Read the *Exam Close-up*. Then complete the questions that the student answered in C.

1 ____________ do you like doing in your free time?
2 ____________ do you usually go ____________?
3 ____________ do you go camping?
4 ____________ do you usually go?
5 ____________ do you like this hobby?
6 ____________ do you do when you camp?

E Now complete the *Exam Task*. Use the *Useful Expressions* to help you.

Useful Expressions

Asking to hear something again
Sorry, can you repeat that?
Can you repeat the question, please?
Sorry, can you say that again?
I'm sorry, I don't understand.

Exam Close-up

Understanding the questions

- The examiner will ask you some questions about yourself.
- Listen carefully to the question words. They will tell you the type of information that the examiner wants.
- If you don't understand the examiner's questions, say *Can you repeat that, please?* or *I'm sorry, I don't understand.*

Exam Task

Work in pairs. **Student A** is the examiner.

Student A: Use the prompts to ask questions about **Student B's** hobbies and free time activities. Make notes in the chart below. Then swap roles.

Hobby? / Free time?	
Why?	
How often?	
When?	
Where?	
Who with?	

- Is having a hobby important to you? Why? / Why not?
- Do you know anyone with a strange hobby? Who? What is it?

Ideas Focus

Writing: responding to an advert

Learning Focus

Identifying who to write to for more information

- An advert (or advertisement) on a noticeboard gives basic information about a product, an event, a class or a job.
- If we want more detailed information we must look on a website or contact the company or person for more information.

A Look at the photo of a noticeboard. Where do you find noticeboards? Why do people look at them? Discuss with a partner.

B Unjumble the types of adverts you find on a noticeboard. The first letter is given. Tick the ones that you often look at.

1 yshlodia
h<u>olidays</u> ☐

2 stpe
p______ ☐

3 cbslu
c______ ☐

4 sessalc
c______ ☐

5 eetnimgs
m______ ☐

6 jectsob
o______ for sale ☐

C Read the adverts. Match one or two adverts to each statement below. Write A, B or C.

1 I can contact them by email. ______
2 It doesn't have a website. ______
3 I don't know the cost. ______
4 I know where the classes are. ______
5 I can phone for more information. ______
6 I know when the classes begin. ______

A

B

C

D Read the email. Which activity does Alex want more information about? Underline the questions.

Email Message

From: Alex
To: Florence Bail

Dear Ms Bail

I am interested in joining your photography classes.
I love taking photos but I am a beginner.

Do you have classes for beginners?
How much is each class? What days do you meet?

I look forward to hearing from you.

Kind regards,
Alex White

E In pairs, complete this advert for a new club. Use the adverts in C to help you.

- Are you ______________________________?
- Do you want to ______________________________?
- Come and join our ______________________________
- We meet ______________________________
- Classes cost ______________________________
- Find out more at ______________________________

F Read the *Exam Close-up* and circle the beginning and the end of the email in D.

Exam Close-up

Writing beginnings & endings in emails

- In a formal email, we begin with *Dear Sir* or *Dear Madam*. We finish these emails with *Yours faithfully*.
- If we know the name and surname of the person we are writing to, we begin with *Dear Mr Smith* or *Dear Mrs Smith*.
- We use *Ms* (Ms Smith) when we don't know if a woman is married or single. We finish these emails with *Kind regards* or *Best wishes*.

G Read the *Exam Task* and underline the three questions you need to answer. Then write the email.

Exam Task

Read the email from the photography class teacher.

Email Message

From: Florence Bail
To: Alex White

Dear Alex
I am very happy that you are interested in our photography classes. Do you have a camera?

The beginner's course costs £20 a month and we meet every Thursday afternoon at 6 p.m.

How often do you go out and take photos? What do you like taking photos of?

Our new course starts next Thursday. I look forward to meeting you then.

Best wishes,
Florence Bail

Write an email to Ms Bail and answer the questions. Write **25–35** words.

H Read through the checklist. Did you remember to do these things?

- ☐ I answered the three questions.
- ☐ I checked my spelling.
- ☐ I checked the beginning and ending of my email.
- ☐ I checked my handwriting.
- ☐ There are between 25 and 35 words.

Useful Expressions

Showing interest
I like / love / enjoy + verb + *-ing*
I'm interested in + verb + *-ing*

Ending an email
I look forward to hearing from you.
Yours faithfully, …
Best wishes, …
Kind regards, …

A group of people taking a photography class in Rostov-on-Don, Russia

Video 2 Yoro, the Fulani Boy

Before you watch

A Look at the photos. What story do you think they tell? Discuss with your partner.

A desert

A pair of oxen ready to travel

A Fulani man

While you watch

B Watch the video. Circle the correct information.

1 Yoro makes a long trip with the cows in the dry / wet season.
2 The trip can take almost a year / eight months.
3 The boys usually drink milk / pick fruit.
4 Ayissa is Yoro's girlfriend / mother.
5 Yoro takes his cows from Mali to Egypt / Mauritania.
6 When he returns it's time to celebrate / get married.

After you watch

C Complete the summary of the video below using these words.

desert fat food man months rain wet year

Yoro Sisse is a sixteen year-old boy from Mali. Every **(1)** ______________, boys like Yoro make a long trip into the Sahel **(2)** ______________ to find **(3)** ______________ for their cows. They go in the **(4)** ______________ season when there is too much **(5)** ______________ and the cows can't stay there. The trip can take many **(6)** ______________. It's not easy for the boys because there isn't much food and they have to keep moving. Yoro's job is to bring back **(7)** ______________ cows, then everyone in the village will say that Yoro is not a boy but a **(8)** ______________.

Ideas Focus

- Do you think deserts are interesting places to visit? Why? / Why not?
- 'Yoro is too young to have this big responsibility'. Do you agree?

Review 1

Units 1 & 2

Vocabulary

A Read and circle the correct word.

1 My grandmother is eighteen / eighty-nine years old.
2 My sister is thirteen / thirty. She's a teenager now!
3 My first name is Rose and my address / surname is Jenkins.
4 My aunt is single / married. She doesn't have a husband.
5 My mum's husband / brother is my dad.
6 My dad's brother is my grandfather / uncle.

B Write the name of some people's favourite things.

1 You use a camera to take this. p_ _ _ _
2 You wear this around your neck. n_ _ _ _ _ _ _ _
3 You write about your everyday life in this book. d_ _ _ _
4 You can chat, text and use the Internet with this. s_ _ _ _ _ _ _ _ _ _
5 You put this picture of a famous person up on a wall. p_ _ _ _ _
6 You always know the time with this. w_ _ _ _

C Complete the sentences with a word from the box.

creative energetic patient organised shy sociable sporty

1 A: Young children are (**1**) ____________________! They don't stop moving!
B: Yes, and teachers need to be so calm and (**2**) ____________________ with them.
2 A: I love our brother's paintings. He is so (**3**) ____________________.
B: But his room is a disaster. There is paint and paper everywhere!
A: It's true. He's not very (**4**) ____________________ .
3 A: You are so (**5**) ____________________ . You know everyone at the party!
B: And you're the opposite. You're (**6**) ____________________!
4 A: Why don't you come and play football with us tomorrow?
B: No thanks! You know I'm not a (**7**) ____________________ person.

D Circle the correct word for each sentence.

1 My cousins do / go / play surfing every summer.
2 We do / go / play drama and dance classes on Saturdays.
3 Hannah does / goes / plays running every day in the morning.
4 Bruno does / goes / plays judo after school on Thursday.
5 I never do / go / play video games on a weekday.
6 I usually do / go / play shopping for clothes with my best friend.

E Choose the best word for each space.

-- for on out to to

Adam is my best friend. We have different hobbies but we get (**1**) ______ really well together. I always meet (**2**) ______ him after school and we walk home together. We often go (**3**) ______ at the weekend too. Sometimes we go (**4**) ______ the cinema with friends and sometimes we go (**5**) ______ a pizza with our families. When we are not together we text or chat (**6**) ______ each other on the phone!

Review 1

Units 1 & 2

Grammar

A **Complete the sentences with *is, are, am, has got, have got*.**

1 My parents ______ at my cousin's wedding today.
2 My favourite food ______ ice cream.
3 My uncle and aunt ______ twenty chickens.
4 I ______ Lizzie's sister.
5 My brother ______ two years older than me.
6 Freddie ______ a lot of friends.
7 I ______ from Argentina.

B **Read the question. Write the short answer.**

1 Has Ryan got a dog? – No, he ______________.
2 Do you do a lot of sport? – Yes, I ______________.
3 Is green your favourite colour? – No, it ______________.
4 Do the students have an art class every week? – Yes, they ______________.
5 Have you both got a diary? – Yes, we ______________.
6 Are the children creative? – Yes, they ______________.
7 Does your tortoise like apple? – No, it ______________.

C **Rewrite the sentences in the correct order.**

1 to get We bus the usually school . ______________
2 children always with patient the She is. ______________
3 go How you swimming often do? ______________
4 ever hardly goes Peter camping. ______________
5 organised sister never My is. ______________

D **Read the conversation. Write the missing question word.**

A: Hey, Phil! Come and join our basketball team!
B: (1) ______ do you play?
A: We play on Sunday mornings.
B: (2) ______ do you play with?
A: I play with some friends and neighbours.
A: (3) ______ is the basketball court?
B: It's next to the park.
A: (4) ______ do you get there?
B: You can walk! It's just five minutes.

E **Complete the sentences with the correct word.**

my his her its our their

1 Emma and ______ sister are good swimmers.
2 My name's Martin and this is ______ brother, Chris.
3 Jess and Moira ride ______ bikes to school every day.
4 'What's your teacher's name?' '______ name is Mr Jones.'
5 We walk ______ dogs in the park at the weekend.
6 This is my rabbit and ______ favourite food is apple!

3 My Home Town

Reading: matching, using words you know to understand signs
Vocabulary: places, people, activities, verbs for travelling, word completion, reviewing vocabulary
Grammar: *there is*, *there are*, prepositions, present continuous, open cloze, using prepositions
Listening: gap-fill, reading & listening to instructions
Speaking: asking & answering about travel, practising saying numbers
Writing: an email, recognising verb patterns, writing a postcard, using clues

A common road sign found in Svalbard, Norway

Reading

A Work with a partner and write down all the places in a town, e.g. school, hospital, etc.

B Quickly read through the leaflet. What is different about this town? Underline any places in the leaflet that were not on your list in A.

Bekonscot Model Village

A Very Small Town

Come and spend a day in a 1930s model village and feel like a giant!

Near the city of Oxford, there is a town that is smaller than you and me. In fact, there are four miniature villages that make up Bekonscot Model Village.
There are 200 buildings, 3,000 inhabitants and several different forms of transport. There is a miniature railway that connects all the areas.

The Villages

Greenhaily Village has a zoo where you can see lions, tigers, elephants and penguins. There is also a castle and a windmill.

Bekonscot Village has lots of shops, schools, a church, a cinema, a fire station and police station.

Southpool Village has a harbour with boats and also many bridges.

Hanton Village has a racecourse, a sports club and swimming pool. There is also a hospital with two ambulances and a farm with a tractor and many sheep.

The Inhabitants

You can observe the inhabitants in their everyday routines: a couple is getting married in the church, a firefighter is putting out a fire, children are having fun at the fair, ladies and gentlemen are watching a horse race and fishermen are arriving on their boats.

There is so much to see. Come and visit us soon!

Word Focus

miniature: very small
inhabitants: people who live in a place
windmill: a building that uses the wind to make flour for bread
harbour: a place on the coast where boats are kept
racecourse: a place where horses race each other
observe: watch carefully

Opening Times

Open 7 days a week from February to October

10 a.m. to 5.30 p.m.

Price

Adults: £10.00
Children (2-15): £6.00
Under 2s: FREE
Family (2 adults / 2 children): £29

Facilities

- Cafés and picnic area with tables
- Ice-cream vans

Transport

- By train: Beaconsfield station only five minutes away.
- By bus: frequent buses from Oxford, London, Luton and Reading
- FREE car park

C Match the signs (A–D) with the places (1–4). Then read the leaflet again and write the name of the correct village.

1 ☐ the swimming pool: __________ village.
2 ☐ the school: __________ village.
3 ☐ the cinema: __________ village.
4 ☐ the zoo: __________ village.

A

B

C

D

D Read the *Exam Close-up*. Then read the *Exam Task* and decide what the signs mean.

E Now complete the *Exam Task*.

Exam Close-up

Using words you know to understand signs

- In this part of the exam there are always five sentences and seven signs you need to match.
- Look for words you know in the signs. Don't worry if you don't know some words.
- Compare each sentence with each sign before you choose your answer.

Exam Task

Which notice (**A – G**) says this (**1 – 5**)?

1 You can only cross the road here. ☐
2 You cannot play in this area. ☐
3 The shop isn't open on this day. ☐
4 Cars can only go in this direction. ☐
5 It's important to keep our streets and parks clean. ☐

A

B

C

D

E

F

G

F Find these words in the leaflet. Then complete these sentences with the correct words.

buses train ambulances car boats tractor ice-cream van

1 There are two __________ in front of the hospital.
2 You can buy ice cream from the __________.
3 You can see fishing __________ in the harbour.
4 There is a __________ at the farm.
5 You can park your __________ for free.
6 Many __________ come to Bekonscot from different cities.
7 There is a __________ station very near the model village.

Ideas Focus

- Does your town have everything that you want and need? Why? / Why not?
- 'It's better to live in a big town than in a village.' Do you agree? Why? / Why not?

3 My Home Town

Vocabulary

A Match a photo with the words below. Write the letter.

a town ☐
a city ☐
a village ☐

B How is each photo similar or different to where you live? Tell your partner.

C Match the words in the three columns. Use the example to help you.

Where?	Who?	What?
1 fire station	police officer	a football match
2 hospital	waiter	serves food
3 library	actor	meat, fruit and vegetables
4 police station	firefighter	books
5 restaurant	spectator	helps in an emergency
6 stadium	nurse	helps when you are sick
7 supermarket	librarian	a play or musical
8 theatre	shop assistant	helps stop criminals

D Write the correct words under each photo.

meat pills and medicine books fish fruit and vegetables bread and cakes

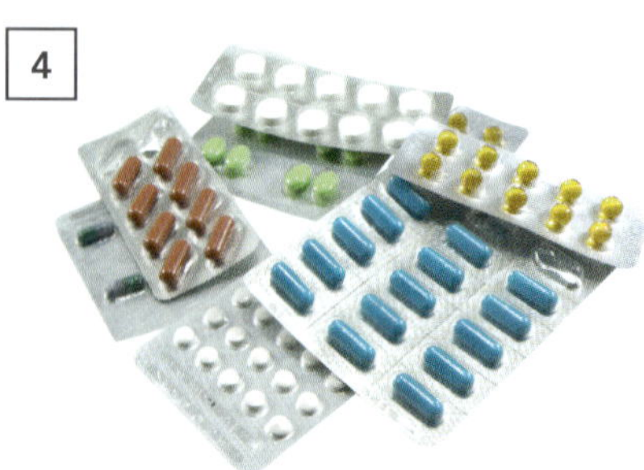

E **Complete the sentences with the correct words from D.**

1 You buy ______________ at the chemist's or pharmacy.
2 You buy ______________ at the greengrocer's.
3 You buy ______________ at the bookshop.
4 You buy ______________ at the butcher's.
5 You buy ______________ at the fishmonger's.
6 You buy ______________ at the bakery.

F **Complete the expressions in the description with the correct words.**

arrive   arrive at   catches   drives   turn   get off   get on   miss   ride   take

How I travel around

Every day I **(1)** ______________ the bus. I **(2)** ______________ the bus outside my house and **(3)** ______________ at the school gate half an hour later. Once or twice a month I **(4)** ______________ the bus because I am late. Then I have to walk to school! I usually **(5)** ______________ school at 8.30 a.m. and **(6)** ______________ home in the afternoon at 3.30 p.m.

My dad **(7)** ______________ the train to work every morning but my mum **(8)** ______________ her car. She is a cook at a village restaurant.

At the weekend, I often **(9)** ______________ my bike to the town centre and meet friends there. It's not far, you **(10)** ______________ left at the end of my road and then go straight on for three kilometres.

G **Read the *Exam Close-up*. Then work with a partner and take turns to define words from these two Vocabulary pages.**

'It's a person who works in a hospital.'

'Is it a nurse?'

'It's a place where you buy ...'

'It's something you ...'

Exam Close-up

Reviewing vocabulary

- You will read five definitions for words on the same topic. You will know the first letter and the number of letters in each word.
- Review vocabulary from each unit as you study it and create word maps for each topic in your notebook.
- Test yourself or a partner on spelling.

H **Now complete the *Exam Task*.**

Exam Task

Read the descriptions of some words about places and transport. What is the word for each one? The first letter is already there. There is **one** space for **each letter** in the word.

1 Some people travel in this to hospital. a _ _ _ _ _ _ _ _
2 You can borrow a book here. l _ _ _ _ _ _
3 This is the best place to see a play or musical. t _ _ _ _ _ _
4 You can get on this at a railway station. t _ _ _ _
5 This person serves you in a restaurant. w _ _ _ _ _

Ideas Focus

- What's your favourite place in your home town? Why?
- How do you travel to school? How long does it take?
- What is your favourite kind of transport? Why?

3 My Home Town

Grammar

There is / There are

A Look at the examples and complete the rules.

There are fantastic cakes in our local bakery.
There's a new librarian at the library.
There is a bus stop near the stadium.
There isn't a hospital in the village.
There aren't beaches near my town.
Is there a bookshop opposite the school?
Are there good restaurants near your house?

- With singular nouns we use *there* ______ or *there* ______. We use *there* ______ in the negative and ______ *there*? for questions.
- With plural nouns we use *there* ______. We use *there* ______ in the negative and ______ *there*? for questions.

B We use *there is / there are* to say what we can find or see. We use *it is / they are* to identify things. Look at the examples, then choose the correct words to complete the sentences.

'Excuse me, where can I find a chemist's?' 'There's one on Penge Road.'
'What's that?' 'It's a library'.

1 There's / It's a fishmonger's on the left.
2 Who's that? There's / It's my sister.
3 There are / They are great cakes at the bakery. Do you want one?
4 There isn't / It isn't my school. My school is in a different village.

Grammar Focus p. 162 & 163 (3.1 & 3.2)

Prepositions

C Look at the photos. Use the words to complete the captions.

behind in in front of near next to on opposite under

1 _ _ _ _ _ _ an umbrella

2 _ _ the street

3 _ _ a bridge

4 _ _ _ _ _ _ _ the tree

5 _ _ /_ _ _ _ _ /_ _ the shop

6 _ _ _ _ the finish line

7 _ _ _ _ /_ _ his girlfriend

8 _ _ _ _ _ _ _ _ his grandfather

D Work with a partner. Think about your city, town or village and complete the sentences.

1 There ______________ a supermarket near our school.
2 There ______________ good Chinese restaurants.
3 There ______________ interesting books in the library.
4 There ______________ a train station.
5 There ______________ a greengrocer's.
6 There ______________ more than three bus stops.

E Circle the correct option.

1 Is / Are there any new students in your class?
2 Is / Are there a chess club in your town?
3 Is / Are there a famous actor from your town?
4 How many people is / are there in your class?

F Circle the correct option.

1 We put food on / under the table at dinner time.
2 My aunt lives in the house opposite / on my house.
3 My books are behind / in my bedroom.
4 I always sit next to / on my best friend in maths class.

Present Continuous

G Add the missing verbs to the text.

You can observe the inhabitants in their everyday routines: a couple **(1)** are getting married in the church, a firefighter **(2)** ______ putting out a fire, children **(3)** ______ having fun at the fair, ladies and gentlemen **(4)** ______ watching a horse race and fishermen **(5)** ______ arriving on their boats.

H Look at the verbs you inserted in the text in G. Choose the correct options to complete the rules.

- We make the present continuous with the verb *be (am, are, is)* / *do (do, does)*. Then we add *-s* / *-ing* to the end of the main verb.
- We use the present continuous to talk about things that happen every day / we can see, hear, etc. at the moment.
- The key word for the present continuous is NOW / ALWAYS.

I Tick the sentences that contain the present continuous.

1 He isn't taking the bus to the supermarket.
2 What are the police doing at school?
3 Do you work at the library?
4 I'm not reading many books these days.
5 She doesn't usually come to this bakery.
6 Is she looking for the hospital?
7 Does your dog like going to the park?
8 You aren't helping very much!

J Find two examples in I to complete the rules.

- The negative form of the present continuous is formed using *'m not*, *aren't* or *isn't*. For example: ______________________
- The question form is formed by putting *am*, *are* or *is* in front of the subject.
  For example: ______________________

Grammar Focus p. 163 (3.3)

K Complete the dialogues with the Present Continous.

1 **A:** What book are you reading at the moment?
  B: I ____________ (read) *Oliver Twist*.
2 **A:** Can Julie come to my house?
  B: No, sorry. She ____________ (do) her homework.
3 **A:** Where are your parents?
  B: They ____________ (walk) into the town centre right now.
4 **A:** Where is your brother?
  B: He ____________ (make) a cake in the kitchen.

Exam Close-up

Using prepositions

- In the exam, there is a short text with eight spaces. There are three options for each space.
- Often the gap in the text needs a preposition.
- After choosing an answer, check the other two options and decide why they are wrong.

L Read the *Exam Close-up*. Then look at these prepositions from C. Are they prepositions of *time* or *place*?

behind in in front of near next to on opposite under

M Now complete the *Exam Task*.

Exam Task

Read a student's description of a painting. Choose the best word (**A**, **B** or **C**) for each space.

My favourite painting

I love this painting of a village **(1)** ______ winter because it is very different **(2)** ______ my town at this time of year. The painting is called *Ice-skating* **(3)** ______ *a Village* and it's by the Dutch painter, Hendrick Avercamp. People are walking and chatting **(4)** ______ each other on a frozen river **(5)** ______ the centre of the village. The scene is quiet, but cold. Many people **(6)** ______ and playing a game. There are simple houses **(7)** ______ to the river and boats aren't moving because the river is frozen. There is a wooden bridge in the background and near it, on the right, **(8)** ______ is a simple windmill.

	A	B	C
1	at	in	on
2	from	by	as
3	under	in	at
4	-	next	to
5	in	at	from
6	skate	is skating	are skating
7	behind	next	opposite
8	there	it	they

Oil painting by Dutch artist, Hendrick Avercamp

3 My Home Town

Listening

A **Look at the photos on this page. With a partner, answer the questions.**

1 What do you know about this place? Say at least three things.
2 What can you visit near here?

The Hollywood Walk of Fame in California, USA

B 3.1 **Listen to five conversations and choose the correct answers to the questions.**

1 What are they looking for?
  a a place b a street c a taxi
2 Where are they going?
  a a shop b a hotel c a restaurant
3 Who is talking to the boy?
  a police officer b a waiter c an actor
4 Who wants to take a selfie?
  a police officer b the boy c an actor
5 What time does the film start?
  a at four o'clock b at six o'clock c at seven o'clock

C 3.1 **Listen again and answer the questions.**

1 Conversation 1: What is the telephone number for taxis?
2 Conversation 2: What time is it?
3 Conversation 3: What is the boy about to eat?
4 Conversation 4: Where is the boy from?
5 Conversation 5: How many tickets are they getting?

D **Read the *Exam Close-up* then read the *Exam Task* instructions. What do you have to do? Complete these sentences.**

1 You will hear __________ people speaking.
2 They are speaking about a __________.
3 You need to __________ and complete the notes.
4 You hear the conversation __________ times.

E 3.2 **Now complete the *Exam Task*.**

F 3.3 **Listen again and check your answers.**

Exam Close-up

Reading & listening to instructions

- In this part of the exam you listen to a dialogue between two people.
- Before the task begins, listen carefully to the instructions because they tell you who is speaking and what they are speaking about.
- Then look at the type of information you need to listen for.

Exam Task

You will hear a visitor asking a man about a bus tour for tourists. Listen and complete each question. You will hear the conversation twice.

Jolly Hollywood Tours

Days:
(1) __________

Starting time:
(2) __________

Starting place:
(3) __________ the office.

Must bring:
(4) __________

Cost of Family ticket:
(5) __________

Speaking

A **Number these types of transport from 1 (your favourite) to 6 (least favourite) and from 1 (fastest) to 6 (slowest). Discuss your answers with a partner.**

	Favourite	Order of speed
bike	☐	☐
bus	☐	☐
car	☐	☐
foot	☐	☐
plane	☐	☐
train	☐	☐

B **Look at the postcard of California. Can you find San Francisco and Los Angeles?**

C **Work with a partner. Decide if the sentences refer to travelling to San Francisco from Los Angeles by car (C) or by plane (P).**

1 It takes about six hours. ☐
2 About $40 for the petrol. ☐
3 It costs $190. ☐
4 There are two or three every hour. ☐
5 It's about an hour. ☐
6 It's a good idea to leave in the morning. ☐
7 It arrives at 10.45 a.m. ☐
8 It leaves at 9.35 a.m. ☐
9 You take San Fernando Road then follow the C-25 Road. ☐

D **Match the sentences in C to the questions.**

a How much does it cost? ______ ______
b How do I get there? ______
c How often are they? ______
d How long does it take? ______ ______
e What time do you leave? ______
f When do you arrive? ______

E **Read the *Exam Close-up*. Then practise saying the following numbers.**

30 minutes	£8.99
50 minutes	Number 11 bus
twelve o'clock	the A66 road
7 p.m.	171 Bath Road, Flat 11
$25	0795 36 88 42

F **Now complete the *Exam Task*.**

Exam Close-up

Practising saying numbers

- You need to be able to say times, prices, addresses, telephone numbers, etc.
- Practise saying your own telephone number, your address, and your age.

Useful Expressions

Asking about travel
How often are the buses/trains/planes from X to X?
How long does it take?
How much does it/a ticket cost?
When does the train leave/arrive?

Answering about travel
There are a lot of buses/trains/planes between X and X.
The journey takes 2 hours.
A ticket costs $150.
The train station is on York Road.

Exam Task

Work with a partner. **Student A:** Look at your role cards below. **Student B:** Look at your role cards on page 183. Take turns to be the hotel receptionist and the tourist. Each use Card 1 first.

Student A:

Card 1

Prepare your **questions** about going to San Francisco **by train**.

Tourist

- How often … ?
- How long … ?
- How … cost?
- When … leave?
- When … arrive?

Card 2

Prepare your **answers** about going to San Francisco **by bus**.

Hotel receptionist

- A lot (of buses)
- 12.35 p.m.
- Bus station on East 7th Street
- 8 hours 30 minutes
- About $70

Writing: an email

Learning Focus

Recognising verb patterns

- When you learn a new verb, look at the type of word that comes after it. For example:

I need to go to English class.	**need + to** + verb
You can visit the city.	**can** + verb
I want to read that book.	**want + to** + verb

A **Look at both photos on the page. Can you find any similarities with your own town or city? Tell a partner.**

B **Look at the photos again. List things you might find in this city.**

Example: "There's a river."

C **Read Sonya's email to Josh. What can you find in the city? Were you correct in B?**

D **Circle all the places and all the forms of transport in Sonya's email.**

email

Hi, Josh!

Look! I'm in Dublin! It's great! There's a castle, a lot of shops and restaurants, and the river is beautiful. You can explore the city by boat, but you can explore on foot too – it's a 'big village'. People are very friendly, too.

You know I love books – well, there are two fantastic libraries! The library in Trinity College is incredible; it's very big, and it closes at 10 p.m.! I love this city! It has got museums and art galleries, and Temple Bar isn't a bar, it's a lovely part of the city. There aren't any cars in Temple Bar, but there are a lot of bicycles. I want to go around the city by bike tomorrow.

There's a restaurant with delicious breakfasts and you can listen to a guitar player! There's also a shop with great doughnuts. It opens at 7.30 a.m. and closes when there aren't any doughnuts left!

There's a big cinema too – I want to see a film there, this afternoon.

So, tell me – where are you?

Love,

Sonya

E **Underline sentences with *want* or *can* in Sonya's email.**

F **Complete the sentences with *want* or *can*.**

1 You ______ have doughnuts for breakfast at 7.30 a.m.
2 You ______ find hundreds of interesting books there.
3 I ______ to walk to the castle tomorrow.
4 I ______ to go and see *Starman*.
5 I ______ walk in the centre at night and there isn't a problem.

G **Read Sonya's email again. Where can you put each of the sentences in F?**

Ha'penny Bridge in Dublin, Ireland

H **Think about your own town or city and answer the questions below. Use the verbs in brackets.**

1 What places are there in your town or city? For example, a castle, shops …
There ______________________________ (be)

2 How can you explore your town or city?
You ______________________________ (can)

3 What place do you like best to visit?
I ______________________________ (love)

4 Where can you eat your favourite food?
I ______________________________ (eat)

5 What do you want to see or visit?
I ______________________________ (want)

Useful Expressions

Writing a postcard
I'm in London/Berlin/Paris.
There's so much to do.
There's a great museum/shopping centre/beach …
This city has got so many …
There's also a …
Tomorrow I want to …

I **Think of your favourite holiday place. Imagine you are there right now and write an email or postcard to a friend. Use the *Useful Expressions* to help you.**

J **Read the *Exam Close-up* then read only the messages and the poster in the *Exam Task*. Circle all the clues (numbers, symbols) and underline the most important information.**

K **Now complete the *Exam Task*.**

Exam Close-up

Using clues

- The content of the two texts will help you complete the missing information in the third text.
- Use clues to help you understand the information. Symbols tell you if there are prices (€, $, £).
- Clues like *a.m.* (morning), *p.m.* (evening), and *st*, *nd*, *rd* and *th* (e.g. 2nd, 3rd, 4th) after numbers tell you a date or the order of actions.

Exam Task

Read the instant message chat and the cinema poster. Sonya is a 12-year-old school girl. Fill in the information in Sonya's email to her aunt.

SONYA – Hi! There's a fantastic film at the cinema tonight. Do you want to come?

TASHA – What film is it?

SONYA – *Starman*. It's on at 5.30.

TASHA – *Starman*? I don't know…

SONYA – Go on! You love Chris Boot.

TASHA – How long is it?

SONYA – It finishes about 7.45 p.m.

TASHA – OK. Meet at 5 p.m.?

SONYA – 👍

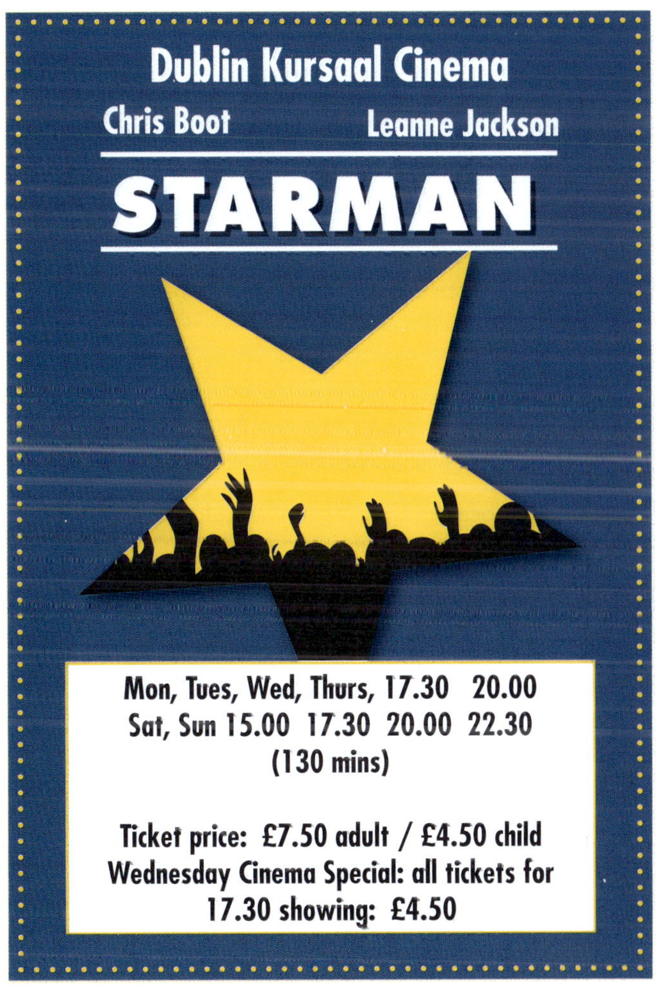

Wednesday 20th November
Dear Aunt Anne,
I am at the cinema called **(1)** ______________________ with Tasha.
We want to see **(2)** ______________________, the new film with **(3)** ______________________ - Tasha's favourite actor.
It starts at **(4)** ______________________ and finishes at 7.45 p.m., so see you at 8 p.m.
Sonya.
P.S. I've got £**(5)** ______________________ to pay for my ticket.

Video

3 Town Rescue

Before you watch

A **What do you know about puffins? Look at the photos and circle the correct answer.**

1 A puffin lives in burrows (holes) / trees in the cliffs.
2 It can / can't fly.
3 It can / can't swim.
4 It eats fruit / fish.

While you watch

B **Watch the video. Decide if these statements are T (True) or F (False).**

1 People help the puffins every summer. ☐
2 The lights of the town confuse the young puffins. ☐
3 People look for puffins in the morning. ☐
4 They use flashlights to find them on the streets. ☐
5 They take the puffins out to sea in a special boat. ☐
6 There is a special way to throw puffins. ☐

After you watch

C **Complete the summary of the video below using these words.**

Families home night puffling seashore streets sea town

There is a local tradition in Heimaey, Iceland. **(1)** ____________ from the town take part in a **(2)** ____________ rescue. When the pufflings are old enough they leave their **(3)** ____________ in the cliffs and fly out to sea. But sometimes they get confused. They fly towards the **(4)** ____________ and land on the **(5)** ____________. So puffin patrols look for the puffins at **(6)** ____________. The next day, families take all the puffins that arrived in the town to the **(7)** ____________. The children then throw the puffins back to the **(8)** ____________.

Ideas Focus

- Does your town have enough green spaces for birds and animals? Why? / Why not?
- 'We need to protect our wildlife'. Do you agree?

4 Celebrate!

Reading:	multiple-choice, identifying the main ideas
Vocabulary:	seasons, prepositions, clothes, food, verbs for celebrations
Grammar:	present simple & present continuous, countable & uncountable nouns, quantifiers
Listening:	gap-fill, listening for specific & detailed information
Speaking:	asking & answering about a celebration, describing a celebration, giving dates, practising pronunciation
Writing:	a recipe, using sequencers, reading carefully

A woman performing with a hula hoop at a Drum Circle party. Treasure Island, Florida

Reading

A **Look at the photographs with a partner. Which one is similar to your New Year celebrations? In what way is it similar?**

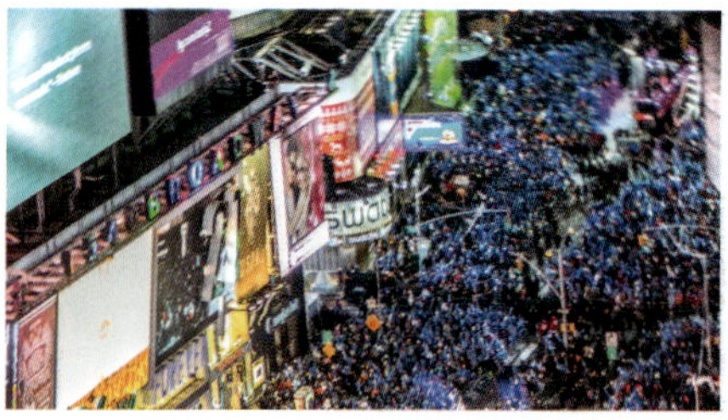

B **Look at the photos in A again. What cities are the celebrations in? Quickly read Part 1 of the text below and find out.**

C **Read Part 1 of the text again and answer these questions.**

1. What are Nathalie's photos for?
2. Why is Nathalie in Singapore?
3. Why is Times Square Nathalie's favourite place on 31st December?
4. What do people do before midnight?
5. What happens at midnight?
6. What do the people do when they hold hands?

Word Focus

fireworks: something that explodes and makes colourful displays in the sky
confetti: small pieces of coloured paper to throw
balloon: a rubber bag you fill with air at parties
'Auld Lang Syne': a traditional New Year song
procession: a line of people walking or dancing
lantern: a light inside a container

New year celebrations!

Part 1

Nathalie

Do you like my photos? They are for my class project on Special Days, and they show three New Year celebrations. I'm from New York but I'm living in Singapore now. My Dad has got a new job so he's working here for two years. It's a new adventure!

In New York, there are lots of celebrations but my favourite is New Year's Eve. There are parties all over the city and incredible fireworks, but the best place is Times Square. It's cold and the weather is sometimes bad but there are lots of lights, colours and people – I love it! Before midnight, we all count – ten, nine, eight, seven ... It's exciting! At midnight, there's a lot of confetti and balloons, and people kiss their family, their friends, their boyfriend or girlfriend; they even kiss the police! Then we hold hands and sing 'Auld Lang Syne'. I'm looking forward to New Year in New York next year, but this year I'm in Singapore.

Part 2

New Year in Singapore is also great – and we celebrate it twice! First, we celebrate New Year's Eve on 31st December, like in New York. The fireworks are fantastic here, too, but the best thing is the hot weather. We eat dinner at a restaurant next to the sea – we have fish, meat, and a lot of tropical fruit, and then we go for a 'snow ice' – it's like ice cream but made with fruit or green tea. Later we watch the fireworks at Marina Bay. The colours are amazing and you can see the fireworks in the sky and in the water – similar to New York, but different, too.

Then, in February, we celebrate the Chinese New Year. I love it! Everything is red and gold, because they're the lucky colours. People give children money in red packets, and they also give friends mandarin oranges for good luck. There are processions and lion dances in the street. There are lanterns and flowers everywhere and people eat pineapple tarts, coconut cookies and other special cakes. Eating with your family is very important. It's definitely my favourite celebration.

D **Now read Part 2 of Nathalie's project work and tick the best summary.**

1 Nathalie likes New Year in Singapore but she loves it in New York. ☐
2 Nathalie thinks New Year in Singapore is the best in the world. ☐
3 She thinks there are similarities and differences between the two cities at New Year. ☐

E **Read the *Exam Close-up*. Then read the *Exam Task* and underline the main ideas in each sentence.**

F **Now complete the *Exam Task*.**

Exam Close-up

Identifying the main ideas

- In this type of exam task, read the complete text quickly to help you understand the topic.
- There are seven sentences in the task. Read them and underline the words that express the main idea in each., e.g. *She's from New York, but she's living in Singapore now.*

Exam Task

Read **Part 2** of the project about New Year in Singapore. Choose the best answer (**A**, **B** or **C**) for each question.

1 In Singapore, Nathalie doesn't celebrate New Year in December.
 A Right
 B Wrong
 C Doesn't say

2 Nathalie likes hot weather on New Year's Eve.
 A Right
 B Wrong
 C Doesn't say

3 'Snow ice' is a traditional dessert for New Year.
 A Right
 B Wrong
 C Doesn't say

4 A New Year tradition is to give friends fruit as a special present.
 A Right
 B Wrong
 C Doesn't say

5 The lion in the lion dance is usually red and gold.
 A Right
 B Wrong
 C Doesn't say

6 There are pineapples, flowers and coconuts at the special markets.
 A Right
 B Wrong
 C Doesn't say

7 In Singapore, people celebrate New Year with their friends, not with their family.
 A Right
 B Wrong
 C Doesn't say

G **Underline all the adjectives you can find in Nathalie's project work. Then complete these sentences with the correct adjective.**

1 I don't like h______ weather. I prefer c__________ weather.
2 Do you like fireworks? I think they're f__________!
3 The colours of that costume are a__________.
4 In many countries, red is a l__________ colour.
5 Starting a new year is always e__________.
6 I like to be with my family at New Year. I think it's really im________ to spend time with each other.

Ideas Focus

- Do you enjoy celebrations? Why? / Why not?
- 'New Year celebrations are the best celebrations of the year'. Do you agree? Why? / Why not?

4 Celebrate!

Vocabulary

A **Write the correct season under each photo.**

winter spring summer autumn

1 ______

2 ______

3 ______

4 ______

B **Complete the sentences with the correct season.**

1 You need to wear warm clothes when you get married in ______.
2 In Australia, December and the New Year are in ______.
3 I love Halloween. It's the time when leaves on the trees change colour and fall because it's in ______.
4 My mum's birthday is in ______ so we often give her flowers.

C **Complete the table by asking your classmates when they have their birthdays. Write their name in the correct column.**

Spring	Summer	Autumn	Winter

D **Circle the correct preposition.**

1 We celebrate Halloween in / at October.
2 For / In the morning, we buy and prepare the pumpkin.
3 We make our costumes at / in the afternoon.
4 Our friends arrive for / in the evening and we dress up.
5 We go 'trick or treating' by / at night to collect sweets from neighbours.
6 It's more fun when Halloween is at / by the weekend.

E **Complete the sentences with *at* or *in*.**

1 On my birthday, we don't eat cake ______ the morning.
2 When it's my birthday, my grandparents sometimes visit ______ the evening.
3 The day before my birthday, I can't sleep ______ night; I'm too excited!
4 I like it best when my birthday is ______ the weekend.
5 We usually have a party ______ the afternoon, and I invite my friends.
6 We always eat cake ______ June because that's the month when I was born!

F Work with a partner. Match these images with the correct words.

1	birthday cake	☐	4	lights	☐
2	decorations	☐	5	Halloween	☐
3	fair	☐	6	wedding cake	☐

A

B

C

D

E

F

G Work with a partner. Match the words below with the four celebrations. Then add your own ideas.

barbecue cards ~~Christmas tree~~ ~~decorations~~ fancy dress flowers pumpkin spiders balloons confetti fireworks presents singing traditional songs special food sweets tricks

Christmas	Halloween	Wedding	Birthday
Christmas tree decorations			

H Choose the correct verb to make phrases.

1 have / give a barbecue
2 wear / make a cake
3 make / have a party
4 do / wear a wedding dress
5 give / do a card and a present
6 wear / make decorations
7 sing / get traditional songs
8 have / give a bonfire
9 wear / give fancy dress
10 go / make special food

I Complete the sentences with the correct form of the verbs. Some of the verbs will fit more than one gap. Which celebrations are they?

dance eat have hold sing visit watch wear

1 In Scotland, everybody __________ hands and __________ a traditional song, then they __________ a typical cake. In the morning, on the first day of January, people __________ each other.
Celebration: ______________________________

2 In India, families and friends __________ a party for three days! The bride __________ a special red dress and __________ with her new husband. They __________ traditional food and they __________ fireworks.
Celebration: ______________________________

Ideas Focus

- Is it a good idea to learn about celebrations in different countries? Why? / Why not?
- Do you like wearing fancy dress or costumes? Why? / Why not?

Grammar

Present Simple & Present Continuous

A Read these sentences. Underline the verbs in the Present Simple and circle the verbs in the Present Continuous.

Nina: Are you celebrating Diwali?
Ankit: No, we celebrate Diwali in October or November.
Nina: Those fireworks are making a lot of noise!
Ankit: Yes, we use them at important celebrations. Today my sister is getting married.
Nina: Is your sister wearing a white dress?
Ankit: No, in India many women wear red saris.
Nina: She's arriving now with lots of people. You have got a big family!

B Circle the correct tense in these rules. PS (present simple) or PC (present continuous).

1 We use the PS / PC to talk about actions that are happening now, at the moment.
2 We use the PS / PC to talk about habits and routines.
3 We use the PS / PC to talk about facts or things that don't change.

Countable & Uncountable Nouns

C Read the sentences. Underline *some* or *any*.

1 'Is there any bread?' 'Yes, there's some on the table.'
2 'Have you got any flowers to put on the table?' 'You can find some in the garden.'
3 Is there any rubbish to take out?
4 Are there any children playing in the street?

D Complete the rule with *some*, *a/an*, or *any*.

1 We use ______ with singular countable nouns.
2 We use ______ with singular countable nouns that begin with a vowel *a*, *e*, *i*, *o*, *u*.
3 We use ______ / ______ with plural countable nouns.
4 We use ______ / ______ with uncountable nouns.

E Choose the correct words to complete the rules.

- We use *any* in negative / positive sentences and questions.
- We use *any* with countable and / not uncountable nouns.

F Look at C. Find an example of each type of noun.

An uncountable noun: ______________
A countable singular noun: ______________
A countable plural noun: ______________

Grammar Focus pp. 163 (4.1 to 4.2)

G Complete the sentences with the present simple or present continuous form of the verbs in brackets.

1 A: What are you doing?
B: We ______________ (celebrate) the water festival!
2 A: What things do Chinese people do at Chinese New Year?
B: They ______________ (visit) their families and ______________ (take) them presents.
3 A: Where's Pablo?
B: He's there on stage! He ______________ (sing) karaoke!
4 A: Can you see Victoria?
B: Yes, she ______________ (wear) a colourful costume and a purple mask.
5 A: What do you do on New Year's Day?
B: I ______________ (swim) in the sea with friends! It's a tradition!
6 A: What are you doing?
B: I ______________ (put) some candles in the garden.

H Complete the conversation with *a*, *an* or *some*.

Dad: Is everything ready for the party?
Sam: Yes, Fiona is putting ______ balloons around the door.
Dad: We have ______ music to play, too.
Sam: Yes, and there is ______ area outside for dancing.
Dad: Great! There is ______ food on the table and ______ big cake in the fridge. Now we just need ______ juice and ______ glasses.
Sam: And ______ people …
Dad: Here's someone now. I hope they have ______ invitation!

I Choose the correct answer.

1 It's a holiday. There isn't ______ traffic on the road.
a a   b an   c any
2 Have you got ______ invitation to the party?
a a   b an   c some
3 We have ______ cousins who live in America.
a a   b some   c any
4 Can I have ______ juice, please?
a an   b some   c any
5 They don't give the children ______ sweets.
a a   b some   c any

Grammar

Quantifiers

J Underline *much, many, a lot of/lots of* in sentences 1–6. Then complete rules a–c with *much, many, a lot of/lots of.*

1 There are many New Year celebrations.
2 There isn't much snow this winter.
3 I can see lots of fireworks near the fair.
4 There are many people dancing on the beach.
5 There isn't much news about the carnival.
6 People throw a lot of water during the water festival!

a We use it with countable plural nouns. ___________

b We use it with negative verbs and uncountable nouns. ___________

c We use them with uncountable nouns and countable plural nouns. ___________ / ___________

K Read the sentences. Circle the correct words.

1 'How much / many people are going to the wedding?' '150 people.'
2 'How much / many pizza do you want?' 'One slice.'
3 'How much / many time do you have?' 'Ten minutes!
4 'How much / many children are wearing costumes?' 'Lots of children.'
5 'How much / many money have you got?' 'Not much!'
6 'How much / many fruit do you eat?' 'Three pieces of fruit a day.'

L Circle the correct words.

- We use how much / how many in questions with countable nouns.
- We use how much / how many in questions with uncountable nouns.

The New Year Water-Splashing Festival in China

Be careful
Watch out when you are talking about whole pieces of food:

*Do you want **a** cake/pizza?* (the whole thing)

*Do you want **some** cake/pizza?* (a slice)

Note that we can use **some** in a question, when we offer food.

Grammar Focus p. 164 (4.3)

M Rewrite the sentences with *much* or *many* instead of *a lot of* or *lots of*.

1 The dancers don't have a lot of time to get dressed.
____

2 There isn't a lot of light. We need candles.
____

3 Lots of people are going to the concert.
____

4 We've got lots of relatives coming to visit us.
____

5 There isn't a lot of food. We need more sandwiches.
____

6 We don't have a lot of decorations. Let's make some more.
____

N Complete the questions. Write *much* or *many*.

1 How ______ cake is there in the fridge?
2 How ______ cousins do you have?
3 How ______ balloons are there on stage?
4 How ______ time do you spend on the Internet?
5 How ______ information do you know about the activities?
6 How ______ languages do you speak?
7 How ______ water do you drink every day?
8 How ______ children are coming to the party?

4 Celebrate!

Listening

A **Look at the photo on this page. What are the children celebrating? Do you ever dress up in a national costume?**

B **Work with a partner. Can you name a country for each letter of the alphabet?**

'A'

'Australia!'

Exam Close-up

Listening for specific & detailed information

- Make sure you listen carefully for detailed information, e.g. times, dates, days and numbers.
- Before the listening starts, quickly look at what type of information you need to listen for.
- Write down your answers the first time you listen.
- Check your answers the second time you listen and make any changes.

C 4.1 **Listen to a student talking about international week at his school. Circle the information that you hear.**

Month:	March	April	May
Country:	America	Australia	Austria
Day:	first day	Friday	last day
Nationality:	Brazilian	British	Bolivian
How long:	half an hour	an hour	five hours
Place for lunch:	library	playground	gymnasium
Time:	1.30 p.m.	2.30 p.m.	3.30 p.m.

D **Read the** ***Exam Close-up*****. Then read the** ***Exam Task*** **and match the missing information below with each question.**

a a time ______
b a number ______
c a country ______
d a date ______
e a colour ______

E 4.2 **Listen and complete the** ***Exam Task*****.**

Exam Task

You will hear a teacher talking to her class about preparing for international week.
Listen and complete each question.

You will hear the information twice.

International week

When: 2nd June until **(1)** ____________________

Country: **(2)** ____________________

Days for preparation: **(3)** ____________________days

Flag: Yellow, **(4)** ____________________ and red.

Presentation: last evening, at **(5)** ____________________ p.m.

F 4.3 **Listen again and check your answers.**

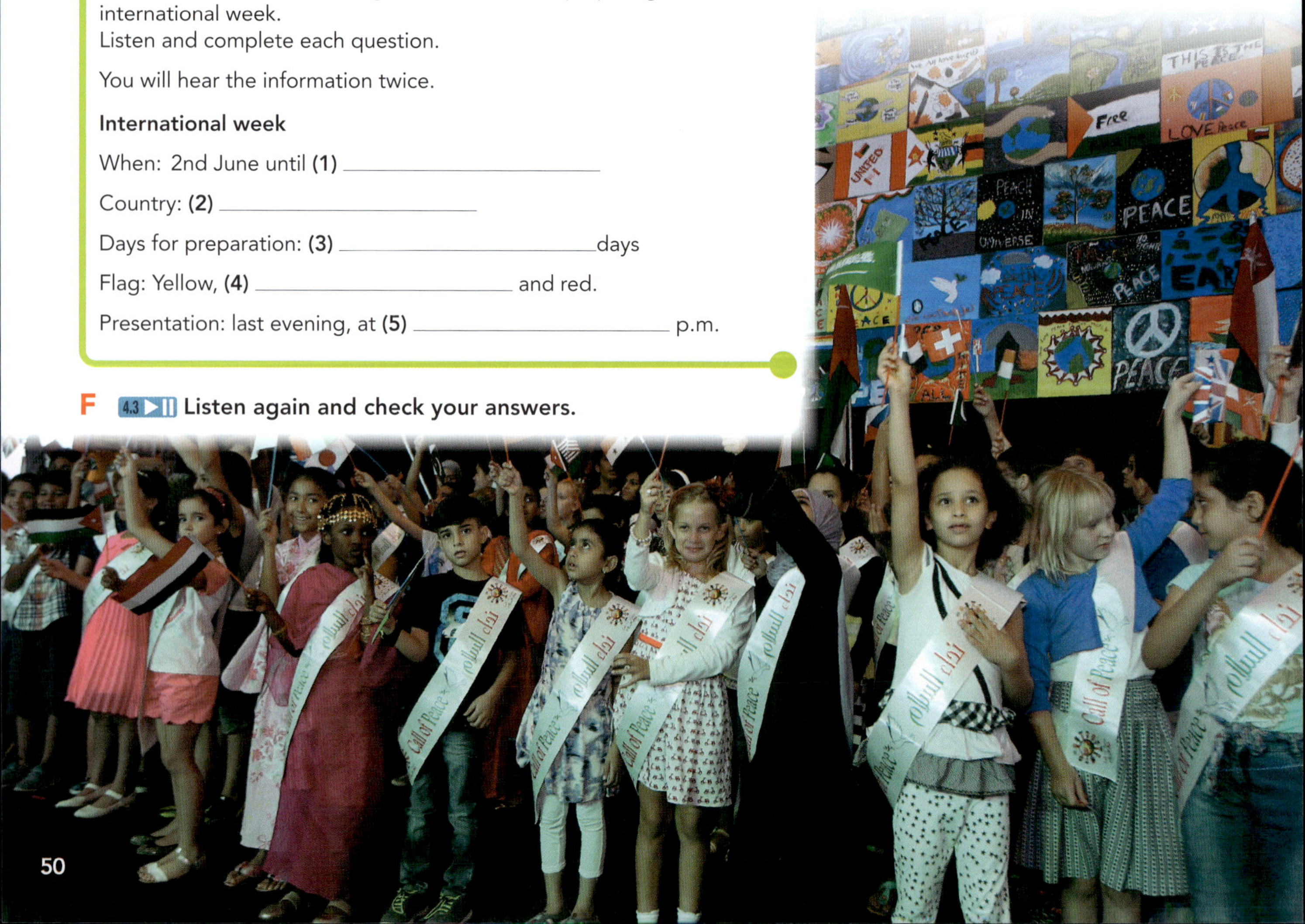

Speaking

A **Match the photos with the celebrations and dates. Compare your ideas with a partner.**

Photo	Celebration	Date
4	Thanksgiving	14th February
	San Juan	between February and March
	Halloween	31st October
	Diwali	fourth Thursday of November
	Carnival	23rd June
	Valentine's Day	between November and December

B 4.4 **Now listen to check your answers.**

C **Work with a partner. Student A: choose one of the celebrations in the photos, but don't tell Student B which one. Student B: ask yes/no questions to find out which photo Student A chose. Then swap roles.**

"Are there people on the beach?"
"Are people looking at a fire?"

D **Work with a partner. Which activity in sentences 1–6 sounds most fun? Why? Do you know which celebration each sentence is about?**

1 I love sharing a special dinner with my family at home.
2 It's a traditional festival. There are many candles, lights and fireworks everywhere.
3 We make big bonfires and have barbecues on the beach at night.
4 It always feels special. He sends me chocolates and flowers and I take him to a restaurant.
5 I like seeing all the costumes in the procession, especially the masks.
6 It's fun making pumpkin faces and collecting sweets.

E **Read the *Exam Close-up*. Then practise saying these words.**

barbecue	delicious	fireworks
candle	favourite	restaurant
chocolate	February	procession
		traditional

Exam Close-up

Practising pronunciation

- Always check and practise the pronunciation of new or long words. Use a dictionary to help you, or ask your teacher.
- Keep a list of tricky words that are difficult to pronounce.
- Don't be afraid of these words! Use them as much as possible so they become easy to say!

F 4.5 **Listen to the words in E and underline the stressed syllable as in the example. Practise saying them again with a partner.**

G **Now work with a partner to complete the *Exam Task*. Use the *Useful Expressions* to help you.**

Useful Expressions

Describing a celebration
It's very special.
I like it because it's special.
I love the food, especially the cakes!
It's fun/exciting.

Giving dates
on **the** 14th **of** February

Exam Task

Work with a partner. Use the prompts to find out about your partner's favourite celebration.

Favourite celebration

- Favourite / celebration?
- When / celebrate?
- Why / special?
- What / do?
- What / eat?
- Give / presents?
- Wear / special clothes?
- Who / celebrate with?

Ideas Focus

- It's important to eat together with your family. Do you agree? Why / Why not?
- What is the worst party or celebration you can remember? What happened?

4 Celebrate!

Writing: a recipe

Learning Focus

Using sequencers

- Use *First, Then, Next, After that* and *Finally* at the beginning of sentences, to help your reader understand the order of the actions.
- When you write a recipe, directions or instructions you can use the imperative (the verb without the subject 'you'). For example: *cut the apple, fry the fish, turn left, press the button.*

A huge seafood paella is served in Barcelona, Spain

A **Many countries have typical foods. With a partner, match these foods and their nationalities.**

1	Sushi	☐	a	Mexican
2	Fish and chips	☐	b	Italian
3	Paella	☐	c	Spanish
4	Pizza	☐	d	British
5	Curry	☐	e	Japanese
6	Guacamole and nachos	☐	f	Indian

"I think Sushi is from ..." "I agree / don't agree."

B **What is a typical food in your country? Do you like it? Why? / Why not?**

C **Look at the photo below. Which is the correct shopping list?**

A russian salad

Shopping list A

one green pepper
one red pepper
two tomatoes
200g. pasta
Jar of mayonnaise

Shopping list B

three carrots
four potatoes
300g. frozen peas
one egg
Jar of mayonnaise

D **Now read the recipe for the Russian salad. How is a recipe different from a shopping list?**

First, cut the carrots and potatoes into small cubes.
Then, boil the potatoes, the carrots and the peas together until soft.
Next, boil the egg for ten minutes. When it is cool, take off the shell and chop.
Mix the vegetables and the egg together and add salt.
After that, add the mayonnaise and mix.
Finally, leave the salad to cool a little before serving.

E **Underline the words in the recipe in D that help to order the instructions.**

F Complete the recipe with these verbs.

add cut and chop mix serve

Guacamole

1. First, ____________ the avocado, onion, garlic and tomato.
2. Then ____________ these ingredients together.
3. Next, ____________ some lime juice and mix again.
4. Finally, add some salt and pepper and ____________ immediately with nachos.

Useful Expressions

Instructions	Sequencing
Bring …	First, …
Buy …	Then …
Make …	Next, …
Don't forget …	After that, …
Don't bring …	Finally, …

Exam Close-up

Reading carefully

- There is often more than one *date*, *time*, *number*, etc., so make sure you read carefully to select the correct information.
- Focus on what information is needed in each gap. For example, if you see a time, e.g. *6 p.m.*, and read information about *an hour earlier*, you know this will be *5 p.m.* You also know that *p.m.* refers to the afternoon and evening.

G Read the *Exam Close-up*. Then read all the information in the *Exam Task* carefully.

H Now complete the *Exam Task*.

Exam Task

Read Andrea's email and shopping list.
Fill in the information on her 'To Do' list.

Email Message

To: Gina From: Andrea
Subject: Carolina's 18th birthday

Hi Gina,

Thank you for your rice salad recipe.

I have onions but I still need to buy the vegetables!

Don't bring any fizzy drinks. David is buying Carolina's favourite juice.

Everyone is arriving at eight o'clock tomorrow. Can you come an hour earlier to help me?

Don't forget the candles for the cake!

Thanks a lot!
Andrea

Shopping list

carrots, peppers and peas
one chicken
candles ✓ Gina
apple juice ✓ David

To Do list.

Buy one chicken and (1) ________ vegetables.

Make a (2) ________ salad.

No (3) ________ drinks! Just (4) ________ juice.

Gina bringing (5) ________ candles

Gina coming at (6) ________ o'clock to help me!

Video 4 The Magic of Diwali

Before you watch

A Label the pictures with these words.

coloured sand fireworks market garland temple

1 ______________

2 ______________

3 ______________

4 ______________

5 ______________

While you watch

B Watch the video. Circle the correct information.

1 Diwali celebrates light / darkness.
2 People visit the Taj Mahal / flower markets and temples.
3 People decorate the ground / walls.
4 Shops are open / closed.
5 It is a time for sharing / singing.
6 There are presents / lights everywhere.

After you watch

C Complete the summary of the video below using these words.

celebration clothes decorate family flowers food fireworks temples

Diwali is an important **(1)** ______________ in India. It takes place in autumn (fall). At this time of year, people **(2)** ______________ their homes with garlands of **(3)** ______________ . They also use coloured sand to make designs in the shape of the lotus flower. This is a symbol of welcome. Families wear new **(4)** ______________ and visit the **(5)** ______________. People make and share plates of delicious **(6)** ______________ with neighbours. You can see and hear **(7)** ______________ in the sky. It's a time to celebrate life and be with **(8)** ______________.

Ideas Focus

- Are celebrations important? Why? / Why not?
- Would you like to celebrate Diwali? Why? / Why not?

Review 2 Units 3 & 4

Vocabulary

A Complete the sentences with the words.

actor   librarian   nurse   shop assistant   spectators   waiter

hospital   library   restaurant   stadium   supermarket   theatre

1 40,000 ________ are watching the football match tonight in the ________.
2 Eddie is an ________. He's in a new play at the National ________.
3 My aunt is a ________. She looks after sick children at the Radcliffe ________.
4 Ask the ________ where the Harry Potter books are in the ________.
5 The food is really good at the new Italian ________ and my brother is a ________ there!
6 The ________ says the ice cream is on the left side of the ________, near the milk.

B Complete the words in the sentences.

1 Are you going to wear f_ _ _ _ dress to the party?
2 Leia loves all her birthday p_ _ _ _ _ _ _.
3 Look up! Can you see the f_ _ _ _ _ _ _ _ _ in the sky?
4 Can you help me put the d_ _ _ _ _ _ _ _ _ _ on the Christmas tree?
5 My sister is getting married. I'm going to the w_ _ _ _ _ _ tomorrow.
6 Let's cook some hamburgers on the b_ _ _ _ _ _ _.
7 There are big orange p_ _ _ _ _ _ _ everywhere at Halloween.

C Circle the correct words.

1 I'm having / making a special cake for my grandmother's birthday.
2 Many Japanese men and women wear / hold traditional clothes at their wedding.
3 My mum has / takes a big birthday party every year.
4 You pay when you drive / get on the bus.
5 My dad catches / drives me to school every morning.
6 Georgia sometimes misses / gets off the bus and is late for school.
7 Go along Peacock Road and arrive / turn right.
8 We usually take / get on the train when we visit our cousins in London.

D Complete the sentences with *in*, *at* or *on*.

1 We often have picnics ______ spring.
2 I have a judo competition ______ the weekend.
3 My brother goes jogging ______ the morning.
4 Children celebrate Halloween ______ 31st October.
5 I never study ______ night. I'm too tired.
6 It's my grandmother's 80th birthday ______ March.
7 People light candles ______ Christmas and Diwali.

E Read and write the season.

1 People often go to the beach at this time. ________________
2 It's cold and people wear boots, hats and gloves. ________________
3 Trees change colour and pumpkins are popular. ________________
4 You see many baby animals. Flowers start to grow again. ________________

Review 2 Units 3 & 4

Grammar

A **Write *is* or *are* to complete the sentences.**

1 There ______ 150 people at the wedding.
2 There ______ a new hotel opposite the beach.
3 ______ there a train station in your town?
4 ______ there good sports centres in your town?
5 There ______ lots of traditional sweets to share.
6 There ______ a chocolate cake in the bakery window.

B **Choose the best answer a, b or c.**

1 There are ___ celebrations around the world for New Year.
a much **b** a lot of **c** a
2 There aren't ___ red balloons at the party.
a some **b** a **c** any
3 There's ___ party at the weekend. Let's go!
a lots of **b** many **c** a
4 There are ___ beautiful flowers at the local market.
a much **b** many **c** a lot
5 There isn't ___ light. We need more candles.
a much **b** many **c** some
6 Families give children ___ money for Chinese New Year.
a many **b** any **c** some
7 I don't like sweets. Can I have ___ apple instead?
a an **b** a **c** any
8 Are there ___ good songs we can sing at midnight?
a much **b** any **c** lots

C **Complete the dialogue with the Present Continuous tense.**

A: Hi Maria, what (**1**) ____________________ (you / do)?
B: Oh nothing much. I (**2**) ____________________ (look) out of the window.
A: What can you see from your window?
B: Well, Mr Harris, my neighbour, (**3**) ____________________ (sit) at the café. He (**4**) ____________________(read) the newspaper.
A: Oh, yes, I remember Mr Harris.
B: School children (**5**) ____________________ (get) on the bus but they (**6**) ____________________ (not wear) uniform today!
A: What (**7**) ____________________ (they / wear)?
B: They (**8**) ____________________ fancy dress.
A: That's because it's carnival today!

D **Underline the correct tense, Present Simple or Present Continuous.**

1 We usually celebrate / are celebrating carnival in March.
2 Every April, people throw / are throwing water at the water festival.
3 This year, the children make / are making their own costumes.
4 People call / are calling the fire station when there is an emergency.
5 Shh! I talk / am talking to my girlfriend on the phone.

5 A Perfect Day

Reading:	multiple-choice, thinking about possible responses
Vocabulary:	nouns and verbs for activities, word combinations, multiple-choice sentences, using your knowledge of vocabulary
Grammar:	past simple *to be*, regular & irregular forms, questions & negatives, *yes/no* questions & short answers, time expressions, open cloze, checking verb tenses & endings
Listening:	multiple choice (pictures), noticing differences
Speaking:	asking & answering about the perfect day, talking about activities with *to go*, showing interest, extending your answers
Writing:	a diary, adding details, expressing positive feelings, giving reasons, planning a draft

A pet iguana fishing from the back of a boat. Palm Beach, Florida

5 A Perfect Day

Reading

A **Think of a perfect day. Tick the things that would be part of your perfect day.**

1 food ☐
2 a surprise ☐
3 a new or special place ☐
4 a new or favourite activity ☐
5 an animal ☐
6 a present ☐
7 family and friends ☐
8 a good book or film ☐
9 a journey ☐
10 a celebration ☐

B **Quickly read the descriptions below in a school magazine. Which things from A were part of each teenager's perfect day?**

C **Which description (1–5) matches the photos? What did that teenager do?**

"The boy went ... "

D **Read the descriptions again and choose the correct answers.**

1 Monica's mum built a snowman / made lunch / bought a toboggan.
2 Becky wore seaweed / got married / went to a wedding.
3 Nico swam in the sea / caught a whale / ate fish.
4 Charlie celebrated in bed / at the cinema / at a restaurant.
5 Adira travelled to Dubai / to the desert / to see her mum and dad.

Word Focus

toboggan: a board used for sliding on snow or ice

bridesmaid: the sister or friend of the woman who is getting married

turquoise: a colour between green and blue

seaweed: a type of plant you find in the sea

lighthouse: a tower with a light on for boats to know their location

waterslide: a slide you go down that ends in a swimming pool

Such a perfect day!

1 My perfect day was when it snowed last winter. I woke up and everything was white! School was closed so my brother and I put on warm clothes and went out to explore. Our neighbours joined us outside and we built snowmen. We had a snowball fight, too. Mum made us a delicious hot soup and roast potatoes. My dad bought us a toboggan so after lunch we went out again and took turns to slide down the road. It was great fun and a perfect day! **Monica**

2 My perfect day was my sister's wedding. Everybody I knew was there; even my great-grandmother! I was a bridesmaid and I wore a beautiful turquoise dress. I spent an hour in the hairdresser's and when I came out my sister gave me a pair of earrings that looked like seaweed. They were so special. The reception was in a garden full of candles and I danced all night. **Becky**

3 On my perfect day I went fishing for the first time with my uncle. We left really early. The sunrise was beautiful. We caught some big fish and later we built a small fire on the beach to cook them. They were delicious. We walked along the beach and suddenly I saw a humpback whale and its baby in the distance – I couldn't believe it! We passed the lighthouse and the lighthouse keeper, who knows my uncle, gave me a tour. It was the end of a perfect day! **Nico**

E **Read the *Exam Close-up*. Then read the first line in each conversation in the *Exam Task*. Think about your own responses. Do NOT look at the options A, B, C.**

F **Now complete the *Exam Task*.**

Exam Close-up

Thinking about possible responses

- In this task there are five, two-line conversations.
- Read the first line of each conversation and think about possible responses.
- Look at the options and decide which is best. Then read the conversation to make sure it makes sense.

Exam Task

Complete the five conversations. Choose **A**, **B**, or **C**.

1 It was a perfect day!
  A Today is not possible.
  B What's the date?
  C How brilliant!

2 We didn't catch any fish.
  A I'm sure they were delicious.
  B That's a pity.
  C Were they big?

3 Why don't you come with us?
  A I can't.
  B She's coming.
  C No, I don't.

4 Who did you go with?
  A With everybody.
  B We went by taxi.
  C I went there yesterday.

5 Do you like that colour?
  A I like colours.
  B Yes, it's my favourite.
  C No, I don't like them.

G **Find these compound nouns in the texts. Then use some of them to complete the sentences.**

bridesmaid hairdresser earring humpback lighthouse quad bike seaweed snowmen snowball waterpark waterslide

1 A good place for fish to hide is in some ______________ . Some fish eat it, too!
2 Don't forget you need to wear a helmet when you ride a ______________.
3 How can you see with all that hair in your eyes? Go to the ______________.
4 A ______________ doesn't hurt if it hits you, but it's very cold.
5 I lost an ______________ yesterday at the party. Now I only have one!
6 ______________ whales have a very strange body shape.

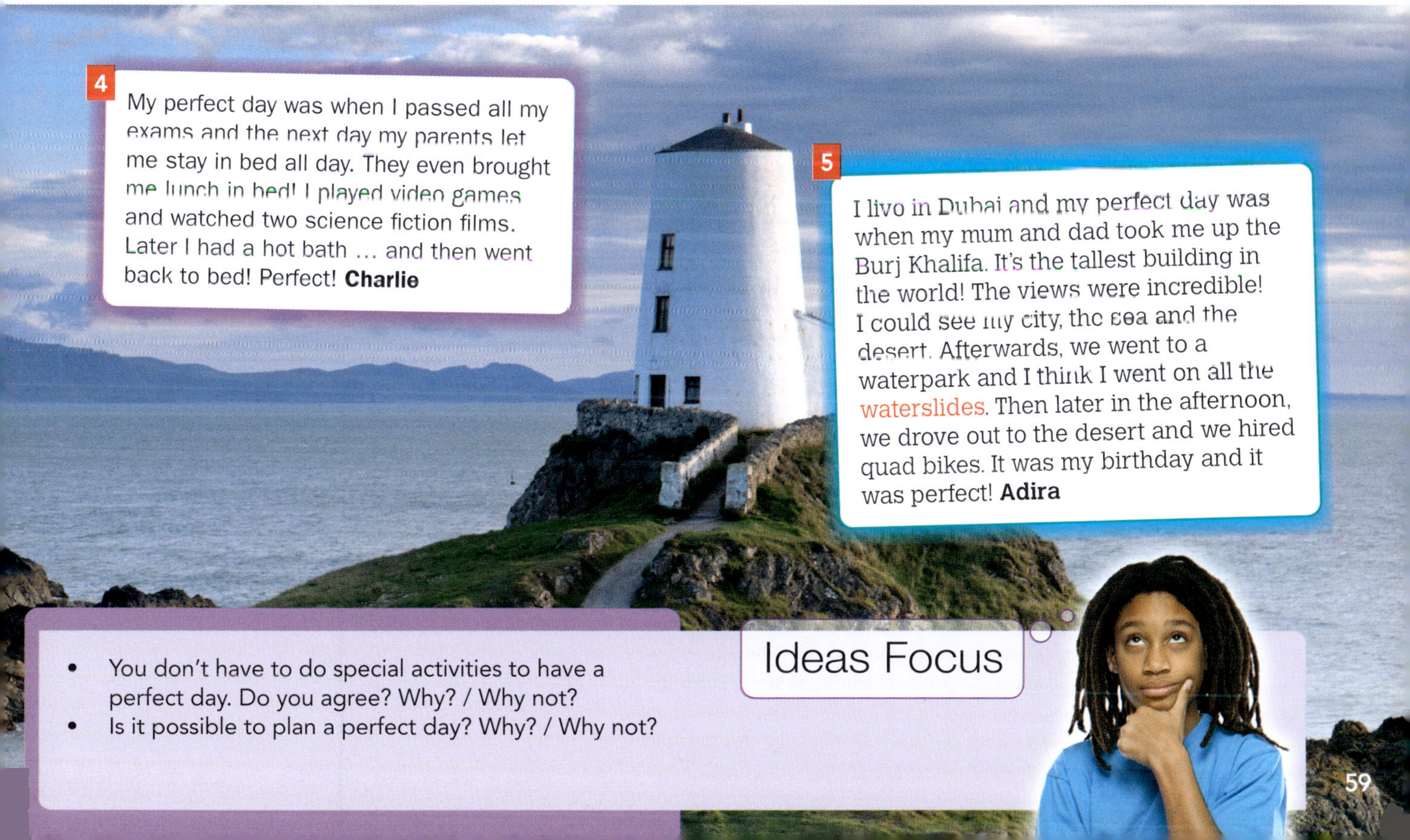

4 My perfect day was when I passed all my exams and the next day my parents let me stay in bed all day. They even brought me lunch in bed! I played video games and watched two science fiction films. Later I had a hot bath … and then went back to bed! Perfect! **Charlie**

5 I live in Dubai and my perfect day was when my mum and dad took me up the Burj Khalifa. It's the tallest building in the world! The views were incredible! I could see my city, the sea and the desert. Afterwards, we went to a waterpark and I think I went on all the waterslides. Then later in the afternoon, we drove out to the desert and we hired quad bikes. It was my birthday and it was perfect! **Adira**

Ideas Focus

- You don't have to do special activities to have a perfect day. Do you agree? Why? / Why not?
- Is it possible to plan a perfect day? Why? / Why not?

5 A Perfect Day

Vocabulary

A **Write the name of each park under the picture.**

snow park   waterpark   amusement park   wildlife park

1

2

3

4

B **Match each activity to a park in the photos in A. Write the number.**

skiing	☐	surfing	☐
seeing wild animals	☐	riding a Ferris wheel	☐
going on a water slide	☐	feeding baby llamas	☐
snowboarding	☐	going on a rollercoaster	☐

C **Work with a partner. Tell each other what type of park in A you like and why.**

"I like wildlife parks because ... "

D **Match a word from Box A with a word from Box B to make ten compound nouns. Write them in your notebook.**

A
sun   roller   hill
water   Ferris   wild
snow
foot   boat   fun

B
ride   animal   run
slide   rise   coaster
wheel   board
top   path

E **Complete the sentences with the correct verbs.**

attend   go   have   ride   take part   visit   walk   watch

1 It's a beautiful day. I want to ____________ on a boat ride on the river.
2 We can sit on the beach and ____________ the sunrise.
3 Why don't we ____________ an amusement park? They're great fun.
4 We can't ____________ the music concert tomorrow.
5 Let's ____________ a picnic on the hilltop!
6 They ____________ in the five km. fun run every year.
7 Make sure you ____________ on the footpath through the forest.
8 I don't want to ____________ on the rollercoaster. It's scary!

F **Circle the correct verb in the sentences.**

1 The children love having / taking an ice-cream on a hot day.
2 Selena has / takes lunch with her family every Sunday.
3 Phil is having / taking lots of photos so he remembers his perfect day.
4 Let's have / take turns to fly the kite.
5 We had / took a great day today. It was perfect!
6 Karima and Julie want to have / take a go on the Ferris wheel.

Exam Close-up

Using your knowledge of vocabulary

- There are many words that often go together. Sometimes one of the words in these word groups is taken out in the exam.
- Use your knowledge of word groups to help you fill in the gap.
- Make word maps to help you remember word groups.

G **Read the *Exam Close-up*. Then look at the word maps in H. Have you ever made your own word map?**

H **What verb can you write in word map 1 that goes with all the words? What words can you write in word map 2 that go with *take*?**

1

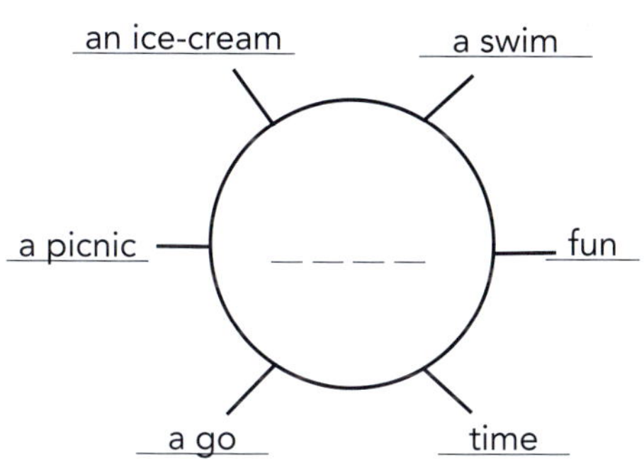

2

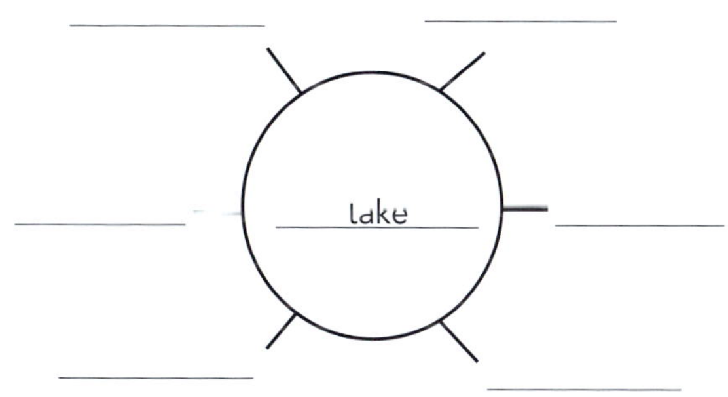

I **Now complete the *Exam Task*.**

Exam Task

Read the sentences about Tom's day out. Choose the best word (**A**, **B**, or **C**) for each answer.

1 A new skating rink ______ in our town last year.
  A opened B began C arrived
2 The first time I went ______ I was nervous.
  A skate B skated C skating
3 Now I go all the ______ with my friends.
  A way B day C time
4 We usually ______ two hours there when we go.
  A spend B waste C count
5 We always ______ a great time!
  A enjoy B have C pass

Ideas Focus

- Are outdoor activities always better than indoor activities? Why? / Why not?
- 'Amusement parks cost too much money. Going to a park with friends is better.' Do you agree? Why? / Why not?

Grammar

Past Simple *to be*

A Match the questions with the answers.

1 When was the wedding? ☐
2 Where were the students last week? ☐
3 Why were you late? ☐
4 Were there lots of people at the concert? ☐
5 Was Tim in the photo? ☐

a There was a lot of snow on the roads.
b No, there weren't.
c It was a year ago.
d No, he wasn't.
e They were on a school trip.

B Underline the Past Simple forms of the verb *to be* in A. Then complete the sentences.

1 The two Past Simple forms of the verb *to be* = ___________ and ___________
2 The two negative Past Simple forms of the verb *to be* = ___________ and ___________

Regular & Irregular Forms

C Read and underline all the verbs in the Past Simple.

Yesterday morning, we took our umbrella and walked in the rain. Of course, we wore our boots and jumped in every puddle. When the rain stopped, we went home and drank hot chocolate. I read a book and Helen studied for her music exam. I took my music exam two months ago and passed!

D Write examples from C for 1–4.

1 a regular Past Simple verb (ending *-ed*)
____
2 a regular Past Simple verb that changes a *-y* to *-ied*
____
3 a regular Past Simple verb that doubles the last letter before *-ed* ___________
4 an irregular Past Simple verb
____

Questions & Negatives

E Circle the verbs in the questions and negative forms. Notice how the verb is different in the answers.

A When did you buy those earrings?
B I bought them a week ago.

A Why didn't you and Gita eat at home last night?
B Because we ate in a new pizzeria called *Giovanni's*.

A Where did your friends go last weekend?
B They didn't go anywhere.

F Look again at the sentences in E. Circle the correct answers in 1–3.

1 For a Past Simple question, we use do / does / did + the infinitive verb.
2 For a negative in the Past Simple, we use don't / doesn't / didn't.
3 For questions and negatives in the Past Simple, we also use the Past Simple verb / infinitive verb.

Grammar Focus p. 164 (5.1)

G Complete the sentences with the correct form of the verb *to be*.

was wasn't were weren't

1 Nora ___________ at the festival because she ___________ sick.
2 There ___________ a lot of cars but there ___________ many bicycles.
3 'Why ___________ you here at five o'clock?' 'Because I ___________ on the bus.'
4 '___________ the museums open yesterday?' 'No, they ___________ closed.'
5 '___________ there any cake at the party?' 'Yes, there ___________.'
6 '___________ you happy as a child?' 'No, I ___________ really. I ___________ very shy.'

H Use the Past Simple form of the verbs to complete the sentences.

buy eat read stop study

1 They ___________ popcorn at the cinema.
2 My dad ___________ maths at university.
3 Jo ___________ a new pair of sunglasses.
4 I ___________ a bedtime story to my sister last night.
5 The music ___________ in the middle of the party!

I Circle the correct forms of the verbs to complete the dialogues.

1 A: When did the new snow park open / opened?
B: It open / opened three months ago.
2 A: Petra take / took part in the fun run yesterday!
B: I know. She run / ran ten kilometres.
3 A: What wild animals did the tourists see / saw?
B: They didn't see / saw any because the park be / was closed.

Grammar

Yes / No Questions & Short Answers

J Read the questions and answers. Complete the rules.

1 'Did they have a good time yesterday?' 'Yes, they did.'

2 'Did Robbie pass his exams last week?' 'Yes, he did.'

3 'Did you ride a quad bike last summer?' 'No, I didn't.'

- We use ______ at the beginning of a sentence to ask a *Yes/No* question.
- We use ______ or ______ without the verb in short answers.

Time Expressions

K Work with a partner and write eight examples of time expressions we use to talk about past time.

yesterday *morning*	a ______ ago
yesterday ______	a ______ ago
last ______	two ______ ago
last ______	three ______ ago
last ______	

Be careful

Watch out when you answer these questions in the past.

- 'What did you do last night?' 'I went to the cinema.' NOT: ~~I did go to the cinema.~~
- 'Did they eat ice cream?' 'Yes, they did.' NOT: ~~Yes, they ate.~~

Grammar Focus p. 164 (5.2)

L Look at the calendar. Complete the sentences with the correct information.

1 The date today is *23rd of January*. Yesterday it was ______.

2 The day today is ______. Four days ago it was ______.

3 Last month was ______. Five months ago it was ______.

4 This year I'm 13 years old. Two years ago I was ______.

5 This year is 2______. Fifteen years ago it was ______.

JANUARY 2017

SUN	MON	TUE	WED	THU	FRI	SAT
1	2	3	4	5	6	7
8	9	10	11	12	13	14
15	16	17	18	19	20	21
22	23	24	25	26	27	28
29	30	31				

M Read the *Exam Close-up*. Then read the email in the *Exam Task*.

N Now complete the *Exam Task*.

Exam Task

Read the teacher's email to parents about their children's school trip.

Write **ONE** word for each space.

email

Re: Our school trip

Dear Parents,

As you know, yesterday we (**1**) ______ the children to an exotic animal farm. It (**2**) ______ great fun and they (**3**) ______ seeing many different animals. There (**4**) ______ snakes, crocodiles, parrots and monkeys. The children studied these animals (**5**) ______ week at school so they knew all about them on their visit.

At lunchtime, we (**6**) ______ a picnic under the trees, (**7**) ______ to the river. It was Elliot's birthday two days (**8**) ______ so we celebrated with a cake. We took (**9**) ______ of photos during the day and I (**10**) ______ attaching the photos to the email for you to see. I hope you like them!

Mrs Walters

Exam Close-up

Checking verb tenses & endings

- Read the whole text first to get the general idea.
- Check which gaps need verbs and use expressions in the text to help you decide which tense to use.
- Check who the subject is (e.g. *I*, *you*, *he/she*, etc.) so your verb endings are correct.
- When you have finished, check that your answers make sense.

5 A Perfect Day

Listening

A **Work with a partner. Look at the photos and answer the questions.**

- What does each photo show?
- What do you think the photos all have in common?
- Which activity would you choose to do?

B 5.1 **Listen to Robert and Wendy. Tick the things they talk about.**

1 a day out with their grandchildren ☐
2 the day they met ☐
3 their wedding day ☐
4 dancing classes ☐
5 a bike ride ☐
6 the cinema ☐
7 a cruise in the Caribbean ☐
8 food ☐

C 5.1 **Listen again. Who says these lines? Write R for Robert or W for Wendy.**

1 It rained all day. ☐
2 We cycled along the river. ☐
3 We cycled up a hill. ☐
4 Fruit cakes were always my favourite. ☐
5 We saw a romantic film. ☐
6 We saw a science fiction film. ☐

D **Read the *Exam Close-up*. Then circle T (True) or F (False).**

In the exam …

1 you will hear two couples speaking. T F
2 you will hear five short conversations. T F
3 you need to look at four photos. T F
4 you need to look at three pictures and choose one. T F

E 5.2 **Now listen and complete the *Exam Task*.**

Exam Close-up

Noticing differences

- You will hear five short conversations. For each conversation there are three pictures. You need to choose ONE picture.
- Look carefully at the pictures and notice how they are similar or different.
- Think about how you can describe the differences.

Exam Task

You will hear five short conversations. You will hear each conversation twice. There is one question for each conversation. For each question, choose the right answer (**A**, **B** or **C**).

1 Where did the students go?

A 

B 

C 

2 How old is Fiona's brother?

A 1 B 3 C 13

3 What is Cathy's favourite colour?

A 

B 

C 

4 Which man is Harry's grandfather?

A 

B 

C 

5 When did the teenager go to the concert?

A Last week B Last month C Last summer

F 5.3 **Listen again and check your answers.**

Speaking

A **Look at the activities and decide whether you can do them in the country (Co), in the city (Ci) or both (B).**

1 go fishing ______
2 take photos ______
3 go horse riding ______
4 go sightseeing ______
5 go on a bus ______
6 take a backpack ______
7 buy souvenirs ______
8 go walking ______
9 have lunch at a restaurant ______
10 have a barbecue ______

A

A day in the city

B

A day in the country

B **Work with a partner. Look at the photos. What are the people doing? What other activities from A might they do?**

C **Read the two conversations. Then match each conversation to the correct photo (A or B). Which conversation gives more information?**

Conversation 1

A: What did you do on your perfect day?
B: I went camping by a lake with my cousins. It was beautiful! There was snow on the mountains!
A: Did you go skiing?
B: No, because there wasn't a lot of snow, but we went walking. We also went for a boat ride on the lake. My cousins caught some fish and we barbecued them on the fire for lunch. It was fantastic!
A: That sounds great!

Conversation 2

A: What did you do on your perfect day?
B: I went to a city.
A: Did you enjoy yourself?
B: Yes.
A: What did you do?
B: I went sightseeing.

D **Read the *Exam Close-up*. Then read the two conversations in C again and find examples of the following.**

1 Questions that ask for information.
2 A word used to give a reason.
3 A word used to add information.
4 Adjectives that show a feeling or opinion.

Exam Close-up

Extending your answers

- When talking about yourself, try to give more than one word answers.
- Give extra information and some details.
- Give reasons and examples.

E **Now work with a partner to complete the *Exam Task*. Use the *Useful Expressions* to help you.**

Exam Task

Student A: Use the prompts in 1 to ask **Student B** about his/her perfect day and tick a box in 2 every time you hear a new piece of information.

1

What did you ...? Did you ...?
Where did ...?
Who did you ...?
Why did you ...?

2

☐ ☐ ☐ ☐
☐ ☐ ☐ ☐
☐ ☐ ☐ ☐

Then change roles and **Student B** asks **Student A**. Who gave the most information?

Useful Expressions

Talking about activities with *to go*
We went on a boat ride.
I went camping.
I went for a walk.
We went sightseeing.
I went skiing / swimming / skating / cycling / horse riding.
We went on a ride in an amusement park.

Showing interest
That sounds interesting! / great!
How fantastic!
Did you enjoy yourself?

Ideas Focus

- Photos are the best way to remember events in your life. Do you agree? Why? / Why not?
- Would your perfect day be in the country or in a city? Why?

Writing: a diary

A

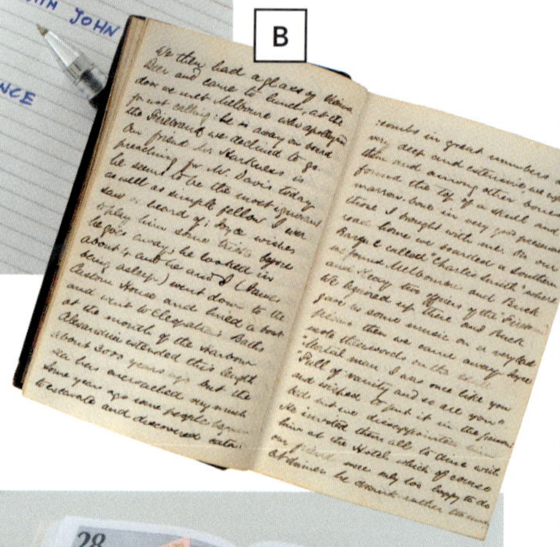
B

Learning Focus

Adding details

- Make your descriptions of an event interesting by adding details.
- Include adjectives and describe how you felt about something, (e.g. *It was amazing!*).
- Give reasons why something was special.
- Remember to use *first, then, next, after that, finally* to show the order in which you did things.

C

A **Look at the photos of the three diaries. Match each diary with a description of how it is used. Write the letters.**

1 To write about experiences and feelings. ☐
2 To remember to do things. ☐
3 As an organiser for appointments and meetings. ☐

B **Complete the spellings for the adjectives. Then choose an adjective to complete the sentences below.**

___ m ___ z ___ ng   ___ ncr ___ d ___ bl ___
f ___ nt ___ st ___ c   w ___ nd ___ rf ___ l
gr ___ ___ t   th ___ b ___ st

1 I flew in a hot air balloon. It was ____________________!
2 I went skiing for the first time. It was ____________________!
3 I loved the show. It was ____________________!
4 I came first in the competition. It was ____________________!

C **Add details and some adjectives to make these sentences more interesting. Use your imagination.**

1 I visited a castle.
"I visited a really interesting castle on a hill. The views were great!"

2 I rode a horse.
____

3 I went to a beach.
____

4 My parents bought me a dog.
____

5 I ate cake.
____

D **Read and circle the TWO correct options in each sentence.**

1 When we write a diary we can talk about our emails / experiences / feelings.
2 We use diaries to remember important days / video games / moments.
3 We can use the past simple / present simple / past continuous to write about what we did.
4 We can use words like *incredible / how / the best* to describe how we feel.

E **Complete the diary page using the Past Simple tense. Then underline the adjectives and circle the words that show the order of events.**

Today I **(1)** __________ (have) the best day ever! Mum and dad **(2)** __________ (take) me and Alex out for the afternoon. First, we **(3)** __________ (stop) for tea and cakes. I love chocolate cake! Then they **(4)** __________ (give) me a present, a new camera, because I **(5)** __________ (pass) all my exams. It's amazing! Next, they **(6)** __________ (drive) us to a field full of hot air balloons … and this was another present, a ride in the sky! It **(7)** __________ (be) incredible! The views **(8)** __________ (be) fantastic and I took lots of photos with my new camera. It was a very special day!

F **Read the *Exam Close-up* then complete activity G.**

G **Write a draft of your own diary page about a special day. Use the *Useful Expressions* to help you. When you have finished, read your draft. Have you remembered to:**

- use different verbs and the correct tenses? ☐
- use words to show the order of events? ☐
- use adjectives to describe how you felt? ☐
- include details? ☐
- use the *Useful Expressions*? ☐

Exam Close-up

Planning a draft

- Write a draft of the message on rough paper first.
- Answer the three questions simply.
- Read your draft and make any changes.

H **Now complete the *Exam Task*.**

Exam Task

Read the email from your grandmother.

email

Re: School trip

Hello there!

I wanted to write and ask you about your school trip.

Where did you go yesterday? What did you see? What did you do?

Write and tell me all about it! I hope you have photos you can show me when I see you!

Lots of love,

Granny

Write an email to your grandmother and answer the questions. Write **25–35** words.

Useful Expressions

Expressing positive feelings
It was amazing!
It was great!
It was incredible!
It was the best!
I loved it!
It was really special.

Giving reasons
It was brilliant because …
It was fantastic because …
I want to go there again because …

5 Laughter Yoga!

Before you watch

A **What do the three photos have in common? Tick.**

1

2

3

Everyone …

1 is laughing. ☐
2 is talking. ☐
3 has a problem. ☐
4 is an adult. ☐
5 is doing yoga. ☐
6 is enjoying themselves. ☐

While you watch

B **Watch the video. Decide if these statements are T (True) or F (False).**

1 Laughter yoga is only for children. ☐
2 You can do laughter yoga in big groups. ☐
3 Laughter is only good for you in hospital. ☐
4 Laughter is one way people communicate. ☐
5 Children laugh as soon as they are born. ☐
6 Laughter helps a mother and child communicate. ☐

After you watch

C **Complete the summary of the video below using these words.**

born energy fun healthy heart months parent people

Laughter yoga is a lot of **(1)** __________! It helps people to feel good and positive. Laughing is a **(2)** __________ activity because it keeps our blood vessels and **(3)** __________ in good condition. It's the same as taking medicine!

Laughter is also a way of communicating and sharing positive **(4)** __________. It is a social activity that connects us to others and brings **(5)** __________ together.

We don't laugh when we are **(6)** __________. We start laughing when we are about three to four **(7)** __________ old. It is one of the first ways a child communicates with a **(8)** __________.

Ideas Focus

- Would you like to try laughter yoga? Why? / Why not?
- 'It's important to laugh *with* people not *at* people.' Do you agree?

6 Welcome To The Jungle

Reading: matching, reading the completed dialogue
Vocabulary: nouns and adjectives for animals, word completion, identifying the topic area
Grammar: comparative adjectives, making comparisons, using adjectives, multiple-choice cloze, reading before & after
Listening: multiple-matching, listening for false information
Speaking: asking & answering about pets, talking about pets, giving reasons
Writing: a fact file, writing facts, expressing animal facts, asking about animals, checking your spelling

An imperial moth hiding in leaves at Yasuni National Park, Ecuador

6 Welcome To The Jungle

Reading

A **Work with a partner. Look at the photos. Which is the strangest?**

B **Read the comments. Match them to the photos. Do you agree?**

1 It looks like a monkey! ☐
2 It looks like a leaf! ☐
3 It looks like a ball! ☐
4 It looks like a star! ☐
5 It looks like a butterfly! ☐
6 It looks like a snake! ☐

I don't agree. I think it looks like a small bear.

C **Try to match each animal with its photo in A.**

1 The Southern three-banded armadillo. ______
2 The snake-necked turtle. ______
3 The sunbittern. ______
4 The leaf-tailed gecko. ______
5 Linne's two-toed sloth. ______
6 The greenbottle blue tarantula. ______

D **Read the introduction. Why does Joel Sartore want to photograph animals in zoos?**

E **Write an animal from C as a heading for paragraphs 1–6.**

A

B

C

D

E

F

Word Focus

endangered species: a type of animal that is close to disappearing from our planet

camouflage: a disguise to help an animal hide

predator: an animal that kills and eats other animals

prey: an animal that other animals attack to eat

poison: when you harm or kill a person or animal with a substance

claws: sharp nails on an animal's foot

UNUSUAL ANIMALS!

Photographer, Joel Sartore, is visiting zoos around the world to take pictures of 12,000 endangered species as part of a new project called PhotoArk. He photographs the animals up close on black or white backgrounds because he wants to get our attention and make a small animal look as big as an elephant! He is photographing as many animals as he can before they disappear and hopes his photos make people want to save these species.

1 ______________________
This is a reptile that is very good at hiding. Its home is in Madagascar, and it is not easy to see with its amazing camouflage. When it is in danger from a predator, it can lose its tail to trick the predator and help it get away.

2 ______________________
This mammal is native to South America. It is a herbivore and it's nocturnal, so it comes out at night. It moves very slowly, just one or two metres a day, then rests for 20 hours! Its toes help it to hang upside down in trees.

3 ______________________
This animal lives in the waterways of Australia. Its neck is as long as its shell and helps it to get food. It has webbed feet, the same as a duck, and these help it to swim.

4 ______________________
This spider is native to Venezuela. It is very colourful with bright blue legs, and turquoise and orange body hairs. It is bigger than an average spider and some can be 15cm long. They are carnivores and like to jump on their prey to poison it.

F **Read the *Exam Close-up*. Then read the dialogue in the *Exam Task* and think about possible responses. Don't look at the options A–H yet.**

G **Now complete the *Exam Task*. Remember to read through the whole dialogue after you have chosen your answers.**

Exam Close-up

Reading the completed dialogue

- Think about possible responses for the dialogue before looking at the options.
- Make sure you read the line after the gap as well as the line before.
- After you choose your answers, read through the whole dialogue and check that it makes sense.

Exam Task

Complete the dialogue between two friends. What does Chloe say to Liam? Choose the correct answer **A – H**. There are three letters you do not need to use.

Liam: Look! There's a photo competition in the local newspaper.
Chloe: (1) ______
Liam: Yes, you have to take an interesting animal photo.
Chloe: (2) ______
Liam: No, it must be an animal that doesn't live with you.
Chloe: (3) ______
Liam: Good idea! There are birds and frogs there.
Chloe: (4) ______
Liam: No, I haven't. Have you?
Chloe: (5) ______
Liam: Oh no!

A No, mine's broken.
B Can I take my camera?
C Which newspaper?
D Let's look by the river.
E That sounds interesting!
F I don't like animals.
G I've got lots of photos of my dog!
H Have you got a camera?

H **These words are underlined in the text. Find them think about what they might mean and then circle the correct animals.**

1 reptile snake / dolphin
2 mammal chicken / elephant
3 herbivore crocodile / horse
4 carnivore lion / giraffe
5 amphibian frog / tortoise

5 ______

This animal is native to Brazil and Bolivia. Its hard shell bends so that it can roll up into a ball for protection. It has a scaly shell but it is a mammal. It can walk on its back legs with only its front claws touching the ground.

6 ______

This bird has long legs and a long neck, but a small head. The red and black feathers on its open wings look like eyes. This helps the bird to look scary to its predators. It likes to feed on fish and small amphibians.

Ideas Focus

- Which animal would you choose to be? Why?
- Is it better to take photos of animals in their natural habitat? Why? / Why not?

6 Welcome To The Jungle

Vocabulary

A **Match the types of animal (1–5) with the correct picture. Write your own example of each type of animal.**

1 ☐ amphibian: ______________

2 ☐ bird: ______________

3 ☐ fish: ______________

4 ☐ mammal: ______________

5 ☐ reptile: ______________

A

B

C

D

E

B **Work with a partner. Do you know these words? Try to label these photos with the words.**

beak claw feather fin fur shell scales skin tail wing

C **Write sentences to describe five different animals using words from B.**

A dolphin has a tail and fin.

1 ______________________________

2 ______________________________

3 ______________________________

4 ______________________________

5 ______________________________

D **Cross out the wrong form of the plurals. The first one is done for you.**

1 The farm has six ~~gooses~~ / geese and 20 ~~sheeps~~ / sheep.
2 Help! There are two mice / mouses in the kitchen.
3 We sometimes ride horseses / horses when we're on holiday.
4 Beeses / Bees and butterflies / butterflys are important for flowers.
5 Rabbits' teeth / tooths never stop growing.
6 Ostrichs / Ostriches can run faster than you or me!
7 Do monkies / monkeys have four feet / foots?
8 Cows have babies / babys called calfs / calves.

E Complete the information with the words.

amphibian babies bodies feet finger skin tail water

Frog Facts

A frog is an **(1)** ________________, which means it can live on land and in **(2)** ________________. A frog lays its soft eggs in water but when the **(3)** ________________ are born they don't look like the adult frog.

Baby frogs are called *tadpoles* and have a big head and a long **(4)** ________________. As they grow, their tail disappears and they develop legs and **(5)** ________________. They also have lungs so they can breathe outside of the water. They can drink water through their **(6)** ________________. There are many different types of frog. Some are smaller than the end of your **(7)** ________________ and some have very colourful **(8)** ________________ but are very poisonous!

F Write an animal from below next to each description. Then add your own animal to each description. Compare with a partner.

puppy leopard frog snake tarantula

1 It's furry and cute: ________________, ________________
2 It's dangerous: ________________, ________________
3 It's poisonous: ________________, ________________
4 It's fast: ________________, ________________
5 It's ugly and scary: ________________, ________________
6 It's tiny: ________________, ________________
7 It's colourful: ________________, ________________
8 It's heavy: ________________, ________________

G Read the *Exam Close-up*. Then read the *Exam Task* and underline the topic.

H Now complete the *Exam Task*.

Exam Task

Read the descriptions of some words for animals. What is the word for each one? The first letter is already there. There is one space for each letter in the word.

1 This type of animal has scales and fins. f _ _ _
2 This type of animal has wings and feathers. b _ _ _
3 Snails and turtles have this. s _ _ _
4 This animal can live on land and in water. f _ _ _
5 Dogs and cats have this on their bodies. f _ _

Exam Close-up

Identifying the topic area

- Underline the topic in the instructions.
- Read the definitions of the words carefully.
- Make sure all your answers connect to the topic.
- Check your spelling.

Ideas Focus

- Which animal would you choose as a pet? Why?
- Some people have exotic animals like snakes and tarantulas. Do you think they make good pets? Why? / Why not?

Grammar

Comparative Adjectives

A Read the sentences. Circle the adjective and underline the comparative adjectives. The first one is done for you.

1 A bee is small. It's smaller than a bird. ______
2 A goose is noisy. It's noisier than a duck. ______
3 An ostrich is big. It's bigger than a chicken. ______
4 A snake is dangerous. It's more dangerous than a tortoise. ______
5 A cat is a good pet. But I think a dog is better than a cat. ______
6 I think tarantulas are bad pets. They're worse than rats! ______

B Match the rules with a sentence in A. One rule matches two sentences.

a change *-y* to *-i* and add *-er*
b it's irregular
c add *more* before the adjective and *than* after the adjective
d just add *-er*
e double the last consonant and add *-er*

C Look at the sentences in A again. Are these sentences true (T) or false (F)?

1 We use *than* before each comparative adjective. ______
2 We use *than* after each comparative adjective. ______
3 We use *more* before all adjectives in the comparative. ______
4 We use *more* before adjectives with three syllables or more in the comparative. ______

D Read the sentences. Then choose the correct words to complete the rules.

A cow is **as** big **as** a horse.
A cat is **not as** big **as** a lion.

1 We use *as* + adjective + *as* to show that two things are the same / different.
2 We use not *as* + adjective + *as* to should that two things are the same / different.

Grammar Focus pp. 164 & 165 (6.1 to 6.2)

E Complete the sentences with *as … as* or *not as … as*.

1 A tiger is ______ dangerous ______ a lion.
2 A butterfly is ______ scary______ a tarantula.
3 A cat is ______ friendly ______ a dog.
4 A hippopotamus is ______ heavy ______ a rhinoceros.
5 A crocodile is ______ soft ______ a rabbit.
6 A tortoise is ______ fast ______ a horse.

F Complete the sentences with a comparative adjective and an animal of your choice.

1 A polar bear is ______ (cute) than a/an ______.
2 A tiger is ______ (scary) than a/an ______.
3 An elephant is ______ (heavy) than a ______.
4 A giraffe has a ______ (long) neck than a/an ______.
5 A parrot is ______ (colourful) than a/an ______.
6 A zebra is ______ (fast) than a/an ______.
7 A brown bear is______ (dangerous) than a/an ______.
8 A polar bear is a ______ (good) swimmer than a/an ______.

Grammar

Making Comparisons

G Read the two examples. Answer the questions.

a Molly's dog is the same as my dog!
b Amphibians are different from/to reptiles.

1 Which sentence shows that two things are not the same? ______
2 Which sentence shows that two things are the same? ______

Using Adjectives

H Underline the verbs and then complete the rules.

1 It looks tiny.
2 It looks like a bee.
3 It sounds beautiful.
4 It sounds like a bird.
5 It feels hard and dry.
6 It feels like scales.

- We use adjectives after the verb to say how something looks, ________, and ________.
- We use *looks like*, ________, or ________ + *noun* to compare something new to something you know.

I Read the sentences and then choose the correct word to complete the rule.

1 How tall is a giraffe?
2 How big is an elephant?
3 How old is your tortoise?
4 How long is a killer whale?
5 How fast is a cheetah?

- We use *How* + comparative adjective / adjective to ask for more information.

J Match these answers with a question in I.

a It can run up to 120 kilometres an hour.
b It's about 30 metres long!
c It can grow up to six metres tall.
d It's very big, but not as big as the blue whale.
e It's ten years old.

Grammar Focus p. 165 (6.3 to 6.4)

K Circle the correct words.

1 Birds are different from / as mammals.
2 The eagle's claws feel like / very sharp.
3 Listen! It sounds as / like a bear.
4 How / What fast is a racehorse?
5 A crocodile is as dangerous as / than a lion.
6 Is a parrot's beak the same from / as a toucan's beak?

L Read the *Exam Close-up*. Then read the text in the *Exam Task* to get the general idea.

M Now complete the *Exam Task*.

Exam Close-up

Reading before & after

- Read the whole text to get the general idea before you look at the options.
- Read the whole text after choosing your answers.
- Make sure the text makes sense.

Exam Task

Read the description of two birds. Choose the best word (A, B or C) for each space.

Puffins and penguins

Last summer I heard puffins on an island in Scotland. They sound **(1)** ______ soft police sirens! People say that a puffin **(2)** ______ a penguin but it's different **(3)** ______ a penguin in many ways. A puffin's beak is more colourful **(4)** ______ a penguin's beak; it's bright orange, yellow and red. Its wings are **(5)** ______ than a penguin's wings because it can fly. Puffins can flap their wings up to 400 times a minute … that's really fast! **(6)** ______ fast can you flap your arms? It's not **(7)** ______ easy as you think! Penguins have got heavier bodies than puffins, so they can't fly. A puffin can swim, like a penguin, but it can't stay as long as a penguin under water. All the same, they are **(8)** ______ swimmers than many other birds!

	A	B	C
1	likes	like	as
2	looks	look like	looks like
3	from	as	-
4	than	that	to
5	strong	stronger	more strong
6	What	How	that
7	as	-	more
8	good	better	best

Listening

A **Work with a partner. Look at the photo and answer the questions.**

1 What part of the world is this?
2 What is the name of the animal?
3 Why do you think these animals are useful?

Peruvian girls in traditional clothing, Chinchero, Peru

B 6.1 **Listen and circle the words you hear.**

1 Feel that fur / shell! How hard / soft.
2 Listen to that bird / bee! How noisy / lovely!
3 Look at that gecko / snake! How beautiful / scary!
4 Look at that dog / rabbit! What cute / long ears!
5 Listen to that mammal / reptile! What an ugly / a strange sound!

C 6.2 **Read the questions. Listen and tick the correct answer.**

1 How far does the sloth move?
a one metre a day ☐ b one kilometre a day ☐

2 How old is the dog?
a eleven months old ☐ b eleven years old ☐

3 How heavy is a baby elephant?
a 3,500 kilograms ☐ b 6,000 kilograms ☐

4 How tall is his brother?
a one metre twenty ☐ b one metre twenty-five ☐

D **Read the *Exam Close-up*. Underline the question in the *Exam Task*.**

E 6.3 **Now listen and complete the *Exam Task*.**

Exam Task

Listen to two students talking. Why are these animals important? For questions **1 – 5**, write a letter **A – G** next to each item. You will hear the conversation twice.

1 Camel	☐	**A**	For riding
2 Horse	☐	**B**	For racing
3 Bear	☐	**C**	For milk
4 Alpaca	☐	**D**	For scarves
5 Eagle	☐	**E**	For a special gift
		F	For coats
		G	For food

F 6.4 **Listen again and check your answers.**

Exam Close-up

Listening for false information

- When you listen, notice any false information you hear. The speaker will correct it and this will help you choose your answer.
- Underline the question in the instructions. Remember the answers will come in the same order as the numbers.

Speaking

A **Work with a partner. Use words from the two lists to compare the pets in the photos. Give reasons.**

big cute dangerous friendly funny heavy scary small soft

dog cat rabbit parrot snake mouse

A: A mouse is cuter than a snake.
B: Why?
A: Because it's small and soft!

B **Work with a partner. Read sentences 1–5. Which pet from A do you think is being talked about? Do you agree with the sentences? Why? / Why not?**

1 This is a good pet for a grandmother because it's good company.
2 This is a good pet for a young child because it's fun and soft, and it's not dangerous.
3 I think this is a good pet for a teenager because it also sleeps a lot!
4 This is a good pet for a busy person because it doesn't need a lot of exercise.
5 I think this is a good pet for you because it's easy to look after.

Yes, I agree. / No, I don't agree. I think X is a better pet because...

C **Read the *Exam Close-up*. Then work with a partner and take turns to tell each other your favourite animal and why you like it.**

D **Work with a partner and complete the *Exam Task*. Use the *Useful Expressions* to help you.**

Exam Close-up

Giving reasons

- Extend your answers by giving reasons with *because*.
- Practise explaining why you like, do or think something.
- You can use *I agree / I don't agree* to respond to other people's reasons and opinions.

Useful Expressions

Talking about pets

It's easy to look after.
It doesn't need a lot of attention.
It needs exercise.
It's fun / soft / cute.
It's not dangerous.
It's good company.
It's a good pet because …
It's better than … because …

Exam Task

1 **Student A** look at some information about your pet.

- goldfish called Bubbles
- smaller than an orange
- swims round and round
- fun to watch / relaxing

Bubbles

Student B turn to page 183. You don't know what pet to get. Ask **Student A** questions about his / her pet.

2 **Student B** look at some information about your pet.

- rabbit called Tobey
- very easy to look after
- sleep / box in bedroom
- eat / vegetables and seeds
- soft and warm / good company

Tobey

Student A turn to page 183. You are going to look after **Student B**'s pet. Ask questions about what you need to do.

Ideas Focus

- What's the perfect pet for you? Why?
- Do all animals make good pets? Why? / Why not?

6 Welcome To The Jungle

Baby mountain gorilla in a nest. Rwanda, Africa

Writing: a fact file

Learning Focus

Writing facts

- Make sure that any facts you write are correct.
- Use the Present Simple to talk about things that are true.
- In formal writing, don't use contractions, i.e. use *It has got* NOT *It's got.*
- Often when we include facts in our writing we explain why something is the way it is. We can use *because* to give a reason. For example: *A puffin needs strong wings because it uses them to fly and swim.*

A **Which of these interesting facts did you already know? Tick the boxes.**

1 Did you know that the heart of a blue whale is as big as a car? ☐
2 Did you know that hippos are born under water? ☐
3 Did you know that gorillas sleep in a nest? ☐
4 Did you know that a crocodile carries her babies in her mouth? ☐
5 Did you know that a baby kangaroo is as small as a paper clip? ☐
6 Did you know that some butterflies have ears on their wings? ☐

B **Write your own interesting fact about anything you like. How many of your classmates know it?**

Did you know that ____?

C **Complete this description using information from the Fact File and the *Useful Expressions* box to help you. Use *because* where possible.**

The panther chameleon

A panther chameleon is a (1) ____________. It has a green and yellow (2) ____________ and big (3) ____________. It lives in the (4) ____________ of Madagascar. We know it is a carnivore (5) ____________ it eats crickets, worms and other insects. It (6) ____________ 63 centimetres long. A male panther chameleon (7) ____________ between 140 and 180 grams, and a female (8) ____________ between 60 and 100 grams. Chameleons are interesting (9) ____________ their tongues are as long as their bodies! They have a long tongue (10) ____________ they need it to catch insects.

FACT FILE

NAME:	Panther chameleon
TYPE OF ANIMAL:	Reptile
DESCRIPTION:	Green and yellow but changes colour. Big eyes.
COUNTRY:	Forests of Madagascar.
ANIMAL DIET:	Carnivore.
SIZE:	63 cms long.
WEIGHT:	Male: 140 – 180 grams Female: 60 – 100 grams
INTERESTING FACT:	A chameleon's tongue is as long as its body! This helps it to catch insects.

D Choose an animal. Do some research and complete the Fact File.

FACT FILE

NAME:	
TYPE OF ANIMAL:	
DESCRIPTION:	
COUNTRY:	
ANIMAL DIET:	
SIZE:	
WEIGHT:	
INTERESTING FACT:	

Useful Expressions

Expressing animal facts

It is native to …

It lives in …

It has (got) …

It weighs … kilograms.

It is … centimetres long / tall.

It can run … kilometres per hour.

Asking about animals

How long can it live?

What does it eat?

Is it poisonous / dangerous?

How big / long / heavy is it?

E Read the *Exam Close-up*. Then look back at the text in C. Can you find any words that are difficult to spell? Write them in your notebook.

F Now complete the *Exam Task*. Remember to check your spelling.

Exam Close-up

Checking your spelling

- Check your spelling after you transfer information from the two texts; it's easy to make mistakes when you are in a hurry.
- Review irregular forms of verbs and plural nouns.

Exam Task

Read the advert and webpage. Fill in the information in the Fact File.

Looking for a new home

Looking for a new home for
Slinky my corn snake because I'm moving to Italy.

She's three years old.

She's 100 cms long and isn't poisonous.

She's easy to look after if you don't have a lot of free time.

She eats mice.

Slinky also has a cage/aquarium.

If interested, please contact: 5022 3741.

FACT FILE

ANIMAL:	Corn snake
COUNTRY / CONTINENT:	(1)
COLOUR:	(2)
MAXIMUM AGE:	(3)
SIZE:	(4)
DIET:	(5)

Corn snakes

Corn snakes (or red rat snakes as they are also called) are reptiles that are native to North America.
They are very pretty with their orange scales.
They are very timid animals and are not dangerous.
They live in fields and forests and they like climbing.
Corn snakes can live for between five and eight years.

Video

6 Tip of my Tongue!

Before you watch

A **How are these body parts important for the panther chameleon? Label the photo.**

tongue foot scales eye

While you watch

B **Watch the video. Circle the correct information.**

1 The panther chameleon can turn its head / eye 180°.
2 The panther chameleon's tongue is long and fast / poisonous.
3 The Komodo dragon is the world's largest reptile / amphibian.
4 It uses its tongue / skin to smell its prey.
5 The horned lizard loves scorpions / ants.
6 The horned lizard sprays blood from its eye / mouth to protect itself.

After you watch

C **Complete the summary of the video below using these words.**

blood deserts island Madagascar prey reptiles smell snake's

Some **(1)** ____________ have amazing ways of hunting their **(2)** ____________ and protecting themselves.

In **(3)** ____________, the panther chameleon can easily see bugs and has a long tongue with a sticky tip to capture them.

The Komodo dragon lives on the **(4)** ____________ of Komodo in Indonesia. It has a tongue like a **(5)** ____________ tongue. It uses this to **(6)** ____________ its prey, which can sometimes be 2 or 3 kms away.

The horned lizard lives in the **(7)** ____________ of North America. It is also good at protecting itself from wild animals. It can spray its enemy with **(8)** ____________.

Ideas Focus

- Which reptile would you like to see in real life? Why?
- 'Animals are cleverer than humans.' Do you agree?

Review 3 Units 5 & 6

Vocabulary

A Complete the sentences with a compound noun. Choose a word from each box.

boat foot fun hill snow sun wild

animal board path rise run top trip

1 My favourite ________ ________ is the polar bear.
2 Aaron's school is organising a 7 km ________ ________ in the park.
3 Why don't we go on a ________ ________ to the island of Formentera?
4 We can walk along the ________ that goes round the lake.
5 I love watching the ________ in the morning and the sunset in the evening.
6 You can take your own ________ to the snow park.
7 The Romans built the castle on the ________ so it was difficult to attack.

B Circle the correct words.

1 Ellie visited / took part in a spelling competition and won!
2 What do you prefer? Going / Attending on a roller coaster or a water slide?
3 Did you take part / have a good time at the water park?
4 I'm hot. Let's have / take an ice cream.
5 The children are having / taking turns to go on the water slide.
6 I want to take / go on the London Eye. It's an enormous Ferris Wheel.
7 Two thousand people attended / visited the concert last night!

C Complete the words in the sentences.

1 A fish swims by using its f_ _ _ and t_ _ _.
2 Most mammals have f_ _ to keep their bodies warm.
3 A bird has a b_ _ _ for a mouth and f_ _ _ _ _ _ _.
4 W_ _ _ _ help a bird fly.
5 A reptile, like a snake or crocodile, has s_ _ _ _ _ all over its body.
6 A frog is an amphibian and has moist or wet s_ _ _.
7 An owl has sharp c_ _ _ _ to help it catch small animals.

D Circle the correct words.

1 A snake's bite can be ugly / poisonous and kill you!
2 Did you know that an ostrich is a furry / fast animal?
3 I don't like roller coasters. They are too scary / fun for me!
4 Looking after animals in a wildlife park can be a dangerous / ugly job.
5 Chris has got a new white rabbit. It's so colourful / cute.
6 My dog, Sasha, is so tiny / heavy, I can't pick her up anymore!

E Write the plural of the words in brackets.

1 Two ________ (baby) born at the same time are called 'twins'.
2 ________ (butterfly) always visit my mum's garden.
3 The dentist said my ________ (tooth) were very healthy!
4 There are lots of crabs on ________ (beach) in the morning.
5 The ________ (mouse) lived under the farm ________ (house).
6 Can we have a rest? My ________ (foot) hurt.
7 My perfect day was full of ________ (surprise).
8 Three ________ (bus) go to the amusement park every hour.

Review 3 Units 5 & 6

Grammar

A Complete the conversation with the correct form of the verb in brackets.

A: Hi, Gaby. Did you (**1**) ________ (have) a good weekend.
B: Yes, I (**2**) ________ (have) a fantastic weekend.
A: What did you (**3**) ________ (do)?
B: I (**4**) ________ (go) to a beautiful hotel in the countryside to celebrate my granny's 80th birthday.
A: (**5**) ________ (be) it a surprise?
B: Yes! My granny (6) ________ (arrive) with my granddad and we (**7**) ________ (be) all at the hotel waiting. My granny didn't (**8**) ________ (stop) smiling the whole weekend.
A: Did you (**9**) ________ (take) lots of photos?
B: My brother (**10**) ________ (take) lots of photos. It was great. We (**11**) ________ (dance), (**12**) ________ (eat) lots of cake and (**13**) ________ (drink) champagne.
A: It sounds like you (**14**) ________ (enjoy) yourselves!

B Write the sentences using the comparative form of the adjective.

1 a plane / fast / ship ________
2 a computer / heavy / a smartphone ________
3 a blue whale / big / a dolphin ________
4 a lion / dangerous / cat ________
5 a waterpark / good / a snow park ________
6 a rollercoaster / scary / a waterslide ________

C Choose the correct answer, a, b, or c.

1 Lucy has the same type of dog ___ you.
a that **b** than **c** as

2 My school is different ___ my sister's school.
a from **b** than **c** -

3 For me, Mondays are worse ___ Fridays.
a to **b** than **c** that

4 A tree frog is ___ poisonous as a snake.
a so **b** as **c** same

5 Driving is ___ so easy as riding a bike.
a not **b** as **c** more

6 ___ fast can an ostrich run?
a Where **b** How much **c** How

7 'What does your new pet look ___ ?' 'It's tiny, cute and furry.'
a as **b** about **c** like

8 '___ you like to go on a picnic on Sunday?' 'That's a great idea!'
a Do **b** Would **c** Shall

9 '___ you like dogs?' 'No, I prefer cats.'
a Do **b** Did **c** Would

10 Bryan ___ going to wildlife parks. He loves wild animals.
a are **b** like **c** likes

7 Invent It!

Reading: right, wrong, doesn't say, checking information
Vocabulary: nouns, verbs & adjectives for objects and devices
Grammar: superlative adjectives, *the one* & *the ones*, expressing purpose, *will* for predictions
Listening: gap-fill, spelling correctly
Speaking: asking & answering about a science fair, giving directions, listening for the question word
Writing: captions, adding information in captions, expressing purpose, completing forms with more detailed information

Robotic jockeys are used in camel racing events. Bidiya, Oman

7 Invent It!

Reading

A Write the correct words under the inventions.

computer car telephone washing machine light bulb camera

A

B

C

D

E

F

B Now match the descriptions (1–6) with the photos in A. Write the correct letter.

1 It takes us from one place to another. ______
2 It takes photographs and helps us remember. ______
3 It washes our clothes. ______
4 It helps us see in the dark. ______
5 We use it for talking to people. ______
6 We use it for looking at the Internet. ______

C Number the inventions in A order of usefulness. Compare your answers with a partner.

"I think B is the most useful because ..."

D Quickly read the article. What do you think is the most interesting invention? Why?

Word Focus

eco-friendly: good for the environment or planet
preserve: keep something fresh
resist: not be harmed by something
biodegradable: living organisms can break it down
hiccups: a repeated sound in your throat when you eat something too quickly
earthquake: a sudden and violent movement of the earth

Young Inventors

Tenith Adithyaa, a teenager from India, won a competition for his eco-friendly invention. Banana leaves normally go bad after two to three days. Tenith invented technology, using UV and other techniques, to preserve the leaves for a year without any chemicals. The leaves become stronger and can resist the hottest temperatures. Tenith thinks that one day the leaves will be used instead of plastic for making plates, cups and containers. The leaves are also biodegradable which means that, unlike plastic, they won't harm the planet.

In 2012, 13-year-old **Mallory Kievman** invented a cure for hiccups. She had a lot of hiccups when she was a child and hated them. She wanted to find a way to stop them and finally invented a special lollipop made of sugar and cider vinegar. The lollipop company thinks that people will love them.

E **Read the *Exam Close-up*. Then, using the text in D, look at the sentences and tick the information you know and put a cross next to the information you don't know.**

We know …

1 … David is a teenager. ☐
2 … Tenith's nationality. ☐
3 … where Mallory is from. ☐
4 … the lollipop ingredients. ☐
5 … how a robotic earthworm can help people. ☐
6 … the first place people used a robotic earthworm. ☐
7 … that Mallory hated having the hiccups. ☐

Exam Close-up

Checking information

- It is important to check that the information in the sentences is in the text.
- Sometimes, some information is NOT in the text. You should then choose 'Doesn't say'.
- Compare each sentence carefully with the information in the text before choosing your answer.

F **Now complete the *Exam Task*.**

Exam Task

Read the article about three young inventors. Are sentences **1–7 'Right' (A)** or **'Wrong' (B)**? If there is not enough information to answer **'Right' (A)** or **'Wrong' (B)**, choose **'Doesn't say' (C)**.

1 Tenith's invention is good for the planet. ☐
2 Technology helped the banana leaves last longer. ☐
3 A company is making plastic cups and plates from the banana leaves. ☐
4 Mallory is the oldest teenage inventor. ☐
5 She found hiccups funny when she was younger. ☐
6 David built his earthworm prototype for a competition. ☐
7 The robotic earthworm will help to find people. ☐

David Cohen, an American teenager, decided to build a robotic earthworm. He thinks his invention will be used for finding people in a fire or an earthquake. The earthworm will be able to go into the smallest places, where humans or dogs can't go. It will also have a camera and will send back photos to help rescue-workers save people's lives.

G **Use a word from the Word Focus box to complete the sentences. Use the plural if necessary.**

1 I can't sing because I've got ______________!
2 ______________ can destroy houses and cities.
3 Plastic is not an ______________ material.
4 You can dry fruit in the sun to help ______________ it.
5 These windows are strong and can ______________ very high winds.
6 Vegetables and fruit are ______________ and don't harm the planet.

Ideas Focus

- Imagine you are an inventor. What would you invent? Why?
- 'Machines make us lazy.' Do you agree? Why? / Why not?

Vocabulary

A **Write the correct words under the photos.**

computer screen door handle earphones remote control phone charger smartphone

1

2
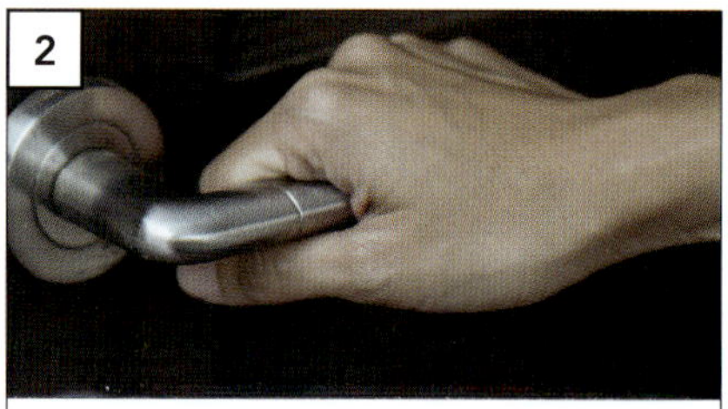

3
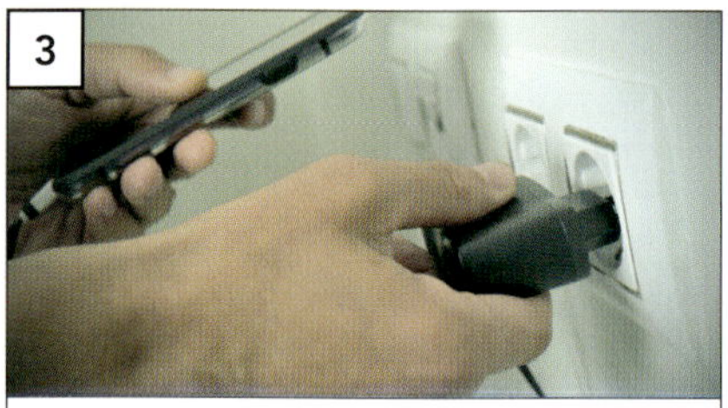

4
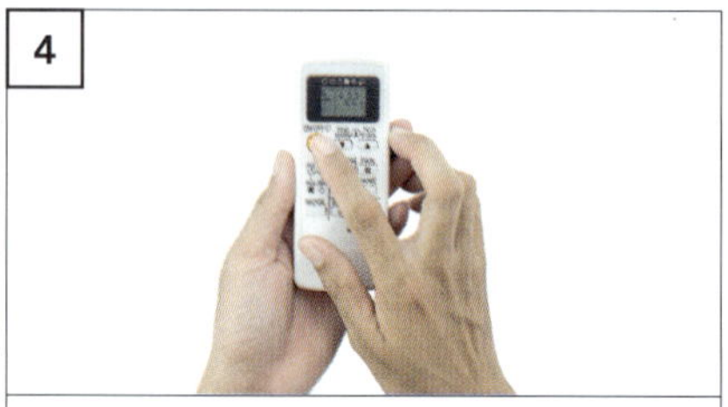

5

6

B **Complete the sentences with these words.**

look at plug in pull switch off turn on wear

1 Let's ______ the website on your computer.
2 Hold and ______ the door handle to come in.
3 Please ______ your smartphone at the cinema.
4 Can you ______ the TV? The remote control is over there.
5 Can you ______ your earphones, please? I'm working.
6 Where can I ______ my phone charger?

C **Complete the sentences with the correct words. Take turns to ask and answer the questions with a partner.**

earphones handle lights phone charger televisions

1 How many ______ do you have in your home?
2 Do you push or pull the ______ of your front door when you come home?
3 Do you remember to switch off the ______ when you go out?
4 Where in your house do you plug in your ______?
5 Do you wear ______? When do you wear them?

D **Unjumble the words and use them to complete sentences 1–6.**

ghtli ionvislete iadro retmocup werosh tramsenohp

1 I want to hear some music. Turn on the ______.
2 It's dark in here. Turn on the ______.
3 Stop playing that game and turn off the ______.
4 Quick! Turn on the ______. That James Bond film is on.
5 To save water you should turn off the ______ after 3 minutes.
6 Stop taking selfies and turn off your ______.

E **Match the objects to the description of what they are made of. Write the letter.**

1 It's made of metal. ______
2 It's made of wood. ______
3 It's made of plastic. ______
4 It's made of glass. ______

A

B

C

D

F **Work with a partner. Discuss what these kitchen objects might be. Underline the adjectives.**

1 It's a tall, rectangular white machine that keeps your food cold.
2 It's a big, square, silver machine with a round plastic window.
3 It's a small, flat, round black object with a handle. We use it for cooking.
4 It's a long, thin, sharp metal object we use to cut food.

G **Write the adjectives from F in the correct columns in the table. Add one more adjective of your own to each column.**

size	shape	colour	material
short	oval	turquoise	glass

H **Follow the order of the adjectives in the columns in G (size, shape, colour, material) to write sentences.**

1 glass window square an enormous
That's ______________________________.
2 turquoise necklace rectangular a small
She's wearing ______________________________.
3 metal a small object round
A compass is ______________________________
4 silver robot a plastic tall
The children have ______________________________.

- What things *can't* you live without? Why?
- 'There is a difference between the things we want and the things we need.' Do you agree? Why? / Why not?

Ideas Focus

Grammar

Superlative Adjectives

A Read sentences 1–4. Underline the superlative forms. The first one is done for you.

1 A pencil sharpener is <u>the smallest</u> object in my bag.
2 A fridge is the easiest invention to use.
3 The Sun is the hottest star in our solar system.
4 The wheel is the most important invention.

B Write the adjective for each sentence in A. Match it with a rule.

1 ________ ☐
2 ________ ☐
3 ________ ☐
4 ________ ☐

a change the *-y to -i* and add *-est*.
b only add *most* before the adjective.
c add *-est*
d double the last consonant and add *-est*.

* We use the superlative to show that something or someone has the most of something.

C Look at the sentences in A again. Are these rules True (T) or False (F)?

1 We use *than* after the superlative adjective. ☐
2 We use *the* before each superlative adjective. ☐
3 We use *the most* before every superlative adjective. ☐
4 We use *the most* before superlative adjectives with two syllables or more. ☐

D Read the sentences. Underline the irregular superlative forms.

1 I think Leonardo da Vinci was the best inventor in the world.
2 *Lost Planets* is the worst video game ever!
3 Is Neptune the furthest planet from the Sun?

E Complete the table.

adjective	comparative	superlative
good	________	________
________	worse than	________
far	further than	________

Grammar Focus p. 165 (7.1)

F What do you think? Complete and answer the questions.

1 What is ________________ (fast) machine? A plane, a car or a rocket?
I think *a rocket is the fastest machine.*
2 Which is ________________ (strong) material for a house? Glass, paper or wood?
I think ________________
3 Which is ________________ (useful) machine in the kitchen? A microwave, a fridge or a dishwasher?
I think ________________
4 Which invention is ________________ (interesting)? A drone, an electric car or a robot?
I think ________________

G Look at the photo of the robots. Complete the sentences with a superlative adjective.

1 Robot A is ________________ (short).
2 Robot B has ________________ (big) head.
3 Robot C has ________________ (long) legs.
4 Robot D has ________________ (interesting) body.
5 Robot E has ________________ (tiny) eyes.
6 I think Robot B can go ________________ (far) distance.
7 I think Robot A is ________________ (good) toy for my brother!

The one, The ones ...

H Underline the noun that is repeated in each sentence.

1 Those robots are the robots that can dance.
2 My invention is the invention with the three screens.
3 These buttons are the buttons we press to select a ticket.
4 Which man is the scientist? The tallest man on the left.

I Rewrite the sentences in H and replace the nouns you underlined with *one* or *ones* to avoid repetition.

1 Those robots are the ones that can dance.
2 My invention is ________.
3 These buttons are ________.
4 'Which man is the scientist?' '________'.

Expressing Purpose

J Read the sentences. Underline *use* or *used* in each sentence. What words come after *use/used*?

1 That machine is used for making bread.
2 It's used for cooking food outside.
3 Drones are used to find people after earthquakes.
4 You use a GPS to get directions.

K Circle the correct option.

1 *is/are used for* is followed by an infinitive verb / *-ing*
2 *is/are used to* is followed by an infinitive verb / *-ing*
3 *I/you/we* + *use* + noun + *to* is followed by an infinitive verb / *-ing*

Will for predictions

L Underline *will* and *won't*.

1 I think robots will make us lazy.
2 More people will drive electric cars in the future.
3 One day planes won't have pilots.
4 'Will cars fly one day?' 'No, they won't!'
5 'Will we live longer?' 'Yes, we will.'

M Complete the sentences with *will* or *won't*.

1 We use ________ and ________ to talk about things we think will happen.
2 We use ________ in positive sentences and ________ in negative sentences.
3 In short *Yes* answers, we repeat ________.
4 In short *No* answers, we repeat ________.

Grammar Focus p. 165 (7.2 to 7.3)

N Complete the sentences with *the one* or *the ones*.

1 Look at those computers! I like ________ with the biggest screen.
2 All the lights are on! Please switch off ________ upstairs.
3 Telephones are smaller than ________ people used 50 years ago.
4 'Which phone charger is yours?' '________ on the table.'

O Choose the correct option.

1 You use a telescope to looking / look at the stars.
2 My invention is used for curing / cure hiccups.
3 I use an old toothbrush to cleaning / clean my shoes.
4 That machine is used for buying / buy train tickets.
5 I use Whatsapp chatting / to chat to my friends.
6 This machine is used for drying / to dry clothes.

P Write a sentence with *use* for each example. The first one is done for you.

1 a fridge / keep food cool
You use a fridge to keep food cool.
A fridge is used for keeping food cool / to keep food cool.
2 a toothbrush / clean teeth
____
3 a handle / pull your suitcase
____

Q Read the predictions. Use *will* or *won't* to say what you think.

1 Robots ________ do all our work at home.
2 Cars ________ fly.
3 People ________ visit other planets.
4 Animals ________ disappear.
5 We ________ use banana leaves instead of plastic.

7 Invent It!

Listening

A **Work with a partner. Describe and compare the three robots. How do you think they help you in your home?**

"Buddy is the smallest but Jibo ..." "I think they will clean the floors ..."

Jibo

Buddy

B 7.1 **Listen to the description. Circle the correct robot.**

1 Jibo 2 Buddy

C 7.2 **Listen to the two descriptions. Write Jibo, Buddy or both.**

You can use this robot:

1 anywhere in your house. ______
2 to wake you up. ______
3 to organise your day. ______
4 to turn lights on and off. ______
5 to teach you and read to you. ______
6 to take photos. ______
7 to show movies and video games. ______
8 with batteries. ______

D 7.3 **Read the *Exam Close-up*, then listen to the first part of the description of the robots. Spell the names of the three robots correctly.**

______ ______ ______

E 7.4 **Now listen and complete the *Exam Task*.**

Exam Task

You will hear a man looking for a toy for his son. Listen and complete each question. You will hear the conversation twice.

Toy Shop

Name of toy: **(1)** ______

Size: **(2)** ______ cms long.

Colour: **(3)** ______ body and black face.

Function: **(4)** finds keys, glasses or ______

Price: **(5)** £ ______

Exam Close-up

Spelling correctly

- Sometimes you will hear the spelling of a word.
- Listen and write the word. Always make sure you check the spelling the second time you listen.
- Always read through all your answers at the end to check your spelling.

F 7.5 **Listen again and check your answers.**

Speaking

A Work with a partner. Look at the maps of the Science Museum and discuss which rooms you would like to visit and why.

"I think in Exhibition G we will learn about Leonardo da Vinci and his inventions."

B Work with a partner. Match questions 1–5 with answers a–e. Use the maps to help you.

1 Excuse me, where is the robot exhibition? ☐
2 Can you help me? I'm looking for the gift shop. ☐
3 Excuse me, where is the Space Travel exhibition? ☐
4 Is there a cafeteria? ☐
5 Are there toilets on the ground floor? ☐

a Yes, on the first floor. Come out of the lifts and it's on the left.
b It's on the ground floor, next to the entrance.
c It's on the first floor. Come out of the lifts and turn right.
d Yes, opposite the gift shop.
e It's between the IMAX theatre and the History of Flight exhibition.

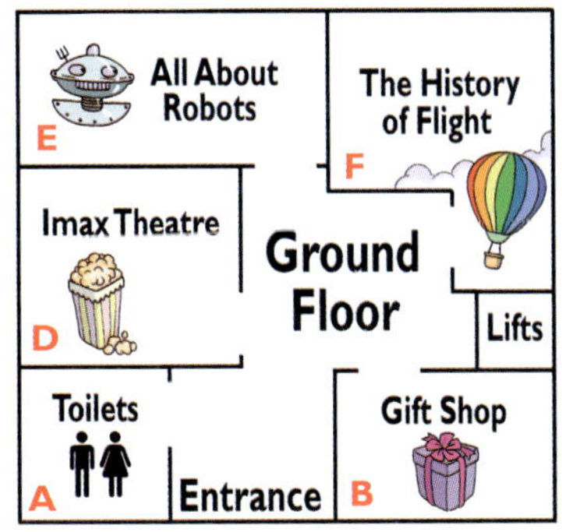

C Read the *Exam Close-up*. Then write two more questions to ask at the Science Museum. Compare with a partner.

D Work with a partner to complete the *Exam Task*. Use the *Useful Expressions* to help you.

Exam Close-up

Listening for the question word

- When talking with a partner, listen carefully for the question word.
- The question word will tell you what information to include in your answer.

Exam Task

Student A: Look at the poster about a Science Fair.
Student B: You are going to the Science Fair with a friend but you don't know the details. Ask **Student A** some questions about it. Turn to page 183.

Come along to this Year's Science Fair at the O2 Plaza in London.
This year's most amazing inventions are there for you to see.
Starts Friday 28th and finishes Sunday 30th April, open from 9 a.m. to 9 p.m.
Entrance: £9.00. Special light show on first floor: £6.50
Call 0795 191 33 74 to reserve your ticket.

Student B: Look at the information about a Science Museum on their website.
Student A: You want to go to the Science Museum with a friend but you don't have any information about it. Ask **Student B** some questions about it. Turn to page 183.

BRISTOL SCIENCE MUSEUM
Come and discover the best inventions from history.
Open every day except 26th to 28th December, from 10 a.m. to 6 p.m.
Entrance: FREE
IMAX movie theatre on ground floor: £4.50
Location: City centre, opposite Queen's Park
Transport: Number 15 bus

Useful Expressions

Giving directions
It's next to / opposite / between …
It's on the ground / first / second / third floor.
Go to X, then turn left / right.

Asking for information
Where is the exhibition?
What floor is it on?
Are the toilets on the ground floor?
How much does it cost?
How can I get there?
What date / time does it open / close?

Ideas Focus

- What type of museum do you like the best? Why?
- Is it a good idea for museums to be free? Why? / Why not?

7 Invent It!

Writing: captions

Learning Focus

Adding information in captions

- A caption is a title or short text that you write to go with a picture, a cartoon or a poster. You often see captions under photos and illustrations in books.
- A caption adds information so that we understand what we are looking at. It explains what people are saying or doing.
- Many people write captions with the selfies they take and put them on social media.

A

B

C

D

A **Match the names of the objects with the photos. Discuss with a partner how they are different from the modern versions.**

"People used a typewriter for / to ..."

1 a pencil sharpener ☐
2 a sundial ☐
3 a typewriter ☐
4 a gramophone ☐

B **Match these captions with the correct machines from A. Write the names.**

1 The ________ was the earliest type of clock people used.
2 The ________ didn't need electricity. You just turned a handle to play a record.
3 Before the ________ people used knives to sharpen their pencils.
4 People still use the ________ in many parts of the world to write formal letters.

C **Complete these funny captions with the correct words. Which machine are they describing?**

pencil case MP3 player fingers wrist

1 People didn't wear these on their ________! ________
2 It's a lot easier to listen to music now with an ________. ________
3 This won't fit in my ________! ________
4 People must have had tired ________ writing with this! ________

D **Look at the photo of a solar cooker. Unjumble the four captions.**

1 older you A is solar cooker than think.
A solar cooker is older than you think.
2 A use solar cooker electricity doesn't.
____
3 sun from for cooking A energy solar cooker uses the.
____
4 planet the and great eco-friendly for is solar cooker A.
____

E Choose one of the items below and write three captions for it. Use the *Useful Expressions* to help you.

- a bike
- a nutribullet®
- a Fitbit
- a walking stick

F Read the *Exam Close-up* then look at the competition poster in the *Exam Task*. Answer the questions on this entry form for your invention.

Why do you want to take part in this competition? (*no more than 50 words*)

I want to take part in this competition because ...

Describe your favourite invention and why? (*no more than 50 words*)

My favourite invention is ...

Exam Close-up

Completing forms with more detailed information

- Some forms ask for more detailed information than just a name, address and telephone number.
- Usually there is not much space so you have to write a clear message using only a few words.
- Write a draft first so you can review and improve your message.

Useful Expressions

Expressing purpose

People / we / you use it to ...
People / we / you use it for ... + -ing
It uses / doesn't use ...
It's good / great for ... + -ing
It's good / great for the planet because ...
It's easy / fun to use because ...

G Now complete the *Exam Task*.

Exam Task

Read the poster and the email. Fill in the information on the student's entry form.

Email Message

To: Daniel Cobson
From: Janice Fields

Hi Danny,
I saw a poster yesterday at my school and I thought of you. It's a competition for inventors and I know you want to be an inventor. Remember that invention you created for my dad's car, called Doglactic, to stop him leaving the dog in the car? The competition is for teenagers and you are 15, so that's great. The deadline is today so write now!!
Janice

Date: (1) ______________

Young Inventor of the Year Competition

Full name: (2) ______________

Age: (3) ______________

Name of Invention:
(4) ______________

How will you spend the
(5) £ ______________ **prize money?**

WATERDALE SCIENCE MUSEUM

Calling all young inventors!

Come and take part in our Young Inventor of the Year Competition.

£100 in prize money for the best inventions.

Plus FREE ENTRY to our museum for one year!

Complete the form on our website before 30th June.

Video 7 An Exciting Invention

Before you watch

A **Match the words to their meanings.**

brakes car engineer roller coaster track wheel

1 ________: something you sit in on a ride
2 ________: an amusement park ride that goes up and down really fast
3 ________: a metal path that some machines travel on
4 ________: a circular object found on some machines to help them move
5 ________: a person who looks after machines
6 ________: something to make you go slower or stop

While you watch

B **Watch the video. Decide if these statements are T (True) or F (False).**

1 This roller coaster is called "The Big One". ☐
2 It is one of the fastest and tallest roller coasters in America. ☐
3 Every year, one million people ride on this roller coaster. ☐
4 It is 67 metres high. ☐
5 Trains can travel at 80 kms an hour. ☐
6 Engineers ride in the train three times a day. ☐

After you watch

C **Complete the summary of the video below using these words.**

engineers roller coaster ride season three track trains wheels

Blackpool has a very big and very fast **(1)** ____________! Every year thousands of people visit and **(2)** ____________ on it. But before the attraction park can open, **(3)** ____________ have to carefully check the track, the brakes and the **(4)** ____________. They need to make sure all the parts are working and are in good condition. They test each car with sandbags instead of people and check that all the **(5)** ____________ can go up and down the **(6)** ____________ at full speed. In the high **(7)** ____________, when there are more tourists, engineers check everything **(8)** ____________ times a day.

Ideas Focus

- Do you like roller coasters? Why? / Why not?
- 'Roller coasters are the most exciting thing ever.' Do you agree?

8 Snap!

Reading: multiple-choice, finding the best connections
Vocabulary: words and expressions for playing games
Grammar: zero conditional, adverbs & other words to show sequence, modals of obligation, models for permission & possibility
Listening: multiple-choice, listening for the answer
Speaking: asking & answering about a game, asking questions about games, forming questions
Writing: instructions, sequencing, making suggestions & responding, making suggestions

Young Buddhist monk plays hide-and-seek in the Ta Prohm Temple hallways. Angkor Wat, Cambodia

8 Snap!

Reading

A Match the games to the pictures. What are they playing?

card game | board game | outdoor game | table game | video game

1

______

2

______

3

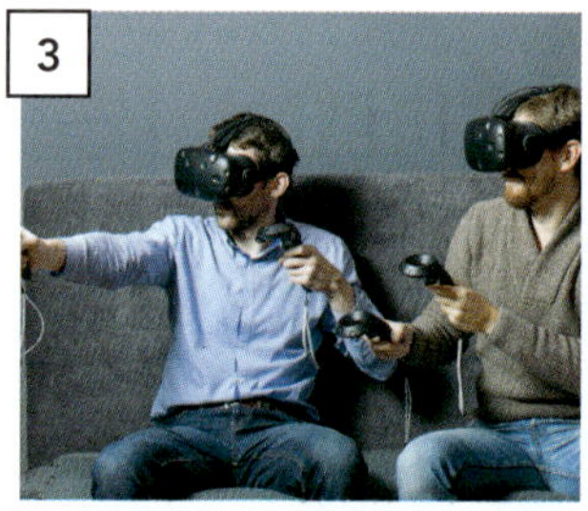

______

4

______

5

______

B Which games in A do you like best? Why? Tell a partner.

C Quickly read Nico's description. How many games does he mention? What are they?

Word Focus

counter: a small object you use to move around a game board

dice: cubes with six sides and dots representing numbers one to six

beat: to win against someone

competitive: wanting to win

THE GAMES I PLAY

My name is Nico and I love playing games. Every weekend my family has an electronics-free Sunday evening. We chat and play music but we also play a game together. We've got lots of games, like *Scrabble™*, *Pictionary™*, *Uno™* … all the classics.

Last year, I learnt to play chess at school. I often play with my granddad. He's really good but I'm getting better! My grandad also likes to play *Jenga™* with us. My younger sister cries if she can't play *Jenga;* she loves it so much! In *Jenga* you take turns to take one block from a tower without it falling.

Sometimes my friends come over on Sunday evening to play *Charades*, a miming game, or a board game like *Monopoly™*. *Monopoly* is my favourite game. The first thing we do when we play it, is choose our counters. I always choose the car.

My best friend, Luca, likes to be the hat and my sister always wants to be the dog. Then we take turns to throw the dice and move around the board. I like to land on the expensive streets because then I

D **Read Nico's description again. Discuss the answers to the questions with a partner.**

1 What does Nico's family do instead of using electronic devices on a Sunday evening?
2 Why isn't Nico as good as his grandfather at chess?
3 When does his younger sister cry?
4 Why do his friends come over on Sunday evening?
5 Which *Monopoly* counter does Luca usually choose?
6 Why is Luca often unlucky when he plays *Monopoly*?
7 What does Nico do when he misses the school bus?
8 What does Nico think is the most important thing about playing games?

E **Discuss these questions with a partner.**

1 Which of the games in the text do you like? Why?
2 Are there any games in the text that you don't like? Why?
3 Do you hate losing? Why? / Why not?

F **Read the *Exam Close-up*. Then read the first line of each conversation in the *Exam Task* and underline the subject.**

G **Now complete the *Exam Task*.**

H **Complete the sentences with the words.**

between from in (x2) on (x2)

1 Hold your counter __________ your hand.
2 Deal the cards __________ the players.
3 Move __________ one square to another.
4 Put the highest number card __________ front of you.
5 If you land __________ a red square, you have to miss a go.
6 Give a card to the player __________ your right.

can buy them - it makes it easier to win. Luca is unlucky - he often lands on the *Go to Jail* square. It's really easy to beat him! My sister doesn't enjoy *Monopoly* as much as us. She thinks it takes too long to play it.

Another game I play with Luca, when we miss the school bus, is *Scissors-Paper-Stone*. You only need your hand!

Playing games is great because they are fun and sociable. I'm quite competitive. I love winning and I hate losing! But I know that I can't always win. And the most important thing about games is to enjoy playing them with friends or family.

Exam Close-up

Finding the best connections

- Notice the subject in the first line of the conversation.
- If the prompt uses the *you* pronoun, the reply may include *I* or *we*.
- If a question asks if something is *yours*, the answer may include *mine* or *ours*.
- Notice how objects can be referred to as *it* or *they*.

Exam Task

Complete the five conversations. Choose **A**, **B**, or **C**.

1 I never win card games!
  A I play games too.
  B At least you have fun!
  C I lost my football.
2 This game is difficult to play.
  A Yes, it is.
  B What about you?
  C It's my turn.
3 We're playing a game.
  A It's ours.
  B It looks fun.
  C No, we can't.
4 I'm bored.
  A That's a great idea.
  B They're boring.
  C Let's play a game.
5 Do you like party games?
  A I love them!
  B Yes, it's my favourite.
  C You must play!

Ideas Focus

- Do you like playing non-electronic games? Why? / Why not?
- 'Games don't need to be competitive.' Do you agree? Why? / Why not?

8 Snap!

Vocabulary

A Match an instruction with a picture. Write the letter.

1 spin the wheel ______
2 deal the cards ______
3 shuffle the cards ______
4 keep/write down the score ______
5 roll the dice ______
6 move the counter two spaces ______

A
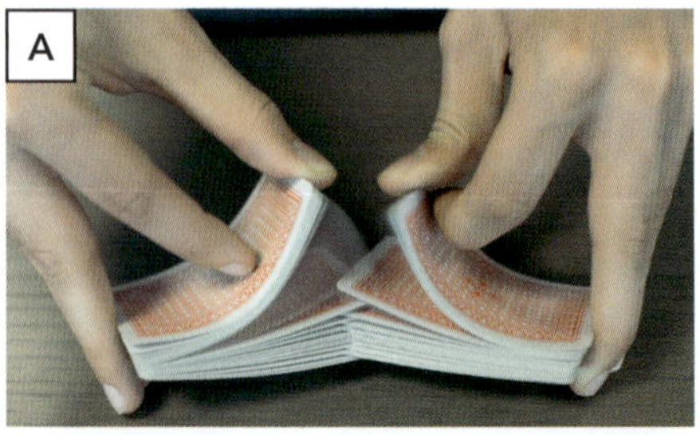

B

C

D

E

F

B Match each expression (1–5) with its meaning (a–e).

1 Miss a turn! ______
2 You cheated! ______
3 I won! ______
4 I lost! ______
5 It's your turn. ______

a I came first in the game.
b You are the next player.
c I came last in the game.
d You weren't fair.
e You can't play this time.

C Choose the correct words.

1 When you play cards you need to spin / shuffle them first.
2 On the board, you move your counter / wheel forwards or backwards.
3 When you roll / jump the dice and get a six, you have another go!
4 You mustn't laugh / cheat in a game. It's not fair!
5 Keep / Draw the score on a piece of paper.

D Look at the scores and then answer the questions.

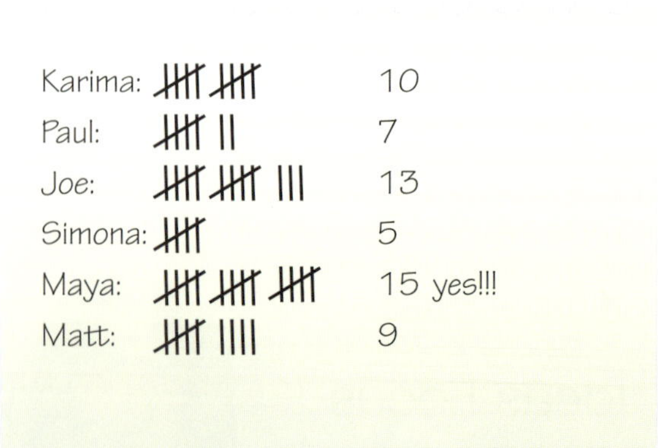

1 Who came 1st? ____________________
2 Who came 2nd? ____________________
3 Who came 3rd? ____________________
4 Who came 4th? ____________________
5 Who came 5th? ____________________
6 Who came 6th? ____________________

E Write the numbers in brackets as words.

1 She came (12th) ______________________ in the tournament.
2 It's her (21st) ______________________ birthday.
3 I'm (32nd) ______________________ in the line.
4 They're celebrating their (25th) ______________________ wedding anniversary.
5 It's the (400th) ______________________ anniversary of Shakespeare's death.

F Circle the correct verb, *lose* or *miss*.

1 I came last and lost / missed the game.
2 It's your turn. I have to lose / miss a go.
3 My dad lost / missed his wallet yesterday. But I found it!
4 Sometimes my brother loses / misses the bus to school.
5 Andrea really loses / misses her grandparents. They live in Argentina.
6 How did you lose / miss one of your football boots?
7 I tried to kick the ball but I lost / missed it!
8 I had to lose / miss school yesterday because I was sick.

G Which verb, *lose* or *miss*, goes in the word map? Create a word map for the other verbs in your notebooks.

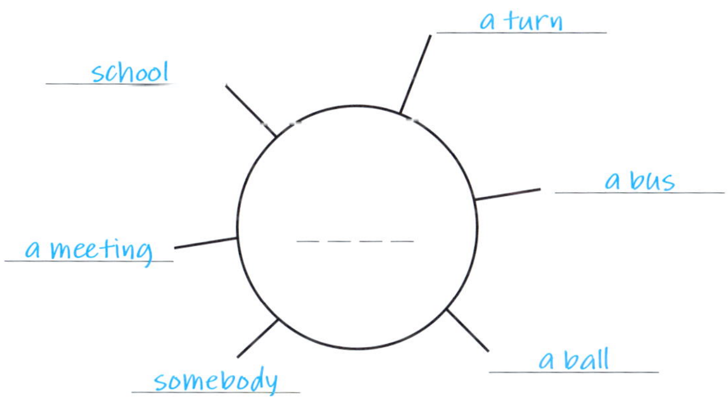

H Complete the conversation with the words. Practise it with a partner.

Why sounds Shall play playing

A Let's **(1)** ________________ musical chairs at your sister's party.
B No, it's very noisy!
A OK. What about **(2)** ________________ an outdoor game?
B There isn't enough space!
A **(3)** ________________ we all play a board game?
B That's impossible with 15 children!
A **(4)** ________________ don't we play a miming game in teams?
B Now that **(5)** ________________ like fun!

Ideas Focus

- Traditional games are very educational. Do you agree? Why? / Why not?
- What can playing games teach us?

Grammar

Zero Conditional

A Underline the verbs in each sentence. Then circle *if* and *when*.

1 If you land on a blue square, you get another go.
2 Games are fun if you follow the rules.
3 When we are bored, we play a board game.
4 You need to sit on a chair when the music stops.

B Choose the correct answer, a or b.

1 We use the zero conditional to talk about ______ situations in the present.
   a real b unreal
2 We form the zero conditional with *If/When* + Present Simple, + ______.
   a Past Simple b Present Simple or Continuous
3 When *If* and *When* come at the beginning of a sentence, a ______ separates the two parts.
   a comma b full stop

Adverbs To Show Sequence

C Underline the adverb in each sentence then complete the rule.

1 After I finish my homework, I play a video game.
2 After playing a game, we tidy up.
3 Before I lost the game, I was happy!
4 Before rolling the dice, choose your team.
5 While waiting for the bus, he plays *Scissors-Paper-Stone*.
6 It's important to keep the score while we play.

After, before and *while* can be followed by the subject + ______________ OR just by the ______________.

Other Words To Show Sequence

D Circle the words in each sentence that show sequence.

1 As soon as the game finishes, I have to go.
2 I want to stay until the party finishes.
3 We played for two hours and eventually I won!
4 At first the game was difficult, but in the end it was easy.

E Match the meanings to a word or words you circled in D.

1 after a long time / finally ______ ______
2 up to a certain moment ______________
3 in the beginning ______________
4 immediately ______________

Grammar Focus pp. 165 & 166 (8.1 to 8.2)

F Match the sentence beginnings 1–6 to the endings a–f.

1 If you press this control button, ☐
2 When one person counts, ☐
3 I never get bored ☐
4 You can't play ☐
5 She misses her dad ☐
6 If you lose your ball, ☐

a when I'm on my own.
b if you are under six years old.
c go and look for it!
d the hero gets more power.
e when he is travelling.
f the others need to hide.

G Choose the correct verb form for each sentence.

1 I always call my friends before visit / visiting them.
2 After we ate / eating dinner, we finished our school work.
3 She listens to music while she plays / playing computer games.
4 After buys / buying the game, he gave it to his best friend.
5 While play / playing hide and seek, Monica lost her shoe!
6 Before you leave /leaving, let's play a game of table football.

H Choose the correct options to complete the sentences.

1 If you land on a black square, you miss / missed a turn.
2 The game doesn't finish in the end / until all players have landed on the last square.
3 If you don't like / are not liking to lose, don't play games.
4 We start the game so / as soon as we hear the teacher say 'go'.
5 If both dice say 'six', you had / have two turns.
6 Don't take / Take not a card if you land on a green square.
7 In the end / Until I beat my dad, after six hours of playing *Monopoly*!
8 If you are the banker in *Monopoly*, you are looking after / look after the money.

Modals of Obligation

I **Underline *must / mustn't / have to / don't have to* in these sentences.**

1. You mustn't cheat in your exams!
2. You must only spin the wheel once.
3. You have to tidy your room. It's a mess!
4. You don't have to eat the whole pizza if you're not hungry.
5. You have to wear a uniform.
6. You mustn't throw your litter on the ground.

J **Use the words you underlined in I to complete the rules.**

- We use ______ and ______ when something is a rule or absolutely necessary.
- We use ______ when something is not permitted.
- We use ______ when something is not a rule or an obligation (not necessary).

Modals for Permission & Possibility

K **Read the sentences. Underline *can* or *can't*, then complete the rules.**

1. You can't phone Natalie until you finish your lunch.
2. I can't go out because I've got no money.
3. We can wear what we want to the school concert.
4. They can play if they read the instructions first.

- We use ______ when we have the possibility of doing, or permission to do, something.
- We use ______ when we don't have permission and/or the possibility.

Grammar Focus p. 166 (8.3 to 8.7)

L **Read sentences 1–6 from I again and match them with the correct option a–f. Write the number.**

a in a park ______
b at a hospital ______
c at home ______
d at school ______
e in an instruction booklet ______
f at a restaurant ______

M **Choose the correct answer and match with a picture.**

1. You have to / don't have to be over seven years old to play. ______
2. You can't / can play with two players. ______
3. You must / mustn't pass 'Go'. ______
4. You must / can miss a turn. ______
5. You can / can't choose any colour. ______

N **Complete the instructions with the words. You can only use each word once.**

can can't has to if to until When While

Rules for Scrabble

Two to four people **(1)** ______ play *Scrabble*.
Each player **(2)** ______ take seven letters from the bag.
The players must take turns **(3)** ______ make words on the board.
(4) ______ you make a word on the board, you replace the number of letters.
For example, **(5)** ______ you put five letters down, you collect five letters from the letter bag.
(6) ______ the other players are playing, think about your options.
The game continues **(7)** ______ there are no more letters in the bag.
You can score extra points on some squares on the board. You **(8)** ______ make words diagonally – only vertically and horizontally.
The player with the highest score wins!

8 Snap!

Listening

A **Look at the photos and discuss the questions with a partner.**

- What type of games are they?
- Which game do you like the best?

B 8.1 **Look at the list of games. Which ones do you know? Listen to five students talk about their favourite game. Complete each question with a game from the list.**

Battleships™ Cluedo™ Chess Table tennis Pass the parcel Sardines Top Trumps™ Trivial Pursuit™

1 How do you play ______________________?
2 How many people can play ______________________?
3 Where do you play ______________________?
4 How old must you be to play ______________________?
5 How long does it take to play ______________________?

C 8.1 **Listen again and write the answers to the questions in B.**

1 ______________________
2 ______________________
3 ______________________
4 ______________________
5 ______________________

D **Read the *Exam Close-up* and read the questions in the *Exam Task*.**

E 8.2 **Now listen and complete the *Exam Task*.**

A

B

C

Exam Close-up

Listening for the answer

- You will listen to just one informal conversation.
- Read the questions before you listen so you know exactly what you are listening for.
- Listen the first time, but don't decide too quickly on the answer. You will usually hear words from the other options too.

Exam Task

Listen to Ryan buying a present with his dad. For each question, choose the right answer (**A**, **B** or **C**). You will hear the conversation twice.

1 When do they go to the toy shop?
A on Martin's birthday
B tomorrow
C today

2 What kind of games does Martin like best?
A card games
B board games
C outdoor games

3 How many games are there in the shop?
A 100
B 50
C 20

4 How old will Martin be on his birthday?
A twelve
B eight
C seven

5 How much is the family game?
A £9.90
B £10
C £6.90

F 8.3 **Listen again and check your answers.**

Speaking

A Work with a partner. What games are people playing in the photos. Which looks more fun? Why?

B Are you good at general knowledge games? Tick the box that applies to you. Tell your partner and give a reason.

Great ☐ Not good ☐ Not bad ☐
Good ☐ Terrible ☐

I'm not bad at general knowledge games because I love facts.

C Work with a partner. Unjumble the question categories. The first one is done for you.

- G — **1** phcgragoy *Geography*
- E — **2** tnmeetnaitrne ______
- H — **3** yrihsot ______
- AL — **4** tar & etalitrrue ______
- SN — **5** incseec & urenta ______
- SL — **6** orstps & erusiel ______

D Write the question word. Which category in C do you think each question belongs to?

How many | What | When | Where | Which | Who

1 ______ was chess invented? In Asia or Europe?
2 ______ board game is a map of city streets and stations?
3 ______ games can you name in one minute?
4 ______ is a famous runner: Lewis Hamilton or Mo Farah?
5 ______ animal did Alice use for an outdoor game in *Alice in Wonderland*?
6 ______ were video games invented? Before or after 1980?

E Read the *Exam Close-up*. Then work with a partner and write four general knowledge questions to ask other classmates.

F Now complete the *Exam Task*. Use the *Useful Expressions* to help you.

Exam Close-up

Forming questions

- Practise asking questions as much as possible.
- Become familiar with the types of question you need for different situations.

Useful Expressions

Asking questions about games

What type of game is it?
How do you play it?
How many people can play?
How old must you be to play?
How long does it take?
Do you need a dice/counters to play?
Whose turn is it?

Exam Task

1

Student A: Look at some information about a game in your toy shop.

Student B: Turn to page 183. You are looking for a game for your sister. Ask **Student A** some questions about the game.

- Card game
- Two to four players
- £5.70
- No dice, just pen and paper to keep scores
- Seven years and up

2

Student B: Look at some information about a party game.

Student A: Turn to page 183. You are organising a party for your younger brother. Ask **Student B** some questions about the game.

- Outdoor team game
- Need to get other team's flag
- Eight to twelve players
- Good fun and exercise
- One hour

Ideas Focus

- Is it important to learn facts? Why? / Why not?
- 'Babies and young children learn by playing.' Do you agree? Why? / Why not?

Writing: instructions

Learning Focus

Sequencing

- We can use *First, Then, Next, After that, Finally* to show sequence, but also words like *before, after, afterwards, while, until, at first* and *eventually.*
- *Before, after* and *until* can be followed by verbs and by nouns: *Before the party, get everything ready; After the game, tidy up; Wait until Jane arrives.*
- We often use the imperative when giving instructions.

A

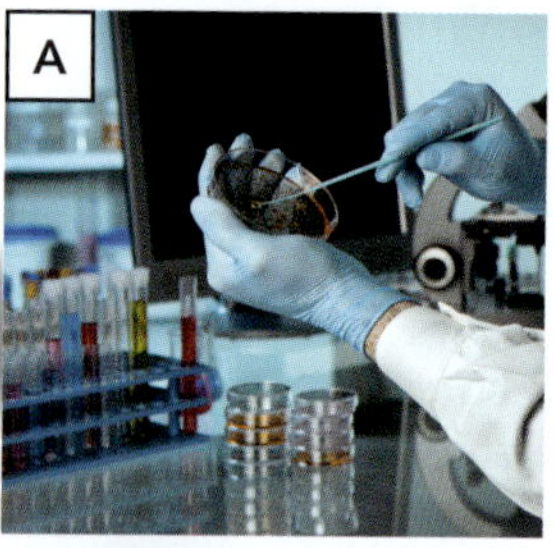

B

C

D

A When do we follow instructions? Match the descriptions to the photos. Write the letter.

1 make a food dish ______
2 fix something ______
3 use a machine ______
4 do a science experiment ______

B When was the last time you followed instructions? Tell a partner.

C Look back at the *Learning Focus*, then underline the sequencing words in these game instructions. Then number them in the correct order.

Eventually one team guesses correctly and scores a point.

The teams keep guessing until the 60 seconds are up.

The two artists throw a dice and take a word card.

After forming the teams, each team chooses an 'artist'.

Before you begin, players must divide into two teams.

As soon as they take a word card, they have 60 seconds to draw a picture.

While the artists draw, the teams must guess.

1 ______
2 ______
3 ______
4 ______
5 ______
6 ______
7 ______

D Think about your favourite game. Use the *Useful Expressions* to help you write the rules.

Game: ______

E Read the three text conversations. Use the words to complete the suggestions for your friend.

How about | Let's | Why don't

1

A I want to buy a new game to play.

B ______________ go to *Juggler's*. It's got lots of new games.

A OK. Shall we go this afternoon?

2

A I need a good party game to play.

B ______________ playing musical chairs?

A Good idea!

3

A Do you know any new video games I can play?

B ______________ you buy *Spacescape?* It's good fun!

A Great! Thanks!

F Read the *Exam Close-up*. Then look back at how the suggestions were made in E.

G Now complete the *Exam Task*.

Exam Close-up

Making suggestions

- Become familiar with the different ways we can make suggestions.
- Be careful about the verb form that follows suggestions.
- Sometimes we can just use the imperative form, i.e. *Buy Spacecraft, it's great!*
- Start noticing different ways of responding to suggestions, too.

Exam Task

Read the email from Rosie.

Email Message

Re: Help

Hi Megan,

My mum's sick and it's my brother's birthday party this afternoon!
What party games do children like to play?
What games can we play outdoors?
What is a good prize for the winners?
Come over and help me if you are free.

Thanks for your help!
Rosie xxx

Write an email to Rosie and answer the questions. Write **25 – 35** words.

Useful Expressions

Sequencing

Before / after / while you throw the dice …

Before / after / while shuffling …

Before / after the game …

Afterwards …

Until …

At first …

Eventually …

Making suggestions & responding

Why don't we / you go …?

Let's go …

How about going …?

Great! / Good idea!

That sounds great!

Video 8 Testing!

Before you watch

A **Look at the photos. Work with a partner and discuss these questions.**

- Which toy do you like best? Why?
- Are these toys dangerous? Why? / Why not?

A

Teddy bear

B

Toy plane

C

Train set

D

Doll

E

Marbles

While you watch

B **Watch the video. Number the tests in the order you see them.**

1 An expert drops a 1 Kilo weight on small toys. ☐
2 An expert burns a teddy bear for three seconds. ☐
3 Two experts test and play with a marble run. ☐
4 An expert tests an elephant's eye. ☐
5 An expert tests the stuffing inside an elephant. ☐
6 A plastic ball is broken by one test. ☐

After you watch

C **Complete the summary of the video below using these words.**

children eyes kilo plastic run strong test Toys

(1) ____________ are an important part of a child's life. They help a child learn to move, coordinate, communicate and be **(2)** ____________. But before **(3)** ____________ can play with toys, experts must **(4)** ____________ them.

Experts test soft toys to make sure parts like **(5)** ____________ don't fall off and that the stuffing inside them doesn't come out. Experts test smaller **(6)** ____________ toys by dropping a one **(7)** ____________ of weight on them. This is to check that the small parts don't break easily. They also burn toys. Soft toys, like teddy bears, must burn slowly. A child who is playing with a soft toy must have enough time to see the fire, drop the toy and **(8)** ____________ away.

Ideas Focus

- What was your favourite toy when you were a child? Why?
- 'Outdoor play is the best kind of play.' Do you agree?

Review 4 Units 7 & 8

Vocabulary

A Match the sentence halves.

1 Remember to switch off
2 All my friends wear
3 Can you turn on
4 Please click the Exit button
5 You can plug in

a at the top of your screen.
b your mobile phone charger next to the computer.
c lights to save electricity.
d the TV? My favourite programme is starting.
e earphones and listen to music on the way to school.

B Write the adjectives in the correct order.

1 We've got a ________________________ clock in our classroom. (black, plastic, round)
2 My brother's got a ________________________ board with wheels. (wooden, big, long)
3 Mr and Mrs Reynolds bought a ________________________ caravan. (big, metal, white)
4 The waiter served the sandwiches on a ________________________ dish. (round, orange, small)
5 The hotel has lots of ________________________ mirrors everywhere! (glass, oval, tiny)

C Circle the correct words.

1 Don't cheat / misplay, Chris! I saw you look at the cards!
2 Danny, can you move / keep the score while we play?
3 Come on, Becky, we're waiting! It's your switch / turn.
4 Don't forget to shuffle / spin the cards before the next game.
5 You need to deal / lose seven cards to each player.
6 Spin / Roll the dice and count the number of spaces on the board.
7 My granddad takes / wins every time we play together. He's always first!

D Complete the sentences with *miss* or *lose* in the correct form.

1 There was a lot of traffic and he __________ his flight to New York.
2 My mum __________ her phone on holiday last month. She bought a new one.
3 If you land on a purple square, you have to __________ a go.
4 It's not fair! I always __________ or come last in games!
5 Joel doesn't like his new school. He really __________ his old school friends.
6 I __________ my dentist appointment yesterday. I didn't write it in my diary!

E Write the numbers in brackets as words.

1 It's my parents' (55th) __________ wedding anniversary.
2 It's their (3rd) __________ visit to Australia.
3 My granddad is celebrating his (71st) __________ birthday this month.
4 This is the (15th) __________ game we've played today!
5 Rio de Janeiro held the (30th) __________ summer Olympic games in 2016.

Review 4 Units 7 & 8

Grammar

A Complete the sentences with the superlative form of the word in brackets.

1 An elephant is an animal with ______ (long) nose and ______ (big) ears!
2 Order the Mediterranean pizza. It's ______ (good) one on the menu!
3 We watched ______ (scary) movie on TV last night. I couldn't sleep afterwards.
4 I think a cooker is ______ (useful) machine in the kitchen.
5 The students thought Tenith was ______ (interesting) inventor.
6 ______ (bad) thing about this computer program is that it isn't easy to understand.
7 Beth lives ______ (far) from the town centre and I live ______ (near) to it.
8 Which animal do you think is ______ (dangerous)?

B Complete the sentences with the words in the correct form.

1 Robots are used for ______ (pick) up heavy objects.
2 Scientists are using a really strong telescope to ______ (look) deeper into space.
3 My granny uses that computer game to ______ (improve) her memory.
4 You have to ______ (spin) the wheel before you can take your turn.
5 After ______ (play) chess for three hours, James won.
6 You can build the machine while ______ (read) the instructions.

C Complete the sentences with a word in the correct form.

be call cry eat go have listen lose miss take read travel

1 I usually ______ to music with my headphones, when I ______ on the bus.
2 If Ana ______ the bus, she ______ her mum on her phone.
3 We always ______ popcorn when we ______ to see a movie.
4 If Poppy, our cat, ______ sick, we ______ her to the vet.
5 Granddad ______ us stories if he ______ time.
6 My little brother ______ when he ______ a game.

D Circle the correct word.

1 You must / mustn't eat during the exam. It's not allowed.
2 Mario lives on the twelfth floor. He won't / has to take the lift every day.
3 I will / mustn't be a writer when I'm older.
4 Sorry, I can / can't go out tonight because I have a lot of work to finish.
5 Can / must you help me build this model? It's difficult.
6 You have to / can't brush your teeth at least twice a day.
7 It's too late. We can / won't have time to finish the game.
8 I can't / can play. I don't know the rules of the game.

9 In The Extreme!

Reading: multiple-choice, comparing the options
Vocabulary: words for sports and sporting equipment, prepositions, adjectives and adverbs, multiple-choice sentences, choosing the missing word
Grammar: present perfect (1), first conditional, multiple-choice cloze, checking for the parts of a tense
Listening: multiple-choice, focusing on specific information
Speaking: asking & answering about an extreme sports class, asking for & giving details
Writing: a blog, thinking about your readers, using adjectives, looking back & checking

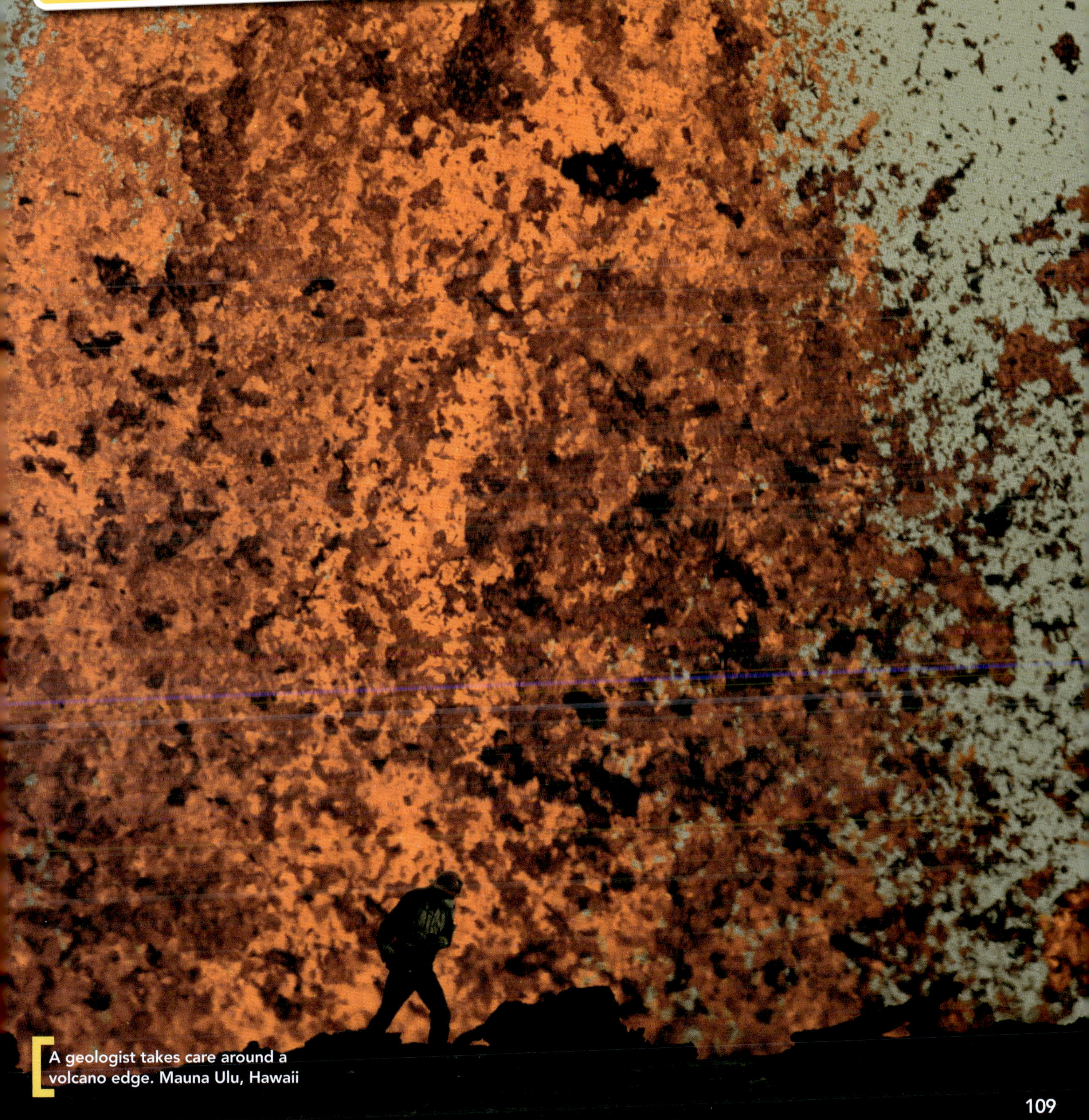

A geologist takes care around a volcano edge. Mauna Ulu, Hawaii

9 In The Extreme!

Reading

A **Match the sports to the pictures. Which sport do you think is the odd one out? Why?**

1 snowboarding ______
2 kitesurfing ______
3 banana boat riding ______
4 ice climbing ______
5 soapbox racing ______
6 paragliding ______

A

B

C

D

E

F

B **What is an extreme sport? Circle the adjectives in the list below that describe this type of sport. Then complete the sentences.**

dangerous boring frightening slow exciting easy careful exhausting

It's a sport that is ______________________.

It can be ______________________.

C **Which is the most/least extreme sport in A? Compare your answers with a partner. Give reasons for your opinion.**

I think ... is the most/least extreme sport because ...

D **Quickly read the four texts and match them to the correct descriptions below. Then write the name of the sport they mention.**

☐	It's an advert.	It's about ______________.
☐	It's a blog.	It's about ______________.
☐	It's a newspaper article.	It's about ______________.
☐	It's a leaflet.	It's about ______________.

Word Focus

compete: take part in a competition
glide: fly without flapping wings
slope: a gentle hill
spin: turn round and round fast
give up: decide to stop
paralysed: not able to move your body

1

Sports | Posts | Home

Today I flew! [Posted Today at 15:45pm]

I usually compete in snowboard competitions, as you know, but today I tried wingsuit flying. I jumped off a mountain and I flew! It's the first time I've ever flown. I was so scared about flying in a wingsuit. Everyone told me how difficult it can be. But when I took off I was like a bird! I opened my wings and started to glide really easily. I've never felt so happy. It was amazing to be up so high and see the ground moving quietly below me. I was having so much fun that I flew past the landing area and it took me two hours to get back! Oh, well … it was definitely worth it!

Geraldine

2

Soapbox Derby Race for Beginners – Saturday 7th July

Come along and try something new! Soapbox racing cars have no motors. You need a hill or a slope to race down. The Derby Race on 7th July will take place at the top of Clifton Avenue from 11.30 a.m. to 3 p.m. You can't go any faster than nine kilometres an hour as you race down the hill or spin round the bends. Racers will be timed to see who wins.

If you are aged between six and 16, come along and try. Entry fee is £22 and includes a car kit and building instructions. We will have experts to tell you all you need to know. See you at the top of the slope!

E **Read the texts again. Decide which sport the sentences describe. Write the name.**

1 You build it and drive it. ________
2 You do it at a beach. ________
3 You have three wheels. ________
4 You feel like a bird. ________
5 It's an Olympic sport. ________
6 It's not very fast. ________

F **Read the *Exam Close-up*. Then read the *Exam Task* carefully.**

Exam Close-up

Comparing the options

- This part of the exam may sometimes have three-option multiple-choice comprehension questions.
- Compare each option carefully with the text.
- Look at the other options and make sure you know why they are wrong.

G **Now complete the *Exam Task*.**

Exam Task

Read the texts about the four sports. For questions **1 – 7**, circle the correct letter **a**, **b** or **c**.

1 When was the first time Geraldine flew?
 a two hours ago **b** today
 c before her snowboarding classes.
2 How did Geraldine feel just before she did it?
 a scared **b** happy **c** quiet
3 What do you need to race a soapbox car?
 a a motor **b** three wheels
 c a hill or slope
4 Why should you book kitesurfing today?
 a classes are free **b** classes are cheaper.
 c the hotel is free
5 Where can I book the kitesurfing classes?
 a on the website **b** at the Boa Mar hotel
 c in Mozambique
6 How many Olympic medals does Karen Darke have?
 a three **b** two **c** one
7 When did Karen start hand cycling?
 a when she was at school.
 b after a car hit her.
 c after she fell and was paralysed.

H **Look at the underlined words in the texts. Complete the sentences with *down*, *off*, *on*, *round*, and *up*.**

1 I get very dizzy when I spin ________ on carousels at the fair.
2 I love surfing. I want to carry ________ with my classes next month.
3 Be careful! You shouldn't race ________ the hill so fast!
4 I want to give ________ snowboarding. It's too dangerous.
5 The plane took ________ on time.

3

4

Printed News — Page 4

Paralympic Hand Cyclist Wins Gold!

Karen Darke is a sportswoman with determination who never gives up.

She has just won her first gold medal here at the Rio Olympics. Karen's story is incredible.

After running and climbing one day, she fell off a cliff and became paralysed from the chest down. She was only 19. Her determination to carry on with sports made her take up hand cycling.

In the 2012 London Olympics, Karen won a silver medal but after the event she was hit by a car and lost sensation in her right arm for a year. Now, here she is, back and very excited that after training so hard, her dreams have come true!

Ideas Focus

- Which extreme sport would you like to try? Which wouldn't you like to try? Why?
- 'Extreme sports should be stopped.' Do you agree? Why? / Why not?

9 In The Extreme!

Vocabulary

A Look at the list of equipment in the table. Complete the table with the name of the extreme sport using the words below.

ice climbing skateboarding skiing skydiving scuba diving surfing

Sport	Equipment
1	wetsuit flippers mask
2	sticks skis goggles
3	board swimwear wetsuit
4	helmet knee pads elbow pads
5	ice axes crampons
6	parachute helmet

B Complete the sentences with equipment from A.

1 Hold on to your ski ______ as you race down the slopes.
2 ______ really help you move through water more easily.
3 I love the moment when my ______ opens and I glide down to earth.
4 ______ and ______ really protect your joints as you do this.
5 You fix ______ onto your shoes so you can walk or climb on snow and ice.
6 Some people wear swimwear but I prefer a ______ to keep me warm in the water.

C Circle the correct words.

1 The instructor jumped into / off the top of the mountain.
2 I love jumping over / off the waves at the beach.
3 We walked along the wall and then jumped down / up.
4 It was so hot, I ran and jumped out of / into the swimming pool.
5 The children jumped into / onto their soapbox car to start the race.
6 One by one, the skydivers jumped out of / into the plane.

D Write the correct adjective for each pair of sentences. The first one is done for you.

1 a After surfing for three hours, she felt ______exhausted______.
  b Surfing is an ______exhausting______ sport.
  (exhausted / exhausting)
2 a Jemma is starting an ______ new extreme sport in the summer.
  b She's so ______.
  (excited / exciting)
3 a He doesn't stop talking about flying. He's very ______.
  b Everyone was ______ by his stories.
  (bored / boring)
4 a I think ice climbing is a very dangerous and ______ sport!
  b Yes, I felt ______ when I was going up.
  (frightened / frightening)

5 a Good morning, I'm ______________________ in buying some new ski boots.
b Those ones there look ______________________.
(interested / interesting)

6 a Lilly was ______________________ she didn't win a gold medal.
b The Olympics were ______________________ for her.
(disappointed / disappointing)

E **Circle the correct words.**

1 The race was easy / easily.
2 Karen Darke is a brave / bravely woman.
3 The skateboard came down the road noisy / noisily.
4 The athlete hurt herself bad / badly on the last slope.
5 The waves today are too dangerous / dangerously for surfing.
6 The divers swam slow / slowly over the coral.
7 Roger is a good / well skier. He skis very good / well.

Exam Close-up

Choosing the missing word

- Read each sentence and see if you know the missing word.
- Then look at the options to see if your word is an option.
- If your word isn't an option, try each option in the gap and see which one seems correct.

F **Read the *Exam Close-up*. Then read the *Exam Task* and guess the missing words without looking at the options.**

G **Now complete the *Exam Task*.**

Exam Task

Read the sentences about Oscar's bungee jumping experience. Choose the best word (A, B, C) for each answer.

1 Bungee jumping was an ______ experience!
A amaze B amazed C amazing

2 I jumped ______ a bridge last weekend; it was like flying!
A into B under C off

3 I was very ______ before I jumped.
A scary B frightened C frightening

4 You don't ______ wear any special equipment.
A must B have to C had to

5 They tie an elastic rope ______ around your ankles.
A carefully B careful C care

Bungee jumping off of Bloukrans Bridge in Western Cape, South Africa

Ideas Focus

- People who do extreme sports love putting themselves in danger. Why?
- 'Taking part in sport is better than winning.' Do you agree? Why? / Why not?

9 In The Extreme!

Grammar

Present Perfect (1)

A Read and underline examples of the Present Perfect. The first one is done for you.

1 <u>I've glided</u> off a volcano.
2 He has climbed to the top of Mount Everest.
3 She's swum from England to France.
4 I have never been to China.

B Look at the sentences in A. Complete the rules.

1 We form the Present Perfect with subject + ____________ / ____________ + past participle.
2 Often we use the contracted form 's or ______.
3 Some verbs have a regular past participle, e.g. ____________ or ____________.
4 Some verbs have an irregular past participle, e.g. ____________ or ____________.

C Complete the table with the correct irregular verb and its forms.

Infinitive	Past Simple	Past Participle
	was / were	
		gone
have		
	saw	
swim		
		flown
		run
win		
	met	
		broken

Paragliding over Koryaksky, a volcano found in Kamchatka, Russia

D Read the conversations. Circle *ever* and *never*.

1 **A:** Have you ever flown in a helicopter?
B: Yes, I have.
A: Where did you go?
B: I flew over the city of New York last year.
A: Did you like it?
B: Yes, it was really exciting!

2 **A:** Has she ever won a competition?
B: No, she hasn't. She's never won anything!

E Circle the correct options to complete the rules.

1 We use the Past Simple / Present Perfect to talk about things we have done at an unspecific time in the past.
2 We use the Past Simple / Present Perfect to talk about things we did at a specific time in the past.
3 We use *have/has* + ever / never + past participle to ask questions about experiences.
4 We use *have/has* + ever / never + past participle to explain we haven't had an experience.
5 We use *have/has* or *haven't/hasn't* in short answers to Past Simple / Present Perfect questions.

Grammar Focus p. 166 (9.1)

F Complete the sentences with the present perfect tense of the verbs in brackets.

1 I ____________ (run) in three marathons.
2 The teams ____________ (cycle) all around the world.
3 George ____________ (jump) off three bridges!
4 We ____________ (climb) Mount Everest.
5 Josie ____________ (not / fly) in a plane.
6 I ____________ (not / sail) in a boat.

G Complete the dialogue with the correct form of the verbs in brackets.

1 **A:** Have you ever ____________ (break) your leg?
B: Yes, I have.
A: When did you ____________ (break) it?
B: I ____________ (break) it last year.

2 **A:** Have you ever ____________ (meet) a famous person?
B: Yes, I have.
A: Who did you ____________ (meet)?
B: I ____________ (meet) the actor, Daniel Craig.

3 **A:** Have you ever ____________ (climb) a mountain?
B: No, I haven't. But I've ____________ (run) a marathon.

H Unjumble the questions and write your own short answe

1 in ever swum Have a you river?
____

2 Has country Olympic the games hosted ever yo
____

3 ever you met famous a Have person?
____

Grammar

First Conditional

I **Circle *if* and underline the verbs in each sentence.**

1 If he has time, he'll teach you how to surf.
2 If you don't wear gloves, your hands will get cold.
3 I'll buy a skateboard if I win some money.
4 You won't fall if you are careful.
5 We won't go rock climbing if the weather is bad.
6 If you enjoy surfing, you'll love kitesurfing!

J **Choose the correct answers, a or b.**

1 We use the first conditional to talk about ______ situations in the future.
   a possible   b impossible
2 We form the first conditional with *If + Present Simple*, + ______.
   a Past Simple   b *will*
3 When *If* is at the beginning of the sentence, a ______ separates the two clauses.
   a comma   b full stop

Grammar Focus p. 166 (9.2)

K **Match the beginnings 1–6 to the endings a–f.**

1 If you try bungee jumping,
2 We won't go skydiving,
3 If she has classes,
4 If you dive now,
5 They'll watch the race,
6 You'll get tired,

a she'll get better at skiing.
b if it rains.
c if they get tickets.
d if you don't rest.
e you'll see lots of tropical fish.
f you'll love it!

L **Correct the sentences.**

1 If you will eat your vitamins, you will stay healthy.
2 If they will wear a helmet, they will protect their heads.
3 We will go skiing if you will come with us.
4 If you will jump, your parachute will open.
5 They will win if they will run fast.
6 You will enjoy this sport if you will try it.

Exam Close-up

Checking for the parts of a tense

- Look at the whole sentence with the gap and identify the tense.
- Check the parts that make up the tense, for example auxiliary words like *do / will / have*.
- Check if the sentence has a negative or a question; this can affect verb endings.

M **Read the *Exam Close-up*. Then read the article in the *Exam Task*.**

N **Now complete the *Exam Task*.**

Exam Task

Read the article about fat biking. Choose the best word (**A**, **B** or **C**) for each space.

Fat biking

Have you ever **(1)** ______ fat biking? It's a new sport that is becoming more and more popular. If you don't like mountain biking, you **(2)** ______ fat biking. It's an easy sport to learn and it's not as dangerous as mountain biking. I **(3)** ______ a group of fat bikers last summer. It was strange at first because fat bikes have very fat tyres! These bikes are popular in places like Alaska where there **(4)** ______ a lot of snow and New Mexico where there are **(5)** ______ sandy areas. The bikes 'glide' across the tracks and I learnt how to ride **(6)** ______. You don't have to worry about falling **(7)** ______ and hurting yourself. I'd never **(8)** ______ like this before and it was great fun. If you try it, I'm sure you'll find it's **(9)** ______!

	A	B	C
1	try	tried	go
2	are loving	love	will love
3	joined	have joined	will join
4	are	was	is
5	many	much	a lot
6	quick	good	well
7	of	off	onto
8	cycled	have cycled	cycle
9	excite	excited	exciting

9 In The Extreme!

A Mermaid swimming

B Trapezing

C Zorbing

Listening

A **Work with a partner. Look at the photos. How are these activities 'extreme'?**

B 9.1 **Listen to the descriptions and number the sports in the order you hear them.**

Mermaid swimming ☐
Trapezing ☐
Zorbing ☐

C 9.2 **Now listen to two students giving their opinions about the sports. Write one positive and one negative opinion about each sport in the table.**

	Mermaid swimming	Trapezing	Zorbing
positive			
negative			

D **Use the expressions below and your notes in the table to talk about the three sports with a partner.**

I think that ...
I agree.
It's interesting but ...
I don't agree.
In my opinion, ...

E **Read the *Exam Close-up*. Then read the *Exam Task*.**

F 9.3 **Now listen and complete the *Exam Task*.**

Exam Close-up

Focusing on specific information

- This part of the exam focuses on understanding specific information.
- Look at the options as you listen so you know the details you are listening for.
- If you are not sure about an answer, leave it and answer it the second time you listen.

Exam Task

Listen to Harry talking to a friend, Victor, about a new hobby. For each question, choose the right answer, (**A**, **B** or **C**). You will hear the conversation twice.

1 What sport has Harry done before?
 A cycling to school
 B skateboarding
 C mountain biking

2 How wide are the fat bike tyres?
 A 15 cms wide
 B 10 cms wide
 C 5 cms wide

3 What is the problem with fat bikes?
 A they're fast
 B they're heavy
 C they're too much fun

4 Where did Victor cycle last month?
 A on beaches
 B along the cliffs
 C on the snow

5 How much did Victor's bike cost?
 A £1,500
 B £550
 C £450

G 9.4 **Listen again and check your answers.**

Speaking

A **Work with a partner. Take turns to ask and answer the questions. Add two more questions of your own.**

Have you ever been surfing?
Yes, I have. / No, I haven't.

	Have you ever …	Me	My partner
1	been mountain biking?	☐	☐
2	been skateboarding?	☐	☐
3	been ice skating?	☐	☐
4	been skiing?	☐	☐
5	climbed a mountain?	☐	☐
6	done an extreme sport?	☐	☐
7	____________?	☐	☐
8	____________?	☐	☐

B **Use the question starters below to ask your partner for more information in A.**

Where did you …? When did you …?
Who did you … with? Did you …?

C **Complete the dialogue with information from the advert. Give full answers.**

HIGH LIFE TRAPEZE

New classes starting 4th February.
Two classes a week for 12 weeks.
8.45 a.m. and 6.30 p.m.
12 people only per class.
Course fee: £75
Join now on our website: www.trapezehighlife.com

A Hi. I'm calling about your trapeze course. When does the next course start?
B (1) The course ____________
A Do you have classes in the morning?
B (2) ____________
A What time are the classes in the morning?
B (3) The classes ____________
A How many people are there in each class?
B (4) There ____________
A How much does the course cost?
B (5) The course ____________
A OK. Great. Can I join online?
B (6) ____________

D **Read the *Exam Close-up*. With a partner, practise the dialogue in C.**

E **Now complete the *Exam Task*. Use the *Useful Expressions* to help you.**

Exam Close-up

Asking for & giving details

- Become familiar with questions that ask for times, prices and dates.
- Use the information in the question to help you give full answers, e.g. *How much does the course cost? The course costs …*

Exam Task

1 **Student A:** You teach at an extreme sports club. Look at the information about your classes. **Student B:** turn to page 184. You want to join an extreme sports class. Ask **A** some questions about it.

The only way is UP! Indoor climbing classes

Classes for beginners and experienced climbers ✓
Classes: 12.00 noon 6 p.m. 8 p.m.
Small classes: Six students per group
Price: £12 per class
Equipment: We have all the equipment you need! Just wear comfortable clothes.

2 **Student B:** You do an extreme sport. Here is the information about it.
Student A: Turn to page 184. You want to take up an extreme sport. Ask **Student B** some questions about it.

Snowboarding

- Every winter.
- Alps in Switzerland.
- Great!
- Go with a group of friends.
- Snowboard, gloves and glasses.

Useful Expressions

Asking for details
I'd like some information about …
What's the address?
When do the classes start?
What time do the classes start?
How many students are there in a class?
How much does it cost?
Do I need to bring …?

Giving details
The address is …
The course starts on/at …
It costs …

Ideas Focus

- Do you think schools should teach more sports? Why? / Why not?
- What things do you find exciting / frightening? Why?

9 In The Extreme!

Writing: a blog

Learning Focus

Thinking about your readers

- A blog is all about connecting with your readers, online. It's like a diary you share with others.
- In a blog, you want your readers to see your personality and what is important to you.
- Blogs normally include a picture and links to websites.
- They often call readers to take action!
- They have short paragraphs with headings and subheadings.
- Readers will make comments on your information and share opinions so it's important to write back or just say thank you.

A Read the blog. Match the parts of the blog 1–6 with a label a–f.

a heading
b subheading
c link to other information
d call to action
e short paragraph
f an image

B Read the blog again and underline the adjectives. Complete the rules and examples.

1 Adjectives ending in ________ talk about how we feel.
For example: *When I felt ________, I stopped for an ice cream.*
2 Adjectives ending in ________ describe characteristics.
For example: *Here's a sport that's ________.*
3 Remember, adjectives make your writing more ____________!

C Complete the table with the missing adjectives.

-ed	-ing
	interesting
	shocking
	surprising
tired	
excited	
disappointed	
	amazing

(1) ☐

(2) ☐ Stefan's Extreme Blog

You know, I've tried lots of extreme sports. So here's a sport that's interesting but not 'extreme'.

(3) ☐ Forget transport

You plan a route carefully with a map and then explore your city! You don't need to visit museums, just walk and enjoy. Look at the trees, the graffiti, the streetlights, statues, etc. When I felt tired, I stopped for an ice cream!

Urban walking

(4) ☐ It's shocking but no one seems to walk anymore! We take buses and trains or drive everywhere. That's why urban walking is so surprising and great exercise!

Check out **(5)** ☐ www.myurbanwalking.com, get excited and **(6)** ☐ walk! You won't be disappointed. And yes, post your amazing pictures here!

D Read the blog. Circle the correct adjectives.

A new experience

Here's a picture of me doing urban walking! It was an amazed / amazing experience and I really enjoyed myself. At first, I was a little confused / confusing because I got lost but then I was fine.

My city

I didn't realise there were so many steps in my city! It was quite tired / tiring but there were beautiful views from a small park behind the bridge. I didn't know it existed! Stefan's right, I wasn't disappointed / disappointing and I want to discover more!

E Write a blog about walking in your city to encourage your friends to try it. Use the *Learning Focus* and the *Useful Expressions* to help you.

F Read the *Exam Close-up*. Then check your spelling in E.

G Now complete the *Exam Task*. Remember to review your answers.

Exam Task

Read the poster and blog. Fill in the information in the student's certificate.

Maggie's BLOG 31st May, 2017

Wow! Just finished my beginner's diving course and got my certificate today to prove it!

It was a relaxing location and the instructor, Bernie Anderson, was amazing!

Take a look at the website: www.pelicandiving.com

Certificate

Try it! If you love fish and swimming, you won't be disappointed!

This is to certify that

Maggie Taylor

has completed

Time: **(1)** ______________ hours

Sport: **(2)** of ______________

Place: **(3)** at ______________

Date: **(4)** on ______________ 2017

Name of Instructor: **(5)** ______________

Useful Expressions

Using adjectives

I was surprised / disappointed …

It was surprising / disappointing …

I got tired.

It was tiring.

I was amazed by this place.

It was an amazing place.

I felt excited.

It was exciting.

I'm interested in street art.

Street art is interesting.

Exam Close-up

Looking back & checking

- After you have completed the notes in the task, look back at the two original short texts.
- Check the information and your answers again.
- Check your spelling, too. Sometimes we make mistakes when we are in a hurry.

BEGINNERS' INTRODUCTION COURSE TO SCUBA DIVING

Ten hours of diving at PELICAN DIVING CENTRE

ROSARIO ISLANDS

Video 9 Extremely Spectacular

Before you watch

A **Look at the photo. Imagine this is you on top of this rock? How do you feel? Why did you climb this rock? Tell your partner.**

While you watch

B **Watch the video. Circle the correct information.**

1. Cedar Wright says China has one of the most diverse / difficult landscapes.
2. The rock formations were formed by hundreds / millions of years of erosion.
3. Cedar wants to climb / paraglide over these formations.
4. Sometimes the experience is adventurous, other times it's dangerous / boring.
5. Many people / Not many people have explored China.
6. This type of landscape / sport can inspire and change you.

Mountain found in Zhangjiajie National Park in Hunan, China

After you watch

C **Complete the summary of the video below using these words.**

climber many explore landscape life
new physically rock years

China has **(1)** ____________ areas with beautiful **(2)** ____________ formations. Cedar Wright is a **(3)** ____________. He says that climbing these formations is one of the most unique and special experiences of his **(4)** ____________.

Climbers and adventurers want to **(5)** ____________ China's landscapes and see something **(6)** ____________ and spectacular. For Cedar, climbing is a way to interact with the **(7)** ____________. He likes exploring and pushing himself mentally and **(8)** ____________. He feels that a landscape like this affects you as a person and inspires you as a climber.

Ideas Focus

- Is rock climbing an extreme sport? Why? / Why not?
- 'The world still has places to explore.' Do you agree?

10 Eat Your Greens!

Reading:	matching, finding words with similar meanings
Vocabulary:	food-related words, expressions and verbs for talking about food and health
Grammar:	past continuous, *should*, imperatives, present perfect (2), reflexive verbs
Listening:	multiple-choice (pictures), listening for specific information
Speaking:	describing photos, asking how someone is feeling, talking about your health, responding to advice, giving advice
Writing:	a note, apologising & making excuses, expanding your answers

A beaver cutting willow branches in Beaver Pond, Alaska

10 Eat Your Greens!

Fruit and vegetable market in Konya, Turkey

Reading

A Work with a partner. List as many fruit and vegetables as you can. You have one minute. Then discuss which ones you like and dislike, and why.

B Do the quiz with your partner and find out how healthy you both are. Do you agree with the quiz results?

Healthy Habits Questionnaire

* one portion = the amount you can hold in your hand.

		a	b	c
1	How much fruit do you eat a day?	1 portion ☐	2 portions ☐	3 + ☐
2	How many vegetables do you eat a day?	1 portion ☐	2 portions ☐	3 + ☐
3	How many glasses of water do you drink a day?	1 glass ☐	2 glasses ☐	3 + ☐
4	How many glasses of fruit juice do you drink a day?	1 glass ☐	2 glasses ☐	3 + ☐
5	How much exercise do you do in a week?	1 hour ☐	2 hours ☐	3 + ☐
6	How many hours do you sleep on a school night?	7 hours ☐	8 hours ☐	9 + ☐

Mostly (a) answers.
You could be healthier! Start eating more fruit and vegetables.
Do more exercise.

Mostly (b) answers.
You're doing well! Add two more portions of fruit and vegetables a day.
Can you do another hour of exercise each week?

Mostly (c) answers.
Congratulations. You are fit and healthy!

Word Focus

headache: a pain in your head
hydrated: with enough water / not thirsty
frozen: kept extremely cold in a freezer
can: a metal container for food
fizzy: with bubbles of gas
tooth decay: a tooth is damaged

C Read the information on the three posters. Why is it important to follow the advice?

DRINK WATER!

Did you know that almost 70 per cent of your body is water?

Your body needs water. Without water your body can't work properly and it's easy to get tired, get headaches and lose concentration.

Check how much water you need to drink.

Age	Males	Females
9–13	6 glasses/day	5–6 glasses/day
14–18	7 glasses/day	6 glasses/day

WATER is wonderful! It contains no sugar that can cause problems for your teeth. You can add a slice of lemon for a different taste.

Remember, when it is hot you need to drink more water to keep your body hydrated.

Five a day to stay ... HEALTHY!

One third (33 per cent) of the food we eat in a day should be fruit and vegetables.

Doctors say we should eat at least five portions a day. This sounds a lot, but just one apple or pear, or a banana, counts as one portion. Three big spoons of vegetables is another portion.

Think about adding a banana to your cereal in the morning, or eating an orange or some grapes instead of a biscuit for your snack. Have some vegetables with your dinner, and strawberries with yoghurt for dessert!

Almost all fruit and vegetables count towards your five a day. They can be fresh, frozen, dried or in a can!

A glass of fruit juice can also count as a portion, but be careful ... some fruit juices contain a lot of sugar.

D **Read the three posters again. Are the sentences true (T) or false (F)? Correct the false information.**

1 More than half of our body is water. ____
2 You can get a stomach ache if you don't drink enough water. ____
3 If you are a 13-year-old boy you should drink seven glasses of water a day. ____
4 We should eat five portions of fruit and vegetables every day. ____
5 A banana is one portion. ____
6 A fizzy drink has less sugar than some cereals. ____

Exam Close-up

Finding words with similar meanings

- Think about where you might see the signs in the *Exam Task*.
- Look for words that are similar in the description and in the sign.
- Underline or circle words with similar meanings: *it's closed/it's not open/it's quiet/don't make a noise.*

E **Read the *Exam Close-up*. Then read the *Exam Task* and underline words that are similar in meaning.**

F **Now complete the *Exam Task*. Use the words you underlined to help you.**

G **Look back at the *Exam Task* and write the word or words that have a similar meaning.**

1 not sweet: ____________________
2 no food permitted: ____________________
3 use again: ____________________
4 needs to stay cold: ____________________
5 reserve: ____________________
6 www.Netgames.com: ____________________

Exam Task

Which notice **(A – H)** says this **(1 – 5)**?

1 It is not sweet. ☐
2 You cannot eat here. ☐
3 You can use the bottle again. ☐
4 It needs to stay cold. ☐
5 You can reserve classes online. ☐

A

B

C

D

E

F

G

H

A spoonful of sugar!

Did you know that sugar hides in our food?

A hamburger has two teaspoons.
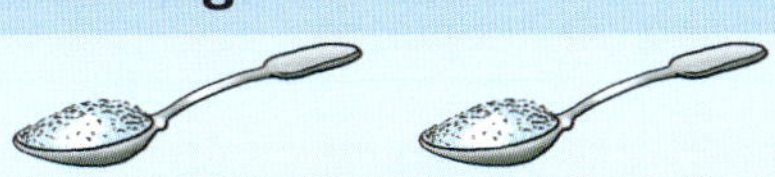

Toast and jam has four teaspoons.

A fizzy drink has seven teaspoons.
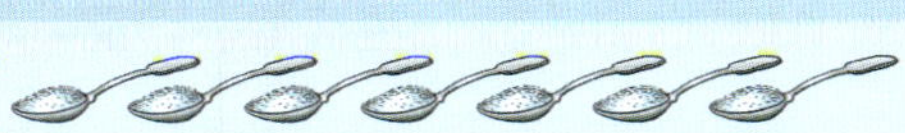

Some cereals have as many as eleven teaspoons per bowl.

Too much sugar is not a healthy option! It causes tooth decay and can make you put on weight.

Ideas Focus

- Do you think you are healthy? Why? / Why not?
- Being healthy is not just about food. Do you agree? Why? / Why not?

10 Eat Your Greens!

Vocabulary

A Match the descriptions to the right photo. Write the letter and the name of the fruit or vegetable.

A

B

C

D

E

F

G

H

I

J

1 It's a green fruit that grows on trees. It has a big seed inside. ☐ ______
2 It's a long, thin orange vegetable. It grows underground. ☐ ______
3 It's a small, red, heart-shaped fruit. It has seeds on the outside. ☐ ______
4 It's an oval, purple vegetable. It's white inside. ☐ ______
5 It's a big fruit that has a rough, brown skin and is yellow inside. ☐ ______
6 It's a vegetable with a big white head. It looks like a flower. ☐ ______

B With a partner, take turns to describe and guess a fruit or vegetable not described in A.

C Put the foods in the correct column in the table. Then think of one extra food for each column.

biscuits carrots cheese eggs pasta fizzy drinks rice watermelon yoghurt fish

VITAMINS	CARBOHYDRATES	PROTEINS	CALCIUM	FATS and SUGAR
… keep your body healthy	… give your body energy	… help your body grow strong	… helps keep your bones and teeth strong	Eat fewer of these foods!
tomatoes	bread	meat	milk	doughnuts
______	______	______	______	______
______	______	______	______	______

D Choose the correct options to complete the descriptions of food and drink.

1 Water is ______. Fizzy drinks are ______.
 a unhealthy b healthy
2 Biscuits are ______. Crisps are ______.
 a sweet b salty
3 Eggs in the supermarket are ______. Eggs in a salad are ______.
 a cooked b raw
4 Fruit at the market is ______. Food in the freezer is ______.
 a frozen b fresh
5 I love ice cream. It's ______. I don't like raw fish. It's ______!
 a delicious b disgusting

E Look at the pictures. Choose the best description.

1 She's tired / thirsty.

2 He's got a toothache / a temperature.

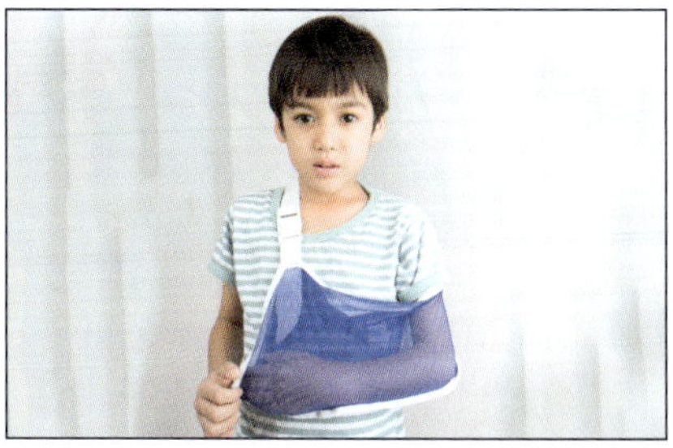

3 He's got a broken arm / leg.

4 She's got a cold / a fever.

5 He's got a headache / stomach ache.

F Use a word to complete each sentence.

brush do drink eat hurt stay take visit

1 If you're thirsty then __________ some water!
2 Do you __________ sport at the weekend?
3 I __________ my teeth after every meal.
4 Don't forget to __________ your medicine.
5 What snacks do you usually __________?
6 You need to rest and __________ in bed.
7 Did you __________ the dentist when you had toothache?
8 My ears always __________ after swimming.

G Circle the correct words.

A healthy granddad

My granddad is 77 years old but he's so energetic and **(1)** healthy / exercise! He never **(2)** is / gets a cold. He goes to bed early and gets up early. He **(3)** sleeps / slept for ten hours every night!

Sometimes he has fruit for breakfast but sometimes he drinks a **(4)** frozen / raw egg! He says it has lots of **(5)** protein / sugar. And then he has toast with lots of **(6)** salty / sweet jam. After breakfast, he walks to the market to buy **(7)** fizzy / fresh meat or fish. If it's a nice day, he walks to the park to read his newspaper. In the afternoon, he cycles to a friend's garden, and looks after the vegetables. There is an apple tree with very **(8)** juicy / cooked apples!

Twice a week my granddad goes dancing. Three years ago, he **(9)** got / broke his leg but as soon as he was **(10)** better / worse, he was dancing again! He says his grandchildren keep him young but I think it's his healthy lifestyle!

Ideas Focus

- 'We should all be vegetarians.' Do you agree? Why? / Why not?
- Do you need to join a sports club to do sport? Why? / Why not?

10 Eat Your Greens!

Grammar

A woman walking her dog along the beach in Saltcoats, Scotland

Past Continuous

A Underline the verbs in the Past Continuous and match the meanings 1–3, to a description a–c.

1. It was raining the day that Carly took her dog to the beach. ☐
2. The children were cycling in the park and their dog was running beside them. ☐
3. I was jumping on the trampoline when I fell off! ☐

We use the past continuous to describe:

a a longer action being interrupted by another.
b two or more actions happening at the same time.
c the background of a situation or story.

B Read and underline the Past Continuous. Then complete the rules with the words below.

A Where were you yesterday morning?
B I was lying in bed.
A Why weren't you in class?
B I wasn't feeling well.

was wasn't were weren't be

- We use the verb ____________ in the past and the *–ing* form of another verb.
- We use ____________ and ____________ + *–ing* to form the negative.
- In questions, ____________ and ____________ change places with the subject.

Should, Imperatives & Other expressions

C Look at the underlined words. What do we use all of these words/phrases for? Choose the correct option a, b, or c.

1. You should stay in bed.
2. You shouldn't go out without a coat. It's cold.
3. If it is hot, you should drink water.
4. Drink more water. Don't drink so many fizzy drinks.
5. Why don't you take an aspirin if you have a headache?

a We use these words to make excuses.
b We use these words to give advice.
c We use these words to express obligation.

Grammar Focus p. 167 (10.1)

D Complete the sentences with the Past Continuous forms of the verbs in brackets.

1. Marta and Lilly ran outside because it ________________ (snow).
2. Felix ________________ (skateboard) round the park and I ________________ (jog).
3. 'What ________________ (you / do) yesterday at midday?' – 'I ________________ (have) lunch with Helen.'
4. The children ________________ (feel) hungry so I made them a sandwich.
5. We ________________ (not / listen) when she gave us advice.
6. I ________________ (chop) onions when I cut my finger.

E Read and choose the correct words to give advice.

Don't Change should shouldn't Why don't you

1. A: I feel sick.
   B: You ____________ go to school.
2. A: My leg hurts.
   B: ____________ do any sport this weekend.
3. A: I've got toothache.
   B: You ____________ go to the dentist.
4. A: I'm hot.
   B: ____________ have a drink of water?
5. A: I got wet in the rain.
   B: ____________ your clothes!

Grammar

Present Perfect (2)

F Circle *just, already,* and *yet* in a–e and then complete the rules for using these words.

a John's just come back from the sports centre. He's tired.

b I've already done my homework. Now I can relax.

c 'Can you wash your hands?' – 'I've washed them already.'

d 'Has Sara had breakfast yet?' – 'No, she hasn't.'

e 'Have you finished your book?' – 'No, I haven't finished it yet.'

1 We use ____________ to talk about a task we haven't done, but still need to do.

2 We use ____________ to talk about something that happened in the very recent past, a few moments ago.

3 We use ____________ to explain that we have completed a task.

4 We use ____________ at the end of questions and negative sentences.

5 We use ____________ between the auxiliary and the past participle, or at the end of a sentence.

6 We only use ____________ between the auxiliary and the past participle.

Reflexive Verbs

G Some verbs have a reflexive pronoun. Read and underline the reflexive pronouns. The first one is done for you. Then complete the table.

1 Dad burnt <u>himself</u> yesterday when he was baking bread.

2 We hurt ourselves when we were climbing the tree.

3 Can your grandparents look after themselves?

4 I cut myself when I was chopping the onions.

5 Do you enjoy yourself when you play basketball?

Subject	Reflexive pronoun
I	____________
you	____________
he/she	____________
we	____________
they	____________

Grammar Focus p. 167 (10.2 to 10.3)

H Read and complete the dialogue with *just, yet* or *already.*

1 A: I've ____________ made a cake!
B: Wow! It looks delicious!

2 A: Have you taken your medicine?
B: No, I haven't taken it ____________.

3 A: Have you done your warm-up exercises?
B: Yes, I've ____________ done them.

4 A: Can I borrow that book?
B: No, sorry, I haven't finished it ____________.

5 A: Something smells delicious!
B: I've ____________ made some vegetable soup.

I Complete the sentences with the correct reflexive pronoun.

1 Dan was making the dinner when he cut ____________.

2 Hi, Jessica! Come in, and help ____________ to a sandwich. They're on the table.

3 My nephews are teenagers now, but they can't look after ____________ – they can't even make toast!

4 We've just booked ____________ a holiday to the Maldives! We can't wait!

5 I've got a terrible cold. I've studied so hard this term, I've made ____________ ill.

J Look at the sports teacher's to-do list for sports day. Answer in full sentences using *yet* or *already.*

1 Has he made the snacks?
Yes, he's already made the snacks/ Yes, he's already made them.

2 Has he got the equipment?

3 Has he bought the prizes?

4 Has he designed the T-shirts?

5 Has he printed the programme?

✓ make snacks
✗ get equipment
✓ buy prizes
✓ design T-shirts
✗ print programme

10 Eat Your Greens!

Listening

A Some people think that lemon juice is a *cure-all* and can cure many illnesses. Do you have any *cure-alls* in your country?

B Work with a partner. Look at the photos and discuss how you think the items can help people be healthy.

A

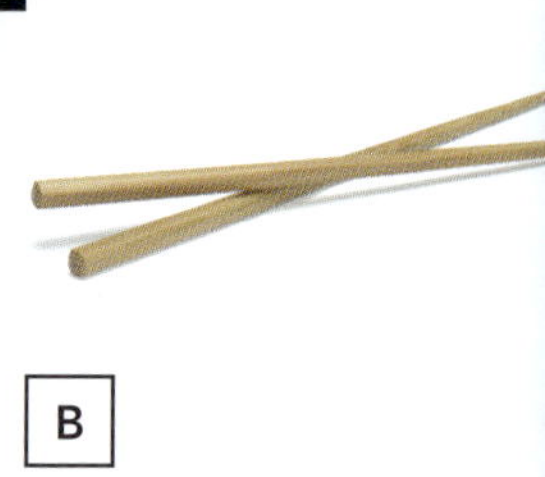
B

C

D

E

C 10.1 Listen to the descriptions and match each one to the correct photo. Write the letter.

1 ☐
2 ☐
3 ☐
4 ☐
5 ☐

D 10.1 Listen again and circle the countries mentioned.

1 Bulgaria / Italy
2 China / Chile
3 New Zealand / Sweden
4 Spain / Britain
5 Mexico / Colombia

E Read the *Exam Close-up*. Then notice the details in each picture in the *Exam Task* and look for any differences.

F 10.2 Now listen and complete the *Exam Task*.

Exam Close-up

Listening for specific information

- Always look for the differences between the three pictures for each question.
- You will hear the description of one or two of the other pictures, too.
- Listen carefully for the speaker's final decision to help you choose the right answer.

Exam Task

You will hear five short conversations. You will hear each conversation twice. There is one question for each conversation. For each question, choose the right answer (**A**, **B** or **C**).

1 What did Mario wear on his feet?

A B C

2 What's Kim's favourite vegetable?

A B C

3 How much exercise does Danny do every day?

A 90 minutes
B 60 minutes
C 40 minutes

4 Which bicycle did Anita buy?

A B C

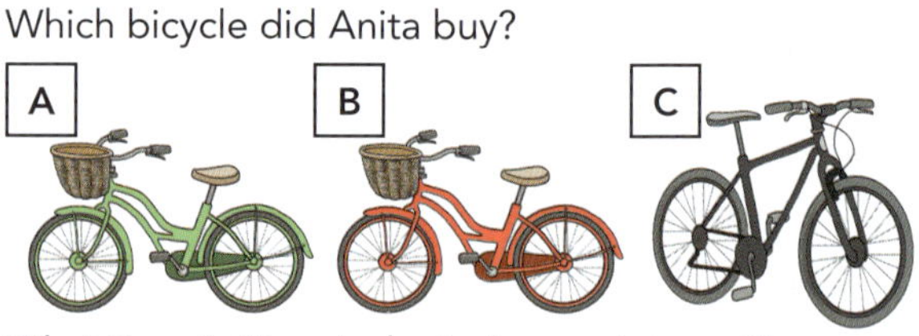

5 What time is Steve's doctor's appointment?

A B C

G 10.3 Listen again and check your answers.

Speaking

A **Work with a partner. Talk about the last time you did these things.**

1 went to the dentist
2 went to the doctor
3 went to a hospital
4 had an injection
5 stayed in bed all day

A: When was the last time you went to the dentist?
B: I went two months ago.

Exam Close-up

Giving advice

- Learn and practise different ways to ask how someone is feeling, and to give advice.
- Notice how to respond to advice; this will help you with conversations.
- Listen carefully to your partner's answers. That way you can respond in the correct way.

B **Complete the conversation between two friends. There are three options you do not need to use.**

Harry: You don't look well. What's the matter?
Lynne: (1) ______________________
Harry: Have you been to the doctor?
Lynne: (2) ______________________
Harry: Why do they hurt?
Lynne: (3) ______________________
Harry: You should warm up and stretch the muscles.
Lynne: (4) ______________________
Harry: And you should buy good running shoes. They can make a difference.
Lynne: (5) ______________________
Harry: Not at all. Why don't you come running with me tomorrow if you feel better?
Lynne: Great!

A No, I'm not healthy yet.
B Really? I didn't know that. Thanks for your help.
C The muscles in my legs hurt.
D That's a good idea.
E No, I haven't been yet.
F I don't look well.
G It hurts a lot. Thank you.
H I've just been running for the first time.

Useful Expressions

Asking how someone is feeling

What's the matter?
What's wrong?
Are you feeling OK?

Talking about your health

I've got a temperature / a fever / a cold / toothache / a headache.
I feel sick / tired / thirsty / hungry.
My … hurts.
I fell down / over / off.
I cut / burnt / hurt myself.

Giving advice

You should …
You shouldn't …
If you feel sick, you should …
Eat / Drink / Go / Do …
Don't eat …
Why don't you …?

Responding to advice

Thanks. That's a good idea.
That's good advice. Thank you.

C **Read the *Exam Close-up* and then work in pairs and complete the *Exam Task*.**

Exam Task

Student A: Look at photos 1 and 2 and tell **Student B** what is happening in both. **Student B:** Look at photos 3 and 4 and tell **Student A** what is happening in both. Then work together and give advice to each person in the photos. Use the 'Notes' and *Useful Expressions* to help you. Don't be afraid to give more than one piece of advice.

Notes

- Doctors / Dentist / Hospital / Bed / Exercise
- Asprin / X-ray / Plaster / Broken / Brush teeth
- Sugar / Fizzy drinks / Sweets / Vegetables

1
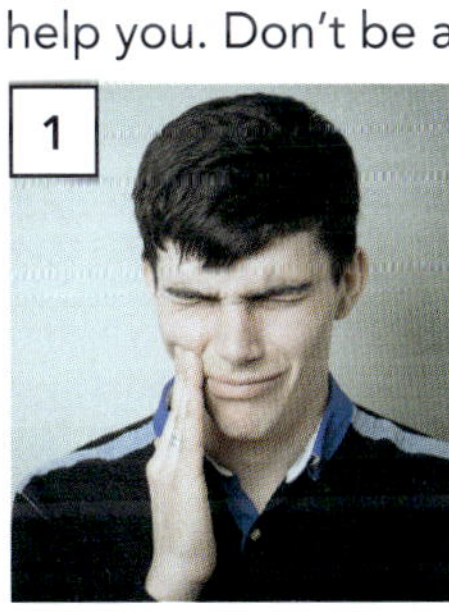
2

3
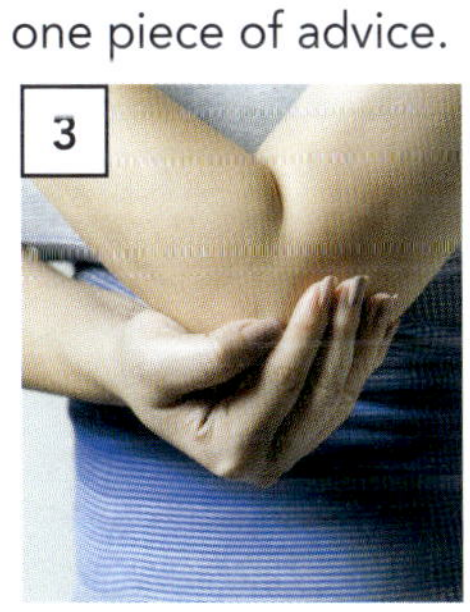
4
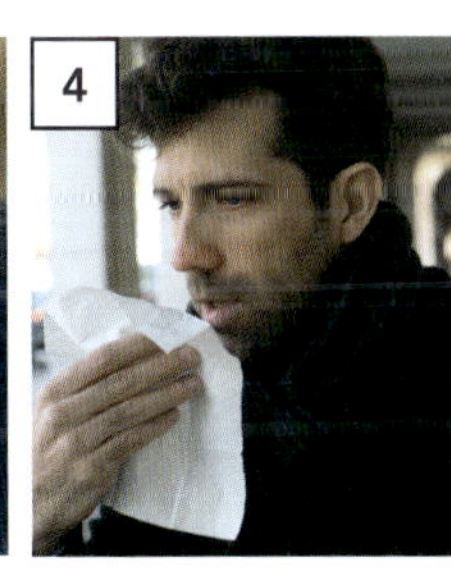

Ideas Focus

- Do you try to eat healthy food? Why? / Why not?
- What should the government do to help people be more healthy?

10 Eat Your Greens!

Writing: a note

Learning Focus

Apologising & making excuses

- When we apologise, we say we are sorry. We often give a reason or an excuse why we can't or couldn't do something when it was expected.
- The types of expressions we use often change depending on the situation, the place or the person.
- For example, if you are talking to someone important, you will use more formal language, e.g. *I apologise …* and we also avoid contractions, for example we say *I cannot* instead of *I can't*. If we are speaking to a friend, we can just say *I'm sorry*.
- We can also use *I'm afraid that …* informally, or *I am afraid that …* formally, when we give an excuse.

Artwork created with more than 100,000 sticky notes

A **Read the questions and match them with an apology or excuse.**

1. Have you taken the dog out yet? ☐
2. Why haven't you finished this project? ☐
3. Have you taken your medicine today? ☐
4. Can I make an appointment for this afternoon? ☐

a. No. Sorry, but I don't like it. It tastes horrible.
b. No, not yet, because it's raining.
c. I'm afraid we're closed.
d. I'm sorry. I couldn't. I've been in hospital.

B **Complete the excuses in the notes with the correct word.**

afraid apologise because but sorry

A
Mike – Really ________ I can't go out on Saturday. My grandparents are visiting. Lorna x

B
Good morning, Miss Burns, I'm ________ Vicky can't attend school today ________ she is sick.

C
Sorry ________ can't go shopping today, got doc's appt. in town.

D
Dear Mr Wright,
I ________ that I could not attend your presentation. I am afraid my plane was cancelled.
Kindest regards,
Joan Potter

C **Work with a partner. Number the excuses in B in order of how formal they are, starting with the most formal (1). How did you decide?**

D Match each situation with the correct excuse. Choose a or b.

1 Email Message

To: Toby Fryer From: Myra Dixon
Subject: Barbecue

Hi Toby,
My cousin is having a birthday barbecue on Sunday afternoon from 4 – 6 p.m.
Why don't you come along?
Let me know!
Myra x

a Email Message

To: Myra Dixon From: Toby Fryer
Subject: Barbecue

Hey Myra,
Sorry but I can't make the barbecue on Sunday. I've got an important football game that afternoon.
Thanks for asking. Have a fun time!
Toby x

b Email Message

To: Myra Dixon From: Toby Fryer
Subject: Barbecue

Dear Ms Dixon,
Unfortunately, I will not be able to join you for your cousin's barbecue on Sunday.
I have an important football game that afternoon.
Please accept my apologies and I hope we will be able to meet soon.
Best wishes,
Toby

2 Email Message

To: Rachel Heath From: Geoff Grant
Subject: Interview

Dear Ms Heath,
We would like to invite you to an interview on Thursday 11th March, at ten o'clock.
The interview will take place at our office in Regent Road and will last approximately 45 minutes.
Please confirm your attendance.
Yours sincerely,
Geoff Grant
HR Manager

a Email Message

To: Geoff Grant From: Rachel Heath
Subject: Interview

Hi Geoff,
That's fantastic news about the interview but I can't make it on Thursday morning because I have a hairdresser's appointment.
Is Friday OK? Hope so!
Can't wait to meet you,
Rachel

b Email Message

To: Geoff Grant From: Rachel Heath
Subject: Interview

Dear Mr Grant,
Many thanks for your offer of an interview.
Unfortunately, I have another appointment and cannot attend an interview on Thursday 11th March.
Would it be possible to arrange an interview for the following week?
I look forward to hearing from you.
Sincere apologies,
Rachel Heath

E Now rewrite the letter below in the correct order in your notebook.

Yours sincerely
Unfortunately, I cannot attend an interview on 26th May.
I look forward to hearing from you.
Dear Ms Thornton,
I'm afraid I have to be in Paris that day.
James Wright
I hope we can reschedule the interview for another day.

Exam Close-up

Expanding your answers

- In the right situation, reasons and excuses can help expand your answers.
- Make sure you know what words come after the expressions you use.
- Check who you are writing to, and what the situation is. Decide if you need formal or informal language.

F Read the *Exam Close-up*. Then read the email in the *Exam Task* and think about your excuses. Will you need to use present tenses or past tenses in your reply?

G Now complete the *Exam Task*. Use the *Useful Expressions* to help you.

Useful Expressions

Saying sorry	Making excuses
I'm sorry!	I'm afraid I can't / couldn't / didn't
I'm sorry, but …	I can't / cannot / couldn't because …
I apologise, but …	I didn't because …
I apologise that I couldn't …	I'm sorry, but I have to / had to …
I'm sorry that I didn't …	

Exam Task

Read the email from Mr Banks.

Email Message

Re: Royal Hedges Riding Competition

Dear Jason,
Could you explain why you did not take part in the riding competition last weekend?
I tried to call you but there was no answer. Were you sick?
When can you come and see me at my office? We need to talk about next month's riding classes.
Many thanks,
Mr Banks

Write an email to Mr Banks and answer the questions. Write **25–35** words.

Video 10 Tasty Snacks!

Before you watch

A What do you think the four photos have in common? Tick the boxes.

honey pot ant(s)

a Huhu grub(s)

the Thai zebra tarantula

a cicada(s)

1 A lot of people don't like them. ☐
2 They are all insects. ☐
3 They are all poisonous. ☐
4 They are all vegetarians. ☐
5 People eat them. ☐
6 They all live underground. ☐

While you watch

B Watch the video. Decide if these statements are T (True) or F (False).

1 Many people have a fear of poisonous spiders. ☐
2 Tourists don't like to eat Thai zebra tarantulas in Cambodia. ☐
3 This tarantula lives in nests in the treetops. ☐
4 People capture the tarantulas with their hands. ☐
5 A bite from a tarantula can kill you. ☐
6 People eat the tarantula raw, without cooking it. ☐

After you watch

C Complete the summary of the video below using these words.

cooks good hands hot hurt nests poisonous snack

In Cambodia, in South-east Asia, the Thai zebra tarantula is a tasty **(1)** ____________ ! The tarantulas live in **(2)** ____________ underground and trackers capture them with their **(3)** ____________ . These tarantulas are **(4)** ____________ ; their bite will **(5)** ____________ but it won't kill you! Local **(6)** ____________ wash and prepare the tarantulas. Then they fry them until they are good and crispy. They are served nice and **(7)** ____________ . In the past, Cambodians ate tarantulas because they had no other food, now they eat them because they like them. Locals say the poison they have is **(8)** ____________ for you!

Ideas Focus

- Have you ever eaten an insect? Would you like to? Why? / Why not?
- What's your favourite snack? Why?

Review 5 Units 9 & 10

Vocabulary

A Complete the sentences with the words.

board flippers helmet parachute ropes skis swimsuit wetsuit

1 The scuba divers put ____________ on their feet before jumping in the sea.
2 You need to wear a ____________ on your head if you go cycling or skateboarding.
3 You need ____________ to go down those mountain slopes. There's a lot of snow!
4 Climbers use ____________ to help them go up a mountain face.
5 A ____________ protects your body and keeps you warm in deep water.
6 I didn't go to the pool party because I forgot my ____________.
7 The skydiver pulled open his ____________ sixty seconds after jumping out of the plane.
8 How long does it take surfers to learn to stand on their ____________?

B Write the adverb form of the word in brackets.

1 The team cycle very ____________ (dangerous) when they are in a competition.
2 The Olympic winner skied down the mountain slopes ____________ (easy).
3 Eat your food ____________ (slow). It's better for you.
4 The children ran ____________ (excited) towards the waves.
5 Marco and Alicia surf really ____________ (good).
6 My brother fell ____________ (bad) and broke his leg.
7 The rescuers jumped ____________ (brave) into the cold sea.
8 We followed the instructions ____________ (careful) to build the soapbox car.

C Circle the correct words.

1 Mayra was disappointed / disappointing with her exam results.
2 Doing a trapeze course will be very excited / exciting.
3 The children were bored / boring when the games finished.
4 My friends are interested / interesting in learning a new sport.
5 Swimming with sharks must be very frightened / frightening.

D Complete the words in the sentences.

1 Fruit and vegetables contain v_ _ _ _ _ _ _.
2 Fizzy drinks are full of s_ _ _ _.
3 You should drink six glasses of w_ _ _ _ a day.
4 Fish and meat contain p_ _ _ _ _ _, which helps your body grow strong.
5 C_ _ _ _ _ _ in milk keeps your bones and teeth healthy.
6 Oliver's head hurts. He's got a h_ _ _ _ _ _ _.
7 Eating a lot of sweets can give you t_ _ _ _ _ _ _ _.
8 I ate too much cake. Now I've got a s_ _ _ _ _ _ a_ _ _.

Review 5 Units 9 & 10

Grammar

A Complete the sentences with the Present Perfect tense.

1 Monica ______ (swim) in all the oceans of the world.
2 I ______ (never / win) a sports competition.
3 ______ (you / fly) in a hot air balloon?
4 Billy ______ (break) his arm twice.
5 Katie and Jess ______ (have) three kite surfing classes this month.
6 We ______ (not / meet) the new flying instructor yet.

B Circle the correct tense.

1 I was having / had a headache last night and didn't sleep.
2 I was surfing / surfed on the waves when suddenly I was seeing / saw dolphins.
3 Suzie was just winning / has just won the national swimming competition!
4 My cousins never went / have never been ice skating before. Today is their first time!
5 My tooth was hurting / has hurt all day yesterday.
6 It was raining / has rained on my birthday last week so we weren't going / didn't go to the amusement park.
7 My brother was knowing / has known Jon, his best friend, all his life!
8 Were you studying / Did you study when I rang you?
9 I was already climbing / have already climbed that mountain. Now it's your turn!
10 Helen and Dave are still here. They didn't go / haven't gone to the stadium yet.

C Write the correct forms of the verbs to make First Conditional sentences.

1 If you ______ (eat) 5 portions of fruit and vegetables, you ______ (be) healthy.
2 If Tania ______ (have) a pool party, I ______ (wear) my new swimsuit.
3 Your brother ______ (feel) better if he ______ (do) some exercise.
4 You ______ (get) a headache if you ______ (sit) in the sun all afternoon.
5 If there ______ (be) a lot of snow, we ______ (go) snowboarding.
6 I ______ (not / jump) out of the plane if I ______ (feel) scared.

D Complete the sentences with *should* / *shouldn't* and a verb from the box.

be go make run take wear

1 'I'm going skateboarding.' 'You ______ a helmet.'
2 'We're going to a wildlife park tomorrow.' 'You ______ your camera.'
3 'My mum cut herself when she was chopping vegetables.' 'She ______ careful!'
4 'Paolo doesn't feel well.' 'He ______ swimming.'
5 'It's my granddad's birthday today.' 'You ______ a cake.'
6 'You have a broken leg.' 'You ______ in the race!'

E Complete the sentences with a reflexive pronoun. There are two you do not need.

myself yourself himself herself ourselves yourselves themselves

1 Zara fell off her bike and hurt ______.
2 We always enjoy ______ at our trapeze class.
3 Did you know it's easy for people to cut ______ on sheets of paper?
4 Look after ______, Alison and Toby. See you both when you return.
5 Jake burnt ______ again when he was cooking hamburgers on the barbecue!

11 Be Creative!

Reading: matching, identifying the type of question
Vocabulary: art, theatre and music-related words, prepositions multiple-choice sentences, choosing the correct option
Grammar: the passive voice: present simple & past simple, narrative tenses, open cloze, reading the whole text
Listening: gap-fill, listening for times & dates
Speaking: asking & answering about preferences, expressing preferences
Writing: a short narrative, using a writing formula, connecting events in a story, writing a draft

An artist uses chalk to create a picture of The Mona Lisa on the pavement. Madrid, Spain

Reading

A **Match the photos to a description.**

art dance literature music theatre

A

B

C

D

E

B **Work with a partner. Talk about the different activities in the photos. What do they have in common?**

C **Look quickly at the article below. Which description in A best describes the subject of the text?**

D **Now read the article and write the correct heading for each paragraph.**

How is face painting important in theatre?
Where does the paint come from?
Your face is the picture.
Why paint your face?
Is face painting art?

Word Focus

canvas: a strong cloth used for painting on

camouflage: a way of hiding or disguising yourself

warriors: brave fighters

enemy: a person that you hate and want to fight

villain: a bad or evil character in a story

dye: a substance that changes the colour of other things

Face Art

1 ______________________

When we think of art, we probably think of painting a picture on a canvas or on special paper; even on walls of a city. However, in many cultures people paint their faces instead.

2 ______________________

In fact, face painting may be the very first form of art. Before humans painted on the walls of caves, they painted themselves! Painting faces in different colours and patterns has been part of people's traditions for 1000s of years. The way that people painted their faces can tell stories and lessons from the past.

3 ______________________

People still paint their faces for lots of reasons. Patterns on faces connect people to a tribal family and can show who is the most important person in the family. Some tribes use face paint as a camouflage when they are hunting animals. For warriors, it is a way to look scary and frighten their enemies. Face painting is also used in many ceremonies and special celebrations.

E **Read the article again and choose the correct answers.**

1 Face painting was popular before / after cave paintings.
2 Some face paint can scare animals / enemies.
3 Face paint can make an actor look scary / friendly.
4 Bird feathers are used / Animal fat is used to add special effects.

F **Read the *Exam Close-up*. Then underline the *Wh-* question words and put a star (*) next to the *Yes / No* questions in the *Exam Task*.**

G **Now complete the *Exam Task*.**

Exam Close-up

Identifying the type of question

- Check if the questions are *Wh-* questions and underline these.
- Look for the information that will answer these types of question.
- Put a star (*) next to *Yes / No* questions. They often have a *yes* or *no* in the answer.

Exam Task

Complete the dialogue between two friends. What does Nina tell Adrian?

Choose the correct answer **A – H**. There are three letters you do not need to use.

Adrian: Have you ever painted your face?
Nina: (1) ____________________
Adrian: Was it for a celebration?
Nina: (2) ____________________
Adrian: What did your face look like?
Nina: (3) ____________________
Adrian: Why was that?
Nina: (4) ____________________
Adrian: Did you wear a costume?
Nina: (5) ____________________
Adrian: What a pity I didn't see you!

A It was a bit scary, actually!
B Yes, my mum wore a dress.
C Yes, but my mum painted it for me.
D Because I had red and black circles round my eyes.
E Because I love painting.
F No, it was for a school play.
G Yes, I dressed up as a comic book villain.
H I don't like face paint.

H **Complete these words from the text. Then match them with their correct meaning.**

1 c_m _ _ fl_g_
2 c_nv_s
3 c_v_
4 c_l_br_t_ _ n
5 c_r_m_ny
6 c_lt_r_

a ideas and customs of a group of people
b a formal event, like a wedding
c a strong cloth that artists paint on
d an underground area in a hill or cliff
e a type of disguise
f an important and happy event

4 ____________________

Face paint was important in Japanese and Chinese ancient ceremonies and was was also used in traditional theatre to transform the actors. Actors in those countries still wear white, black and red face paint today to show feelings and make the villain look dramatic and evil.

5 ____________________

Tribal people make facepaint from the natural colours in plants and earth. Roots, berries and tree bark are all used to make dyes. The ingredients are dried over a fire and then crushed with stones to make a powder. This is then mixed with animal fat. Sometimes, dust or soft bird feathers are also used to create special effects.

Ideas Focus

- Do you think face painting is a form of art? Why? / Why not?
- 'It's important to keep traditions.' Do you agree? Why? / Why not?

11 Be Creative!

Vocabulary

A **Look at the photos. Write the number next to the words.**

☐ aisle
☐ audience
☐ author
☐ back cover
☐ conductor
☐ front cover
☐ orchestra
☐ musician
☐ row
☐ seat
☐ stage
☐ title

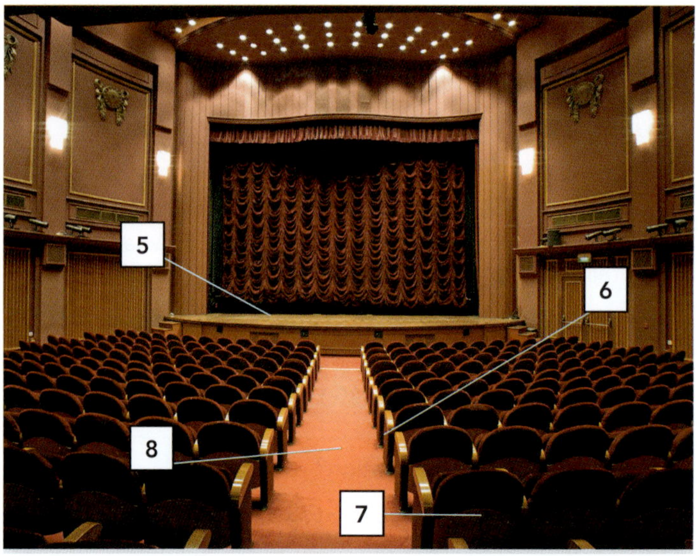

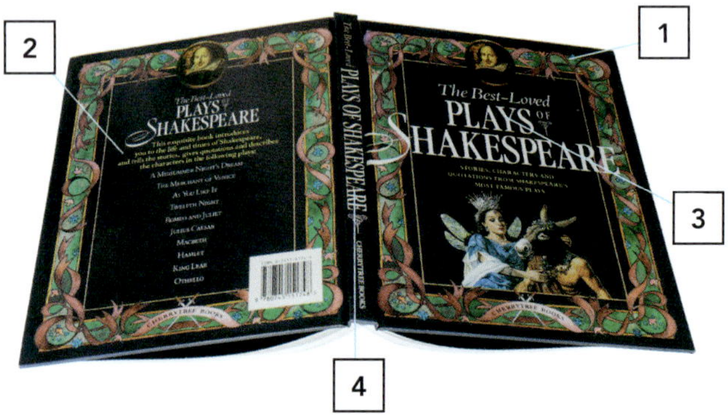

B **Choose a word from A to complete the sentences.**

1 The ________________ clapped at the end of the play.
2 What's the ________________ of her novel?
3 The ________________ stood in front of his musicians.
4 We're sitting in the front ________________!
5 My ________________ number is 14 J. It's next to the aisle.
6 You can read what the story is about on the ________________ of the book.
7 There were 12 musicians in the ________________.
8 Suddenly the curtains opened and the actors walked on to the ________________.

C **Match the beginnings 1–8 to the endings a–h.**

1 The musician played
2 The film
3 He takes
4 The group danced
5 She designs
6 The author types
7 You paint
8 The hero and heroine

a hip hop energetically.
b acted brilliantly.
c the piano beautifully.
d on the canvas so carefully.
e clothes very creatively.
f ended sadly.
g photos too quickly!
h his words very slowly.

D Read the *Exam Close-up*. Then complete E.

E Complete the sentences with the words.

about at for in of on with

1 I'm really bad ____________ painting!
2 My brother's keen ____________ learning an instrument.
3 I'm not very happy ____________ the way I acted on stage today.
4 They were really happy ____________ meeting the famous actor.
5 She's famous ____________ fighting aliens.
6 I'm tired ____________ listening to the same music all the time.
7 We're interested ____________ joining a book club.

Exam Close-up

Choosing the correct option

- Sometimes the option to choose may seem obvious. Other times you may not feel so certain.
- Try each option in the gap and say the sentence to yourself. Choose the word that 'feels' and 'sounds' best.

F Now complete the *Exam Task*.

Exam Task

Read the sentences about Carla's mum. Choose the best word **(A, B or C)** for each answer.

1 My mum ______ that photo exhibitions are always interesting.
A tells B says C speaks

2 She's especially interested ______ bird photography.
A about B because of C in

3 Last year, she ______ a photography club.
A joined B took part C learnt

4 She can now photograph birds ______.
A beautifully B beauty C beautiful

5 Now she has her ______ exhibitions!
A self B one C own

A green-crowned hummingbird flying in the air

Ideas Focus

- Is school a creative place? Why? / Why not?
- 'Technology makes people less creative.' Do you agree? Why? / Why not?

11 Be Creative!

Grammar

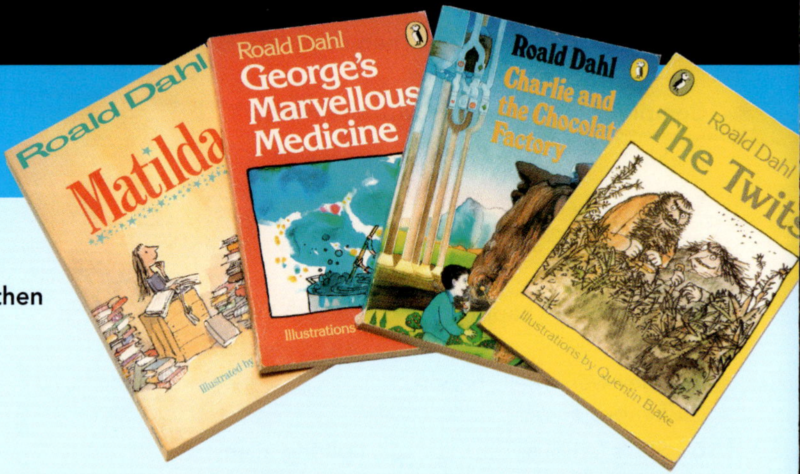

The Passive Voice: Present Simple

A Read the sentences. Underline the verbs and then write *passive* or *active* next to each sentence.

1 Warriors paint their faces. ____________
2 Their faces are painted. ____________
3 The dye is made. ____________
4 People make the dye. ____________

B Look at the sentences in A. Tick the correct rule.

1 We form the passive of the Present Simple with *have / has* + past participle. ☐
2 We form the passive of the Present Simple with *is /are* + past participle. ☐

C Circle the words *faces* and *dye* in A. Are the sentences below true (T) or false (F)?

1 In a passive sentence the object becomes the subject. ______
2 In a passive sentence we are interested in who does the action. ______
3 In a passive sentence we are more interested in the action than in who did it. ______

The Passive Voice: Past Simple

D Read the sentences and underline the verbs.

1 Those stories were written by Roald Dahl.
2 The famous painting, *Sunflowers*, was painted on canvas.
3 The photos in the exhibition were taken in America.
4 The dance was performed by Cirque du Soleil.

E Read the sentences in D again and complete the rules.

We use ____________ or ____________ + past participle to form the passive of the Past Simple. When we want to mention who does the action (the agent), we use ____________.

Grammar Focus p. 167 (11.1 to 11.2)

F Complete the sentences with the Present Simple passive form of the verbs in brackets.

1 Some face paint ________________ (make) from plants and berries.
2 The plates ________________ (paint) by hand.
3 The song ________________ (sing) at the beginning of the football match.
4 The tickets ________________ (sell) at the entrance to the theatre.
5 All these books ________________ (sign) by the author.
6 The art gallery ________________ (visit) by thousands of people each year.

G Complete the second sentences using the passive voice in the correct tense. Use the word *by* if necessary.

1 The hero saved the city.
The city ______________________ the hero.
2 The thief stole all the paintings.
All the paintings ______________________ the thief.
3 They built the castles in 1219.
The castles ______________________ in 1219.
4 The actress Carrie Fisher played the princess in the film.
The princess ______________________ Carrie Fisher in the film.
5 The Queen opened the exhibition.
The exhibition ______________________ the Queen.
6 They made their instruments out of recycled material.
Their instruments ______________________ out of recycled material.

Grammar

Narrative Tenses

H Underline the Past Simple and circle the Past Continuous verbs in the story. The first ones are done for you.

Alice was walking in the garden when suddenly she fell down a hole.

While she was falling, she saw lots of strange objects.

When she got to the bottom, she saw a white rabbit.

She ran after him and followed him through a small door.

As she was going through the door she got stuck.

In the end, the white rabbit rescued her and took her home.

I Read the story in H again and answer the questions.

1 What was Alice doing when she fell down the hole?
____

2 What did she see while she was falling down the hole?
____

3 What did she do when she got to the bottom?
____

J Complete the rules with *Past Simple* or *Past Continuous*.

1 Narrative tenses, for example, _______________ and _______________, help us tell stories in the past.

2 We use the _______________ to describe the background or setting to a story.

3 We also use the _______________ to describe longer activities that are often interrupted by something in the _______________.

4 We often use *while* and *as* with the _______________.

5 We use the _______________ to describe many actions happening one after the other.

Grammar Focus p. 168 (11.3)

K Complete the sentences with the correct form of the verbs in brackets.

1 Sophie _______________ (sleep) in her bed, when suddenly a noise _______________ (wake) her up.

2 When Sophie _______________ (hear) the noise, she _______________ (jump) out of bed.

3 The young wizard _______________ (get) on the train with his owl, and _______________ (sit) next to the window.

4 While he _______________ (learn) about dragons, all of a sudden, one _______________ (fly) in the window!

5 When the students _______________ (see) the dragon, they all _______________ (scream).

6 George _______________ (buy) a chocolate bar, and _______________ (discover) it _______________ (have) a golden ticket inside!

7 The super hero _______________ (arrive) in the city when everyone _______________ (fight).

L Read the *Exam Close-up*. Then read the text in the *Exam Task*.

M Now complete the *Exam Task*.

Exam Task

Read a student's story about playing in an orchestra. Write **ONE** word for each space.

The Rubbish Orchestra

My name is Antonio Rocha and I'm **(1)** _______________ Paraguay. I started to play an instrument when I **(2)** _______________ 12. Instruments are very expensive for **(3)** _______________ lot of children in my country. But my violin is special. It **(4)** _______________ made from recycled rubbish! I joined the Rubbish Orchestra two years **(5)** _______________ and we all have instruments made from rubbish. At first, it wasn't easy but slowly we started to make music. One day when we **(6)** _______________ practising, a famous conductor came to listen **(7)** _______________ us. He loved our music and wanted **(8)** _______________ to travel to Europe and play in front **(9)** _______________ audiences there. We really enjoy **(10)** _______________ our instruments and now we are famous, too!

Exam Close-up

Reading the whole text

- It's important to read the whole text to get the general idea.
- Then read one sentence at a time.
- Identify the type of word you need, e.g. part of a tense, a preposition, an adverb, etc.
- Read through the whole text again with your answers. Do your words sound right?
- Don't forget to check your spelling, too.

Listening

A Work with a partner. Label the pictures with the words. Tell your partner about a time you visited one of these places.

book shop gallery stadium theatre

A

____

B

____

C

____

D

____

B Match the posters and tickets with the type of venue in A.

1

2

3

4

C 11.1 Listen to students talking about the events in B. Circle the correct date and time on the posters and tickets.

D Read the *Exam Close-up*. Then identify where you will write a time or a date in the *Exam Task*.

E 11.2 Now listen and complete the *Exam Task*.

Exam Task

You will hear a radio presenter giving information about a competition. Listen and complete each question.
You will hear the information twice.

Young Writers Competition

Open to young people between: (1) ______________ and 18 years old

Maximum number of words: (2) ______________

Final date for stories: (3) ______________ June

Winner will be announced: on (4) ______________ September

at (5) ______________ p.m.

Exam Close-up

Listening for times & dates

- Practise asking for and telling the time and talking about dates.
- This will make you more familiar with this type of information when you listen.
- Look at the gaps in the *Exam Task* and check where you will need to write a date or a time.

F 11.3 Listen again and check your answers.

Speaking

A **Work with a partner and answer the questions. Give reasons for your answers.**

1. Which painting do you like best? The landscape, the portrait or the abstract painting?
2. What type of books do you prefer?
   Action and adventure   Fantasy   Romance   Mystery
3. Do you prefer the cinema or the theatre? Where do you like to sit?
   near the front   in the middle   near the back   on the balcony above the other seats
4. How do you prefer to study?
   alone   with friends   with music   in silence
5. How do you like to relax?
   with family   with friends   on your own
6. What type of activity do you enjoy doing?
   creative activities   playing sport   reading   playing board games

B **Choose the correct words to complete the conversation.**

because   better   Yes, I prefer   I don't   Me too   What type   Which ones

1 **Steve** Hi Kieran. ______________ of music do you listen to when you're studying?
Kieran I prefer listening to pop music.
Steve Really? ______________. I like classical musical ______________.

2 **Emma** There are so many different paintings!
Vicky ______________ do you like best?
Emma I prefer the modern art paintings.
Vicky ______________ them too!

3 **Eddie** Do you prefer reading the novel or seeing the film?
Dora I prefer reading the novel ______________ there is more information.
Eddie ______________!

C **Read the *Exam Close-up* then read the *Useful Expressions*.**

D **Now complete the *Exam Task*. Use the *Useful Expressions* to help you.**

Exam Close-up

Expressing preferences

- Having a preference means liking one thing or person, more than another thing or person.
- We can use *prefer* + *to* + infinitive or *prefer* + verb + *-ing*.
- We can also use *I like* / *I like ... better.*

Exam Task

Work with a partner. **Student A** is the examiner.
Student A: Use the prompts to ask questions about **Student B**'s preferences. Make notes in the chart below. Then swap roles. Remember to try to give reasons for your preferences.

Type of book?	
Type of music?	
Type of art?	
You / creative?	
Who / favourite artist / writer / musician / actor?	

Useful Expressions

Asking about preferences
What / Which do you prefer?
Which one do you like better?
Do you prefer A or B?
Do you prefer reading the book or seeing the film?

Expressing & responding to preferences
I prefer to read the book.
I prefer reading the book.
I prefer detective novels.
I like fantasy novels better.
I like it too!
Me too!

Ideas Focus

- Do you prefer reading the book or seeing the film of a story? Why? / Why not?
- 'It's important to respect other people's preferences.' Do you agree? Why / Why not?

Writing: a short narrative

Learning Focus

Using a writing formula

- A narrative describes an experience or event.
- Use the following formula to help you organise your writing:

  Divide your story into three paragraphs: a beginning, a middle, and an end.

  The beginning sets the scene. Describe *who* is in your story, and *when* and *where* it took place.

  The middle describes something that happened, or a problem.

  The end describes the solution and the conclusion.
- Use the *Useful Expressions* to make your writing more exciting and interesting.

A Read and choose the correct words.

1 It was a calm day at sea. Suddenly / Eventually, a wave pushed the small boat out of the water!

2 The boy swam across the river after / before the tiger could catch him.

3 In the end / Suddenly, Lyra decided to leave home and start a new life on Planet Bellatrix.

4 As soon as / Meanwhile the children arrived home, they realised something was wrong. Nothing was in the right place.

5 Ben and Katie tried to start a fire. As soon as / Meanwhile, the others ran to collect firewood.

6 Before / Eventually, after three long days at sea, they saw land and knew that their problems were over.

B Read the three short paragraphs of a story. Label them (1) *beginning*, (2) *middle*, (3) *end*.

☐ In the end, he discovered the other end of the rubber made the objects come back.

☐ One day, when he was drawing, he noticed that his rubber erased real objects.

☐ Felix loved drawing. He always carried his sketchbook, pencils and rubber with him wherever he went.

C Read the first two paragraphs of a short story. Underline all the verbs. What tenses are they? Think of a good ending for the story with a partner.

A surprising find!

One day last year, Henry was walking his dog along the beach. It was a beautiful day and all the pebbles were shining in the sun. There were some beautiful shells and he collected some and put them in his pocket.

The next morning his mother's screams suddenly woke him up. He ran downstairs and before he could talk to his mum, he saw the crabs … all over the kitchen table. As soon as he saw them he realised that hermit crabs were living in his shells!

A hermit crab crawls across the sand in the Galapagos National Park, Ecuador

D Use the story frame to write notes for your own short story, then write your story. Use the *Useful Expressions* to help you.

Beginning: The setting	
Middle: The problem	
End: The solution	

E Read the *Exam Close-up* then review the story you wrote in D.

F Now complete the *Exam Task*. Remember to review your answers.

Exam Task

Read the two drafts for the same story. Complete the student's story plan.

Ideas / notes

Every weekend Kevin went fishing at six in the morning on the south coast of England.

He didn't see rocks.

Suddenly ... boat got stuck in the rocks.

Two tourists phoned Land and Sea rescue team!

Ideas / notes

Fisherman? Young teenager?

~~Peter~~ Kevin MacDonald?

Rocks

Emergency Number 211

STORY PLAN

Name of character: **(1)** ____________

Place: **(2)** ____________ coast of England

Time of event: **(3)** ____________ a.m

Problem: Boat got stuck in the **(4)** ____________

Emergency number: **(5)** ____________

Solution: A rescue team arrived.

Useful Expressions

Connecting events in a story

Before ...	Eventually ...	All at once ...
After ...	In the end ...	Meanwhile ...
As soon as ...	Suddenly ...	Later ...

Exam Close-up

Writing a draft

- Get into the habit of writing a first draft of your work.
- Review your draft and think how you can improve it.
- Remember to read your own work and check for capital letters, punctuation, apostrophes and spelling.

Video

11 Creative Recycling

Before you watch

A Label the pictures with these words. How do you think glass is recycled?

bottle bottom label neck pane of glass stained-glass window

1 ______________

2 ______________

3 ______________

4 ______________

5 ______________

6 ______________

While you watch

B Watch the video. Circle the correct information.

1 Plastic / Glass bottles arrive in electric lorries.
2 First the bottles are cleaned / cut.
3 Boiling / Freezing water helps the bottoms fall off.
4 The glass melts in an oven with a temperature of 600 / 766 °C.
5 The window panes are cut into squares / shapes.
6 Coloured glass is also used to make vases / new bottles.

After you watch

C Complete the summary of the video below using these words.

art bottom cleaned create cut melts recycle window

A group of crafts people turn junk, or rubbish, into **(1)** ______________. They **(2)** ______________ old glass bottles and turn them into beautiful stained-glass. Old **(3)** ______________ panes and glass bottles arrive at the warehouse. The bottles are **(4)** ______________ and then the neck and the **(5)** ______________ are removed. The body of the bottle is cut and placed in a special oven. The glass **(6)** ______________ into flat pieces. These pieces and the old window panes are **(7)** ______________ by hand. The artists **(8)** ______________ lots of different things from the recycled glass including vases, bowls and of course, stained-glass windows.

Ideas Focus

- Do you recycle things? Why? / Why not?
- 'We need to reuse and recycle. We need to stop buying new things all the time'. Do you agree?

12 School's Out!

Reading: multiple-choice, thinking about responses
Vocabulary: travel and weather-related words, prepositions and adjectives
Grammar: present continuous for future plans & arrangements, *be going to*
Listening: multiple-choice, reviewing your answers
Speaking: prompt-card activity, asking about holidays
Writing: an invitation, writing & responding to an invitation, understanding language functions

Young boys slide down a cobbled street on wooden boards. Taxco, Mexico

12 School's Out!

Reading

A **Work with a partner. Match the different types of holiday to the pictures. Write the letter. Have you ever been on one of these holidays? Tell your partner.**

1 Adventure holiday ☐
2 Beach holiday ☐
3 Camping ☐
4 Caravan holiday ☐
5 Cruise ☐
6 Volunteering holiday ☐

B **Quickly look at the text. What type of holiday is it about? Why do you think the title of the article is *A Floating City*? Discuss your ideas with a partner.**

C **What questions would you like to ask about the cruise ship? Write two questions here.**

____

____

D **Read the article. Can you answer your questions? What did you find interesting?**

Word Focus

decks: the floors of a ship
neighbourhood: an area or community in a city
promenade: a public walkway, often by the sea
on board: on a ship, plane or train
cabin: the room where you sleep on a ship

A Floating City

The day after school finished for the summer, my mum and dad won a holiday in a competition! I couldn't believe it when they told us what type of holiday it was … a ten-day cruise around the Mediterranean. I wasn't sure how I felt about being on a ship in the middle of the sea for ten days with my parents!

I decided to find out a little more about it. I was quite surprised and shocked to discover that *Harmony of the Seas* is the biggest cruise liner in the world! It's 362 metres long and has 16 decks. It took 2,500 workers over 10 million man hours to build … that's more than two years!

It is a floating city with seven neighbourhoods, restaurants, a shopping centre, a sports zone and a promenade. There's an ice-skating rink, a full-size basketball court and a mini-golf course. There are also two climbing walls. I've never done climbing before, so I want to try that.

The swimming pools look cool! There are 23 of them plus surf machines and it's even got the tallest water slide at sea! I'll have to go on it! There are so many things to do, it will be impossible to get bored!

There will be more than 6,000 passengers on board but the ship is so big, I don't think it will feel crowded. Oh, and there are also 50 trees and 10,000 plants!

The cabins look comfortable. Some don't have windows. Instead they have a real-time view of the outside on a screen. And talking of technology, there is a cafeteria with robotic waiters. You just go along with your pad and order a drink or snack.

E **Find these numbers in the text. What do they refer to?**

1 four ____________
2 16 ____________
3 23 ____________
4 50 ____________
5 10,000 ____________
6 10 million ____________

F **Read the *Exam Close-up*. Then read the *Exam Task*. Which questions are suggestions, which are offers, which ask for advice?**

G **Now complete the *Exam Task*.**

Exam Close-up

Thinking about responses

- Sometimes an answer to a suggestion is not a simple *yes* or *no*.
- We often reply with expressions like *That's great!* or *Good idea!*
- Sometimes a reply to a suggestion might be an excuse, or an opinion, for example: *I can't, I'm busy. / Let's go another day. / Sorry, I don't like the beach.*

Exam Task

Complete the five conversations. Choose **A**, **B**, or **C**.

1 Let's go to the beach!
  A It was a good idea.
  B Can we go after lunch?
  C Yes, we went.

2 Shall we travel in July or August?
  A I don't mind.
  B It's in August.
  C I love the summer.

3 Shall I book the tickets?
  A Now you can book.
  B I'd like to go.
  C Yes, please!

4 Why doesn't Amy come too?
  A I think so.
  B She doesn't want to.
  C She doesn't know.

5 Would you like some sun cream?
  A I've got some, thanks.
  B I often wear some.
  C It was sunny yesterday.

H **Find the underlined words in the text in D. Notice the words that follow these verbs. Then complete the sentences with a verb from the box.**

be book go put stay take

1 This year we decided to ____________ camping.
2 They wanted to ____________ at home this summer.
3 We have to ____________ the tickets in advance.
4 The children stopped to ____________ on sun cream.
5 If you leave the country, you need to ____________ your passport.
6 It's going to ____________ a great holiday!

We'<u>re going to</u> cruise around the Mediterranean and <u>stop to</u> visit four amazing cities along the way: Lisbon, Barcelona, Rome and Naples. I really can't wait ... but I think I will <u>need to</u> have a holiday on the sofa when I get back!

Ideas Focus

- Would you like to travel on the *Harmony of the Seas*? Why? / Why not?
- 'Holidays are fun whatever you do.' Do you agree? Why? / Why not?

12 School's Out!

Vocabulary

A **Match the airport pictures to the information. Write the letter.**

1 Board the plane. ______
2 Wait in the departure area. ______
3 Go through passport control. ______
4 Find your seat on board. ______
5 Go through security control. ______
6 Check in your suitcases. ______

A

B

C

D

E

F

B **Read statements 1–10. Tick the form of transport they refer to. More than one option is often possible.**

	Coach	Cruise ship	Plane	Taxi	Train
1 You often need your passport.					
2 You wait on a platform.					
3 You wear a seatbelt.					
4 You reserve a cabin.					
5 You reserve a seat.					
6 You travel on the motorway.					
7 You take off and land.					
8 You are served food.					
9 You pay at the end of your journey.					
10 You can enjoy outdoor activities.					

C **Read the dialogue. Circle the correct prepositions.**

A: This year we are going to have a holiday **(1)** in / at the mountains.
B: Really? But I thought Thomas and Julia love being **(2)** at / in the beach.
A: Yes, but I don't like lying **(3)** in / on the beach all day.
B: Why don't you borrow our tent and go camping **(4)** by / in a river or a lake?
A: Thank you! Now I can't wait to go **(5)** on /at holiday!
B: There are great walks **(6)** at / in the forests and adventure sports, too.
A: That sounds perfect.
B: You can always camp for one night **(7)** at /on the coast, on your way back.
A: That's a great idea!

D Look at the weather map. Complete the sentences.

cloudy cold hot rainy snowy stormy sunny

1 It's __________ and __________ in Sicily.
2 It's __________ and __________ over the Alps.
3 It's __________ and __________ in the east.
4 It's __________ in the west, over Rome.

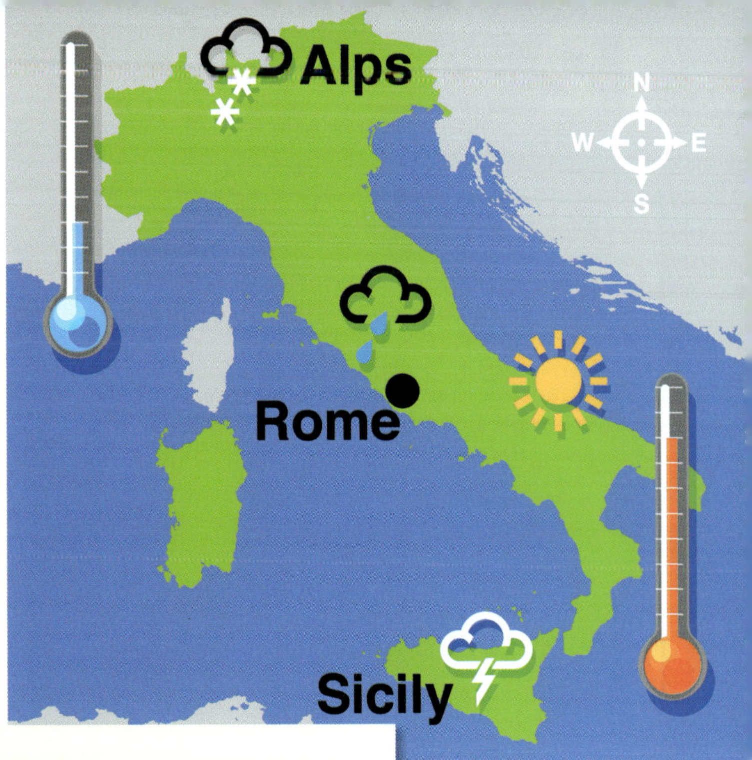

E Complete the postcard with the correct words.

beaches hotel ice cream Fish pool
sightseeing souvenir sun cream three weather

Hi Nana,

We've been in Mallorca for **(1)** __________ days now and it's beautiful!
The **(2)** __________ is very comfortable with great views.
Yesterday the **(3)** __________ was really sunny so we sunbathed by the **(4)** __________. Don't worry, I remembered to pack my **(5)** __________ in my suitcase so I put lots on!
The **(6)** __________ are very clean and everyone is really friendly.
Tomorrow we want to go **(7)** __________ around the old town.
The food is incredible. **(8)** __________ tastes more delicious here …
And the **(9)** __________ is so creamy!
See you soon. I'll bring back a **(10)** __________!

Love, Sara

F Read the postcard again and answer the questions.

1 What is Mallorca like? – It's __________.
2 What is the hotel like? – It's __________.
3 What was the weather like yesterday? – It was __________.
4 What are the beaches like? – They're __________.
5 What are the people like? – They are __________.
6 What is the fish like? – It's __________.
7 What is the ice cream like? – It's __________.

Ideas Focus

- What's your ideal holiday? Why?
- 'You should know your own country before you go on holiday abroad.' Do you agree? Why? / Why not?

Grammar

Present Continuous: Future Plans & Arrangements

A Read the dialogue and underline examples of the Present Continuous.

A: Hi Eric, what are you doing this summer?
B: We're going on a cruise next month.
A: Really? Where are you going?
B: We're sailing round the Mediterranean.
A: Are you visiting Spain?
B: No, we're not. We're sailing straight to France.
A: When are you coming back?
B: We're coming back on 17th August!

B Look at the sentences in A. Are the sentences below true (T) or false (F)?

1 The sentences describe activities in the present. ______
2 The sentences describe plans and arrangements in the future. ______
3 We can use the Present Continuous to ask questions about people's future plans. ______
4 We can use future time expressions, e.g. *next summer / week* and dates. ______
5 We form the Present Continuous with *was / were* + verb + *-ing* ______
6 We form the Present Continuous with *is / are* + verb + *-ing* ______

Grammar Focus p. 168 (12.1)

C Look at the ticket. Complete the information using the Present Continuous.

1 Mr Reyes ____________ (board) at ____________.
2 He ____________ (fly) with Air ____________.
3 The flight ____________ (take off) at ____________.
4 He ____________ (sit) in seat ____________.
5 He ____________ (fly) to ____________.

AIR ANDES FLIGHT AA7188>
NAME: JORGE REYES; **SEAT NUMBER** 11D;

BOARDS AT:	DEPARTURE:
8.20 a.m.	8.55 a.m.

FLYING FROM BOGOTÁ (BOG)
TO MEXICO CITY (MEX).

D Look at the schedule for the cruise. Use the Present Continuous to answer the questions.

HARMONY OF THE SEAS – AUGUST SCHEDULE	
Saturday 7th August	Set sail from Southampton
Monday 9th August	Arrive in Lisbon. 11.00 a.m. tour around historical centre by tram.
Wednesday 11th August	Arrive in Barcelona. See Gaudí's park and cathedral.
Thursday 12th August	Arrive in Rome. Visit the Vatican.
Friday 13th August	Arrive in Naples. Walk up Mt. Vesuvius.

Dalia: When are you setting sail?
Eric: We____________
Dalia: When are you arriving in Lisbon?
Eric: We____________
Dalia: What time are you going on the tour?
Eric: We____________
Dalia: What are you doing on Wednesday?
Eric: We____________
Dalia: When are you visiting the Vatican?
Eric: We____________
Dalia: Where are you going on the last day?
Eric: We____________

E Complete the questions. Then take turns asking and answering the questions with a partner.

1 What ____________ (do) after school today?
2 What ____________ (do) this weekend?
3 Where ____________ (go) in the summer?
4 ____________ (visit) relatives in the summer?
5 ____________ (go) to the beach in the holidays?

Be going to

F **Read the sentences and underline the examples of *be going to* + infinitive. The first one is done for you.**

A: We're going to fly to Australia next summer.
B: Wow. That's far away.
A: I know. We're going to visit relatives there.
B: Are you going to stay with them?
A: We're going to stay with them the first week, then we're going to travel.
B: You're going to have an amazing time!

Be careful
Often, when we use *be going to* and the infinitive of the verb *go*, we lose the second *go*.
For example, instead of saying '*We're going to go swimming at the beach.*' we can just say *We are going swimming at the beach.*

G **Complete the rules with the correct words.**

before what we know future infinitive

1 We form the construction with *is /are + going to* + ________.
2 We use *be going to* to talk about the ________.
3 We use *be going to* to talk about plans we decided ________ the moment of speaking.
4 We use *be going to* to talk about a future event based on ________ / evidence.

Grammar Focus p. 168 (12.2)

H **Complete the sentences with *be going to* and the verb in brackets.**

1 It's too sunny. My ice cream ________ (melt)!
2 I bought a bucket. I ________ (wash) the caravan!
3 They said there are bad storms. The flight ________ (be) delayed.
4 My cousin ________ (teach) me how to surf this summer.
5 You ________ (drop) your camera! Put it around your neck!
6 We ________ (look for) a good place to camp by the river.

I **Complete the question for each answer.**

Dad: How ________? (travel)
Kylie: We're going to travel by train.
Mum: Who ________ with? (travel)
Kylie: I'm going to travel with friends.
Dad: Where ________? (stay)
Kylie: We're going to stay with Coral's cousins.
Mum: What ________? (do)
Kylie: We're going to explore the city
Dad: How long ________ there? (be)
Kylie: We're going to be there for a few days.

J **The school year is almost over. What are your plans for the summer? Tick the boxes. Talk about your plans with a partner.**

I'm going to be bored. ☐
I'm going to have fun. ☐
I'm going to go away. ☐
I'm going to be a couch potato. ☐
I'm going to hang out with friends. ☐
I'm going to learn something new. ☐

12 School's Out!

Listening

A **Work with a partner. Imagine you are going to spend a week on holiday. Discuss these subjects and put them in order of importance for you.**

The journey ______
The accommodation ______
The food ______
The weather ______
The culture ______

B 12.1 **Practise saying the words with a partner. Then listen and underline the syllable that is stressed.**

1 (a) accommodation (b) excursion (c) information
2 (a) adventure (b) departure (c) temperature
3 (a) flight (b) luggage (c) suitcases
4 (a) relaxing (b) sightseeing (c) sunbathing
5 (a) comfortable (b) journey (c) restaurant

C **Read the *Exam Close-up*, then complete D.**

D 12.2 **Listen to a tourist talking about their holiday. Tick the correct boxes on the feedback form.**

Exam Close-up

Reviewing your answers

- Don't choose your answers too quickly.
- If you are not sure of the answer to a question the first time you listen, leave the question and move on.
- The answer will be more obvious the second time you listen.

HAPPY DAYS IN THE SUN – FEEDBACK FORM				
FLIGHT	on time ☐	delayed ☐	cancelled ☐	
HOTEL	comfortable ☐	cheap ☐	expensive ☐	noisy ☐
BEACH	beautiful ☐	clean ☐	crowded ☐	dirty ☐
WEATHER	sunny ☐	cloudy ☐	rainy ☐	stormy ☐
TOWN	interesting ☐	modern ☐	old ☐	boring ☐

E 12.2 **Listen again and check your answers.**

F 12.3 **Now listen and complete the *Exam Task*.**

Exam Task

Listen to Samantha and Zac talking about a holiday activity. For each question choose the right answer (**A**, **B** or **C**). You will hear the conversation twice.

1 What are they going to do?
A go on a boat
B go horse riding
C go swimming

2 Where are they going?
A through the forest
B along the beach
C on the lake

3 What do they need to pack?
A a helmet
B sun cream
C a raincoat

4 How long is the trip?
A one hour
B two-and-a-half hours
C three hours

5 What time will they get back?
A at 3 p.m.
B at 4.30 p.m.
C at 5.30 p.m.

G 12.4 **Listen again and check your answers.**

Speaking

A Look at the two photos. What can you do in each place?

B Work with a partner. Match the beginnings 1–5 to the endings a–e.

1	Where are you going	a	to do?
2	What are you going	b	to go?
3	Who are you going	c	to travel?
4	How are you going	d	to be away?
5	How long are you going	e	to travel with?

C Imagine you are going on holiday. Tick the options you would like. Ask and answer the questions in B with a partner.

Location:
beach ☐ countryside ☐ city ☐

Accommodation:
campsite ☐ hotel ☐ cottage ☐

Companions:
family ☐ friends ☐ alone ☐

Travel:
boat ☐ plane ☐ train ☐

Number of days:
10 ☐ 14 ☐ 21 ☐

Activities:
sightseeing ☐ sunbathing ☐ swimming ☐
horse riding ☐ surfing ☐ canoeing ☐

D Read the *Exam Close-up* then read through the *Useful Expressions.*

E Now work with a partner and complete the *Exam Task.* Use the *Useful Expressions* to help you.

Exam Close-up

Asking about holidays

- Think about the tense you need to use when asking someone about their holiday. Are you asking about plans in the future, or a holiday in the past?
- The same type of questions about holidays appear again and again. Make sure you become familiar with them.

Useful Expressions

Asking about holidays

What was the hotel / beach / weather like?
When did you go?
How long did you go for?
Who did you go with?
Did you have a good time?
Where are you going next summer?
What are you going to do there?
Where are you going to stay?
How long are you going for?

Exam Task

1 **Student A:** Complete the feedback form about your last holiday. Then answer **Student B**'s questions. **Student B:** turn to page 184. Ask **Student A** questions about his/her holiday.

***Great Outdoors Holidays:* feedback form**			
Campsite:	great ☐	too small ☐	too big ☐
Weather:	sunny ☐	cloudy ☐	rainy ☐
Beaches:	beautiful ☐	clean ☐	crowded ☐
People:	friendly ☐	helpful ☐	serious ☐
Food:	delicious ☐	simple ☐	horrible ☐

2 **Student B:** Complete the feedback form about your last holiday. Then answer **Student A**'s questions. **Student A:** Turn to page 184. Ask **Student B** questions about his/her holiday.

Ocean View Holidays: feedback form			
Cruise ship:	amazing ☐	crowded ☐	too big ☐
Cabins:	comfortable ☐	clean ☐	too small ☐
Swimming pools:	fun ☐	deep ☐	cold ☐
People:	friendly ☐	helpful ☐	serious ☐
Food:	delicious ☐	simple ☐	horrible ☐

Ideas Focus

- Do you like discovering new places? Why? / Why not?
- 'Sometimes holidays can be stressful.' Do you agree? Why? / Why not?

12 School's Out!

Writing: an invitation

Learning Focus

Writing & responding to an invitation

- In invitations we often use the Present Continuous for future plans, e.g. *We're having a party.* We can also say, *Would you like to come?*
- Invitations should include information about **who** the invitation is from, **what** the event is, and **when** and **where** the event is.
- We can accept invitations, e.g. *I would love to come to your party,* or refuse invitations, e.g. *I'm sorry, I can't come/make it to the prom.* If you refuse, it is always polite to give a reason.
- Sometimes you can offer to help, e.g. *Shall I make a cake?* or ask permission to do something, *Can I / Is it OK if I bring a friend?*

(1) ____________

Highvale School is having a Prom!

Come along and celebrate the end of term!

(2) ____________

Saturday 30th June From 7 p.m. to midnight.

(3) ____________

The Hilton Hotel, Pinewood Road, San Rafael.

(4) ____________

Contact John (head boy) at:
highvaleschool@internet.com
Let us know if you can make it!
Dress code = black tie (dresses for girls, suits for boys)

A **Look at the invitation. Label the different parts with the correct words.**

who what where when

B **Look at the invitation again. Choose the correct answer, a or b.**

1 When is the event?
   a in the past   b in the future
2 What is the reason for it?
   a end of term   b a birthday
3 What should girls wear?
   a suits   b dresses
4 What time does the it start?
   a 7 p.m.   b midnight
5 Where is it?
   a at a hotel   b on the beach

C **Read the two responses to the invitation. Circle the correct words.**

1

To: highvaleschool@internet.com

From: Leela

Subject: Prom!

Hi John,

Thanks for invite / inviting me to the prom. I'd love to come!

Shall / Will I bring any snacks to the hotel?

Tell / Let me know,

Lots of love,

Leela

2

To: highvaleschool@internet.com

From: Dan

Subject: Prom!

Hi John,

What / How a shame! I'm afraid I can't go / make it to the prom. I'm leaving to go on holiday on that day.

Hope you all have fun.

Look forward to hear / hearing all about it when I'm back!

Dan

D **Unjumble the different responses to the questions.**

Would you like to come to a barbecue on Friday evening?

1 love would to I ____________________!
2 great would be That ____________________!
3 idea That's good a ____________________!
4 not Why ____________________!
5 busy I'm Unfortunately ____________________.
6 make can't Sorry I it ____________________.
7 afraid on Friday I'm can't I ____________________.

E **Write your own party invitation like the one in A. Then swap with a partner and reply to their invitation. Decide if you are going to accept or refuse. Use the *Useful Expressions* and the points below to help you.**

accept
↓
- say thank you
- offer to help or take something

refuse
↓
- say sorry
- give a reason

F **Read the *Exam Close-up*. Then read the email in the *Exam Task* and underline the questions you need to answer.**

G **Now complete the *Exam Task*.**

Exam Close-up

Understanding language functions

- Different situations require different types of language.
- Read and identify the language function: making a suggestion, asking or giving advice, asking permission, offering, inviting, etc.
- This will help you identify the best way to respond.

Exam Task

Read the invitation from your friend, Adam.

email

Re: Leaving Party

Hi Ellie,

I'm having a party on Sunday to say goodbye to Veronica. She's leaving and moving back to Canada. Would you like to come?

It's a barbecue so could you bring something to cook? What is Veronica's brother 's name? Do you have his telephone number? I'd like to invite him, too.

Let me know if you can come. The party starts at 3 p.m.

Adam

Write an email to Adam and answer the questions. Write **25 – 35** words.

Useful Expressions

Inviting
We're having a party!
Join us for a party!
Come along to …
Would you like to come to …?

Accepting an invitation
I would love to …
I'd love to!
That would be great!

Refusing an invitation
Unfortunately, I can't come.
I'm afraid I can't make it.
I'm sorry but …

Explaining why
I have to …
I need to …
It's my brother's graduation

Video 12 Best Summer Job

Before you watch

A Look at the photos. What animal do you think it is?
Where do you think you might find it? Discuss your answers with a partner.

While you watch

B Watch the video. Decide if these statements are T (True) or F (False).

1 Nansen Weber is a diver and swims with the beluga whales. ☐
2 About 2,000 beluga whales visit the island. ☐
3 They visit every winter. ☐
4 Nansen calls it a 'beluga disco'. ☐
5 Nansen identifies the whales that return every year. ☐
6 In the future there will be more ship traffic. ☐

After you watch

C Complete the summary of the video below using these words.

babies future photographer ship summer temperatures travel whales

Nansen Webber works on Somerset Island, Canada. It's not an easy place because of the snow, ice and cold **(1)** ____________ . He is a **(2)** ____________ and takes photos of the beluga whales that visit the island every **(3)** ____________ . The **(4)** ____________ come here to moult (lose their skin), socialise and look after their young **(5)** ____________ . Nansen tries to identify the whales that return every year. He wants to study their behaviour and how they **(6)** ____________ through the Northwest Passage. It is important to make sure that the whales are safe because in the **(7)** ____________ , there will be more **(8)** ____________ traffic and we will need to protect special places like this.

Ideas Focus

- Do you like cold places? Why? / Why not?
- 'Nansen's job is the best job ever'. Do you agree?

Review 6 Units 11 & 12

Vocabulary

A Circle the correct word.

1 JK Rowling is the author / musician of the *Harry Potter* books.
2 My brother plays the violin in a youth conductor / orchestra.
3 'What's the cover / title of the book you're reading?' *'The Lie Tree.'*
4 We're sitting in the front line / row of the theatre, next to the aisle / road.
5 The play was terrible and the spectators / audience didn't clap.
6 When I started acting classes, I was scared to go on the stage / platform.

B Complete the sentences with the words.

about at for in of on with

1 The painter Picasso is famous ______ a style of painting called 'Cubism'.
2 I'm really bad ______ making pancakes!
3 My brother is keen ______ getting married on the beach.
4 Are you interested ______ doing a photography course?
5 I'm not very happy ______ Julie – she's hasn't cleaned her bedroom!
6 Are you tired ______ cooking? Order Jamie's Take Away Meals today!
7 My grandparents were really happy ______ coming on holiday with us.

C Complete the text with the words.

airport departure area passport plane seats suitcases time weather

We arrived at the (**1**) ____________ in a taxi. First we checked in our (**2**) ____________ and got our boarding passes. Next, we went through (**3**) ____________ control and security control. After that, we had to wait for an hour in the (**4**) ____________. Then we boarded the (**5**) ____________ and found our (**6**) ____________, 15 E and 15 F. The (**7**) ____________ was sunny and we took off on (**8**) ____________. School is out for the summer!

D Complete the words in the sentences.

1 You should put s_ _ _ _ _ _ _ on your face and arms when it's sunny.
2 Let's relax on the b_ _ _ _ and listen to the sound of the sea.
3 I'm going to buy some s_ _ _ _ _ _ _ _ at the local shop to remember our holiday.
4 My parents usually go camping, but this holiday they stayed in a h_ _ _ _.
5 Shall we go s_ _ _ _ _ _ _ _ _ _? There are so many interesting places to see!
6 Lemon i_ - is delicious to eat in the summer.

E Choose a word to complete the answers about a holiday.

beautiful comfortable delicious friendly stormy

1 What was the weather like? – It was ____________.
2 What were the beaches like? – They were ____________.
3 What was the food like? – It was ____________.
4 What were the people like? – They were ____________.
5 What was the hotel like? – It was ____________.

Review 6 Units 11 & 12

Grammar

A Rewrite the sentences using the Present or Past Passive voice.

1 The artists use recycled material.
Recycled material __________ by the artists.
2 A group of volunteers clean the beaches every weekend.
The beaches __________ by a group of volunteers every weekend.
3 Every school child reads this book.
This book __________ by every school child.
4 My aunt and uncle organised our summer holiday.
Our summer holiday __________ by my aunt and uncle.
5 First, the tourists checked in their suitcases.
First, the suitcases __________ by the tourists.
6 The actors painted their faces before going on stage.
The actors' faces __________ before going on stage.

B Complete the sentences with the Past Simple or Past Continuous tense.

1 While the tourist __________ (take) a photo, she __________ (drop) her camera.
2 We __________ (buy) a painting and __________(put) it up in the living room.
3 While the family __________(having) a picnic, it __________ (start) to rain.
4 When I __________ (arrive) at the party, everyone __________ (dance).
5 On our holiday to Mallorca, we __________ (visit) a castle, we __________ (buy) some souvenirs and we __________ (relax) on the beach.
6 My plane __________ (take off) while I __________ (wait) in the departure area!

C Complete the sentences with the Present Continuous tense.

1 On Monday I __________ (start) an art course.
2 Sara and Patrick __________ (catch) the 7 o'clock train from Paris tomorrow.
3 We're __________ (sail) to the island on 29th July.
4 My grandfather __________ (not / come) on holiday with us this year.
5 Our neighbour __________ (have) a barbecue in his garden tomorrow night.
6 Vinita and Neel __________ (not / get) married until next year.

D Complete the sentences with the correct form of *be going to* and the verb in brackets.

1 Look at those storm clouds. It __________ (rain).
2 My friends and I __________ (hire) bicycles to see the city.
3 I __________ (be) a pilot when I leave school.
4 We __________ (collect) some shells on the beach. Come with us!
5 My brother __________ (join) an orchestra in the autumn.
6 My class __________ (celebrate) the end of the school year.

Grammar Reference

Unit 1

1.1 *Be*

Affirmative	
I am. we/you/they **are.** He/she/it **is.**	
Negative	
I am not ('m not). we/you/they **are not ('re not /aren't).** He/she/it **is not ('s not / isn't).**	
Questions	
Am I? **Are** we/you/they? **Is** he/she/it?	
Short Answers	
Yes, I **am.** **Yes**, we/you/they **are**. **Yes**, he/she/it **is.**	**No**, I'**m not.** **No**, we/you/they **are not ('re not / aren't).** **No**, he/she/it **is not ('s not / isn't).**

We use the verb *to be*
- with an adjective.
  *I **am** tall. It **is** green. They **are** beautiful.*
- with a noun.
  *It**'s** my pet. They **are** children.*
- to talk about our age or nationality.
  *He **is** 12 years old. She **is** from Mexico. We**'re** Spanish.*
- for a location.
  *It**'s** in the centre of the city. The books **are** in my bag.*
- as part of other tenses (auxiliary).
  *I **am** listening to music. We **are** playing tennis.*
  *My dress **is** made in Spain.*

Note: In short affirmative answers, there is no contraction: *'Is he Italian?'- 'Yes, he is.'* **NOT** *'Yes, he's.'*

1.2 *Have got*

Affirmative	
I/we/you/they **have got**. He/she/it **has got**.	
Negative	
I/we/you/they **haven't got**. He/she/it **hasn't got**.	
Questions	
Have I/we/you/they **got**? Has he/she/it **got**?	
Short Answers	
Yes, I/we/you/they **have**. **Yes**, he/she/it **has**.	**No**, I/we/you/they **haven't**. **No**, he/she/it **hasn't**.

We use *have got* for
- possessions.
  *They**'ve got** a kite. I**'ve got** a camera.*
- relationships.
  We'**ve got** lots of cousins. Ana **has got** three brothers.

Note: In short affirmative or negative answers, we don't repeat **got**: *'Have you **got** a pet?'- 'Yes, I have.'* **NOT** *'~~Yes, I have got.~~' 'Has she got a brother?'- 'No, she hasn't.'* **NOT** *'~~No, she hasn't got.~~'*

1.3 *This, That, These, Those*

We use *this* and *these* to show that something is **near** us in space or time.
We use ***this* + singular noun.**
***This** is my classroom; I sit here.*
***This** party is great. I like dancing.*
We use ***these* + plural noun.**
***These** apples are from my garden. Do you want one?*

We use *that* and *those* to show that something is not so near us in space or time.
We use ***that* + singular noun.**
That castle over there is very famous.
We use ***those* + plural noun.**
***Those** students at the back of the class are my friends.*

We can use ***this, these, that, those*** without a noun.
***This** is my best friend, Kevin.*
***These** are beautiful flowers.*
*I think **that** is my phone.*
***Those** are interesting hobbies.*

1.4 Possessive Adjectives

Subject Pronouns	Possessive Adjectives
I	my
you	your
he	his
she	her
it	its
we	our
you	your
they	their

We use possessive adjectives before nouns to show possession.
*It's **my brother**'s birthday and these are **his** presents.*
***We** live here. This is **our** house.*

1.5 Possessive *'s*

We use *'s* to show that
- something belongs to someone.
  *Sara**'s** dog is big.*
- something has a particular relationship with someone or something else.
  *Peter is my dad**'s** brother.*

We use **'s** after singular nouns.
- *That's the rabbit**'s** carrot.*
- *The teacher**'s** smartphone is on the table.*

We use **'s** after irregular plural nouns.
- *People**'s** hobbies are all different.*
- *The children**'s** kite is red.*

We use **s'** with regular plural nouns.
- *The dogs**'** ears were very long.*
- *My parents**'** names are Debbie and Mark.*

Unit 2

2.1 Present Simple

Affirmative	
I/we/you/they play. He/she/it play**s**.	
Negative	
I/we/you/they **don't** play. He/she/it **doesn't** play.	
Questions	
Do I/we/you/they play? **Does** he/she/it play?	
Short Answers	
Yes, I/we/you/they/**do**. **Yes**, he/she/it **does**.	**No**, I/we/you/they **don't**. **No**, he/she/it **doesn't**.

We use the Present Simple for
- facts.
  *Children **study** at school.*
- routines or habits (often with adverbs of frequency).
  *My dad **goes** to work every day by train.*
- permanent states.
  *My grandparents **live** in Brazil.*

Note: Time expressions that refer to **repeated actions** are often used with the Present Simple. For example, *every day/week/month, once a week, twice a year, at weekends, at night, in the morning*, etc.

2.2 Question Words

We use ***wh- questions*** to ask for more specific information.

We use
- **who** for people.
  Who is your dance teacher?
- **what** for things or ideas.
  What do you do in your free time?
- **when** for time in general.
  When do you start guitar classes?
- **where** for places.
  Where do your aunt and uncle live?
- **why** for reasons.
  Why do you want to be an astronaut?
- **how** for describing in what way you do something.
  How do you travel to school?

Note: the order of the words when you form a question:
Question word + do /does + subject + verb ...?

2.3 Adverbs of Frequency

Adverbs of frequency show how often we do things. They come **before** the main verb, but **after** the verb *be*. We use *How often?* to ask about frequency in a question.

Different adverbs show different frequency.

100% — 0%
always usually often sometimes hardly ever never

*We **usually visit** our grandparents on Sunday.*
*My dad **is never** late for work.*
*It **is always** hot in summer.*

Unit 3

3.1 *There is / There are*

Affirmative	
There **is**. There **are**.	
Negative	
There **is not (isn't)**. There **are not (aren't)**.	
Questions	
Is there? **Are** there?	
Short Answers	
Yes, there is. **Yes**, there are.	**No**, there is not / there isn't. **No**, there are not / there aren't.

We use *there is / there are*
- to describe a place.
  ***There is** a river; **there are** boats on the river.*
- to describe where things are.
  ***There's a** park in the centre of the town.*
- to talk about numbers and quantities.
  ***There are** fifteen students in my dance class.*
  ***There is** a lot of food at the party.*
- to introduce a new topic.
  ***There's** a good film on at the cinema this evening.*

Note: we use *there is* with uncountable nouns.
***There is** cake on the kitchen floor.*

3.2 Prepositions of place

We use ***at*** with
- places in general (not specific):
  at the cinema
  at the restaurant
  at the station
  at the supermarket
  at home
  at school
  at work

We use ***in*** with
- containers:
  in my bag
  in the fridge
  in the cupboard

- rooms, buildings, countries, towns, places with limits:
  in the kitchen
  in my mum's car
  in the park
  in hospital
  in Paris
  in England

We use ***on*** with

- surfaces:
  on the floor/wall
  on the road

- transport:
  on a bus/plane/boat/ship

- left and right:
  on the left
  on the right

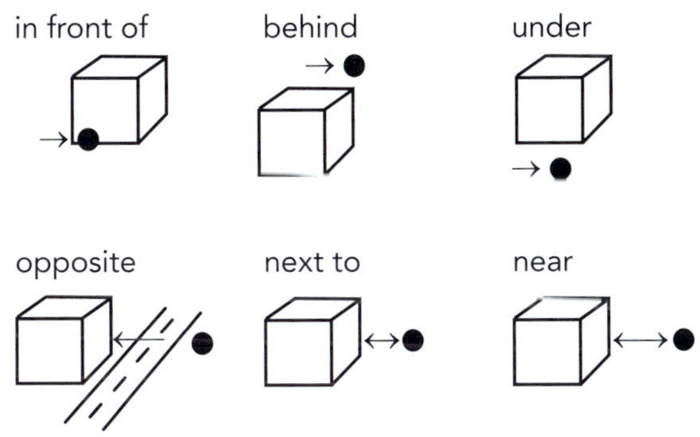

3.3 Present Continuous

Affirmative	
I **am ('m)** visiting. He/she/it **is ('s)** visiting. We/you/they **are ('re)** visiting.	
Negative	
I **am ('m) not** visiting. He/she/it **is not (isn't)** visiting. We/you/they **are not (aren't)** visiting.	
Questions	
Am I visiting? **Is** he/she/it visiting? **Are** we/you/they visiting?	
Short Answers	
Yes, I **am**. Yes, he/she/it **is**. Yes, we/you/they **are**.	No, **I'm not**. No, he/she/it **isn't**. No, we/you/they **aren't**.

Spelling: have → having
get → getting
study → studying

We use the Present Continuous for

- actions that are happening NOW, at the time of speaking.
  *The firefighters **are putting** out the fire now.*
- actions that happen around the time of speaking.
  *I**'m reading** a lot of books at the moment.*
- temporary situations.
  *My dad **isn't driving** to work this week. He's sick.*

Note: We often use phrases like: *now, nowadays, these days, this week, this month* and *at the moment* with the Present Continuous.

Note: We don't use the Present Continuous with verbs like: *have, like, love, know, think.*

Unit 4

4.1 Countable Nouns

Most nouns are countable and have singular and plural forms.
banana → bananas
We usually use *a* with singular countable nouns.
a pear
or *an* with singular countable nouns that begin with a vowel *a, e, i, o, u*
an apple
an egg

We can use *some* or a number (e.g. *three*) with plural countable nouns.
*I have **some** flowers for the wedding.*
*There are **ten** cakes on the table.*

We use *any* in questions and negatives.

*Are there **any** fireworks?*
*There aren't **any** decorations.*

We use singular verb forms with singular countable nouns.
*There **is a party** in the street.*
We use plural verb forms with plural countable nouns.
***Parties are** fun.*

Note: Some countable nouns don't end in *-s*. Remember to use a plural verb form with them.
*The **children are** happy.*
*The **people** next door **have got** three dogs.*

4.2 Uncountable Nouns

Some nouns are uncountable. They do not have plural forms.
bread
cake
food
fruit
rubbish
snow
time
traffic
water

We always use singular verb forms with uncountable nouns.
*Snow **is** white.*
*The rubbish **is** outside.*
*The bread **is** on the table.*

Note: When we are talking about whole pieces of food we use *a / an*:
*Do you want **a** cake/pizza?*

When we are talking about a slice or a piece we use *some*:
*Do you want **some** cake/pizza.*

We can use *some* in a question, when we offer food.
*Would you like **some** water?*

4.3 Quantifiers

We use *a lot of* or *lots of* with both uncountable and plural countable nouns.
*There are **a lot of people** in fancy dress.*
*There is **lots of food** at the barbecue.*

We use *much* in the negative with uncountable nouns.
*You don't eat **much fruit** for breakfast.*
We use *many* with plural countable nouns.
*There are **many festivals** to celebrate New Year.*

We use *much* in questions about uncountable nouns and *many* in questions about countable nouns.
***How much** time have we got?*
***How many** pizzas did the children eat?*

Unit 5

5.1 Past Simple of Verb *To Be*

Affirmative	
I **was**. We/you/they **were**. He/she/it **was**.	
Negative	
I **was not (wasn't)**. We/you/they **were not (weren't)**. He/she/it **was not (wasn't)**.	
Questions	
Was I? **Were** we/you/they? **Was** he/she/it?	
Short Answers	
Yes, I was. **Yes**, we/you/they were. **Yes**, he/she/it was.	**No**, I wasn't. **No**, we/you/they weren't. **No**, he/she/it wasn't.

We use the verb *be* in the past
- with adjectives and nouns.
  *I **was** happy. We **were** late. It **was** a perfect day*
  *It **was** a fun day.*
- location and time.
  *The children **were** at school at 9 o'clock.*
  *She **was** at the beach last weekend.*
- as part of other tenses (auxiliary).
  *The sun **was** shining. Josie and Rob **were** playing in the park.*
  *The house **was** painted by my dad.*

5.2 Past Simple

Affirmative	
I/he/she/it/we/you/they start**ed**.	
Negative	
I/he/she/it/we/you/they **didn't** start.	
Questions	
Did I/he/she/it/we/you/they start?	
Short Answers	
Yes, I/he/she/it/we/you/they **did**.	**No**, I/he/she/it/we/you/they **didn't**.

Spelling: dance → danc**ed**, stop → sto**pped**, stu**dy** → stu**died**, play → play**ed**
Note: Some verbs are irregular and do not follow these spelling rules. See a list of irregular verbs on pages 185–186. It's a good idea to learn irregular verbs with the same pattern in the past tense together, e.g.,
cut, hit, put and *read* all stay the same in the simple past.
Draw, fly, grow, throw all have simple past forms that end *'ew'*, (*drew, flew, grew, threw*).

We use the Past Simple for
- something that started and finished in the past.
  *We **lived** in Dubai three years ago.*
- actions that happened in a sequence.
  *We **walked** on the beach, **built** a fire and then **cooked** the fish.*

Note: Some common time expressions we use with the Past Simple are *yesterday, last night/week/month/summer, a week/month/year ago, twice a week, once a month, at the weekend.*

Unit 6

6.1 Comparative Adjectives

Adjective	Comparative
small	small**er**
cute	cut**er**
big	big**ger**
noisy	nois**ier**
dangerous	**more** dangerous
good	**better**
bad	**worse**

We usually form the comparative by adding *-er* to an adjective. If the adjective has three or more syllables, we use the word *more*. We use the word *than* after the comparative in a sentence.
*A lion is **more dangerous** than a cat.*
*A butterfly is **more beautiful than** a frog.*
Some adjectives are irregular and form their comparative in different ways.
*I like wildlife parks **better than** amusement parks.*

We use the comparatives for
- comparing two people, animals or things.

6.2 Other comparative structures

We use *as* + adjective + *as* to show that two people or things are similar in some way.
A lion is ***as dangerous as*** *a tiger.*

We use *not as/so ... as* to show that two people, animals or things are different, not equal.
A snake isn't ***as cute as*** *a rabbit.*

6.3 *How* + Adjective

We use *How + adjective* in a question to ask for more detailed information.
How long *is your snake?*
How tall *is that building?*
How old *is your grandma?*

6.4 Adjectives and Sense Verbs

We use adjectives after sense verbs to say how something *looks, sounds, smells, tastes* and *feels*.
That bird song ***sounds beautiful****.*
My mum's cakes always ***taste delicious****.*
You ***look sad****.*

We use sense verbs + *like* + noun to compare what we see, hear, smell, taste or touch to something we know.
It ***feels like*** *a rock.*
It ***looks like*** *a monkey.*
It ***sounds like*** *a train.*

Unit 7

7.1 Superlative Adjectives

Adjective	Superlative
small	the smallest
brave	the bravest
hot	the hottest
easy	the easiest
interesting	the **most** interesting
far	the **furthest**
good	the **best**
bad	the **worst**

We use the superlative to compare one person or thing with other people or things of the same type. We usually form the superlative by adding **-est** to the adjective. If the adjective has two or more syllables, we use the word *most*. We use the word *the* before the superlative.
A paper plane is ***the easiest*** *thing to make.*
This is ***the most interesting*** *invention I have.*

Some adjectives are irregular and form their superlative in different ways.
Neptune is ***the furthest*** *planet from the Sun.*

7.2 Expressing purpose

We can use the following expressions to show purpose.
is /are used for is followed by a verb + *-ing*.
is /are used to is followed by an infinitive verb.
I/you/we use something *to* is followed by an infinitive verb.

An oven ***is used for*** *bak**ing** cakes.*
*It'**s used to** transport astronauts into space.*
We ***use*** *a smartphone* ***to*** *talk, text and take photos.*

Note: Sometimes we can leave out *is/are used*. For example: *It's for taking photos.*

7.3 *Will*

Affirmative	
I/he/she/it/we/you/they **will** fly.	
Negative	
I/he/she/it/we/you/they **will not (won't)** fly.	
Questions	
Will I/he/she/it/we/you/they fly?	
Short Answers	
Yes, I/he/she/it/we/you/they **will**.	**No**, I/he/she/it/we/you/they **won't**.

We can use ***will*** for
- predictions about the future and to talk about what we think will happen.
  I ***will*** *be president of my country.*
  Animals ***will*** *learn to talk.*
  We ***won't*** *live under the sea.*

Unit 8

8.1 Zero Conditional

If clause	Main clause
present simple	present simple

We use the zero conditional to talk about real or true situations in the present.
If you ***win*** *the game, you* ***get*** *a prize.*
We can use *when* instead of *if* to talk about things or situations that are more certain.
When you ***play*** *this game, you* ***need*** *four players.*

Note: When *if* and *when* come at the beginning of a sentence, a comma separates the two parts.
It is also possible to say: *You need four players* ***when*** *you play this game.*
In this case, a comma is not necessary.

8.2 Sequencing

There are many adverbs and expressions that help us sequence and show the order of events.
Adverbs like *after, before* and *while* can be followed by the subject + verb or by the verb + *-ing*.
After I have *breakfast, I go to school.*
Before going *to school, I pack my school bag.*

We can also use *as soon as, until, eventually, in the end.*
***As soon as** the teacher arrives, we all take our books out.*
*I can't play video games **until** I finish my homework.*
***Eventually**, the bus arrived after 45 minutes!*
*The children wanted to go swimming but **in the end** they went to the park.*

8.3 *Must*

We use *must* + infinitive
- to say that something is necessary.
  *Players **must be** older than seven to play this game.*
- to talk about obligations.
  *You **must have** a shower before you go into the pool.*

8.4 *Mustn't*

We use *mustn't* + infinitive to talk about something that is not allowed.
*Children **mustn't play** games in the library.*

8.5 *Have To*

We use *have to*
- to say that something is necessary.
  *You **have to** miss a turn if you land on a red square.*
- to talk about obligation.
  *Monica **has to** go home now.*

8.6 *Mustn't* & *Don't Have To*

There is an important difference between *mustn't* and *don't have to*. We use *mustn't* to say that something is not allowed, and we use *don't have to* to show that there is no obligation.
*Players **mustn't** cheat when they play games.*
*We **don't have to** play a board game, we can play a card game instead.*

8.7 *Can* & *Can't*

We can use *can* and *can't* + infinitive
- for possibility.
  *We **can** play a game inside or we **can** play outside.*
  *We **can't** go to the toyshop. It's closed.*
- for permission.
  ***Can** my sister play? - Yes, your sister **can** play too.*
  *No, she **can't** play, she's too young!*

Unit 9

9.1 Present Perfect Simple (1)

The Present Perfect Simple is formed with the verb *have* + the past participle.

Affirmative	
I/we/you/they **have ('ve)** climb**ed**. he/she/it **has ('s)** climb**ed.**	
Negative	
I/we/you/they **have not (haven't)** climb**ed** He/she/it **has not (hasn't)** climb**ed**	
Questions	
Have I/we/you/they climb**ed**? **Has** he/she/it climb**ed**?	
Short Answers	
Yes, I/we/you/they/ **have.** **Yes**, he/she/it **has.**	**No**, I/we/you/they **haven't.** **No**, he/she/it **hasn't.**

Spelling: *jump → jump**ed***
*cycle → cycl**ed***
*stud**y** → stud**ied***
*pla**y** → play**ed***
*trave**l** → travel**led***

Note: Irregular verbs do not follow these spelling rules. See a list of irregular verbs on pages 185–186.

We use the Present Perfect Simple
- for something that happened in the past but we don't say when.
  *I **have been** to school in America.*
- for experiences.
  *My dad **has flown** in a helicopter.*
- with *ever* to ask questions about experiences.
  *Have you **ever** eaten an insect?*
- With *never* to say we don't have a particular experience.
  *We have **never** travelled on a boat.*

Note: When we want to talk about a specific time in the past we can use the Past Simple.
*I He **went** to school in America **in 2010.***

9.2 First Conditional

If clause	Main clause
present simple	*will* + bare infinitive

We use the first conditional to talk about the results of a possible situation now or in the future.

*If you **like** skating, you**'ll love** snowboarding!*
*We**'ll get** better if we **have** skiing classes.*
*If it **rains** tomorrow, Harry **won't go** sailing.*

Note: When *if* comes at the beginning, a comma separates the two parts of the sentence.

Unit 10

10.1 Past Continuous

Affirmative	
I/he/she/it **was** eat**ing**. we/you/they **were** eat**ing**.	
Negative	
I/he/she/it **was not (wasn't)** eat**ing**. we/you/they **were not (weren't)** eat**ing**.	
Questions	
Was I/he/she/it eat**ing**? **Were** we/you/they eat**ing**?	
Short Answers	
Yes, I/he/she/it **was**. **Yes**, we/you/they **were**.	**No**, I/he/she/it **wasn't**. **No**, we/you/they **weren't**.

Spelling: cycle → cycl**ing**, run → run**ning**, stud**y** → stud**ying**

We use the Past Continuous for

- actions that were happening at a specific time in the past.
  *Jon **was cycling** in the park with his brother at 11 o'clock yesterday morning.*
- two or more actions that were happening at the same time in the past.
  *My mum **was making** sandwiches for the picnic and I **was helping** her.*
- giving background information in a story.
  *It **was raining** and the children **were feeling** bored.*
- an action that was happening in the past that was interrupted by another action.
  *We **were snowboarding** down the mountain when we **saw** a bear!*

Note: Some common time expressions that are often used with the Past Continuous are *while*, *all day/week/month/year*, *at 11 o'clock yesterday morning*, *last night*, *last Sunday/week/year*, *this morning*, etc.

10.2 Present Perfect Simple (2)

The Present Perfect Simple is formed with the verb *have* + the past participle.

We can use the Present Perfect Simple with

- *just* to talk about something that happened in the very recent past, a few moments ago.
  *The children have **just** eaten a whole pizza. Now they are full!*
- *already* to explain that we have completed a task (we were expected to do).
  *We don't need to buy fruit. Dad has **already** bought some at the market.*
  *My dad has bought fruit **already**.*
- *yet* to talk about a task we haven't done, but still need to do. We use it at the end of questions and negative sentences.
  *I haven't finished my homework **yet**.*
  *'Have you taken the dog for a walk **yet**?' 'No, not **yet**.'*

Note: We can only use *just* between the auxiliary and the past participle. *Already* can be used between the auxiliary and the past participle or at the end of the sentence. *Yet* must be used at the end of a question or negative sentence.

10.3 Reflexive verbs

Subject	Reflexive pronoun
I	myself
you	yourself
he	himself
she	herself
it	itself
we	ourselves
you	yourselves
they	themselves

Some verbs have a reflexive pronoun.
We can use them when the object is the same as the subject.
*The dog **hurt itself** when it jumped over the wall.*
*The children **enjoyed themselves** at the beach.*
*I **cut myself** when I was making my fancy dress costume.*
*My granddad lives on his own and can **look after himself**.*

Unit 11

11.1 The Passive Voice: Present Simple

The passive is formed with the Present Simple of the verb *be* + a past participle.

Tense	Active	Passive
Present Simple	make/makes	**am/are/is** made

11.2 The Passive Voice: Past Simple

The passive is formed with the Past Simple of the verb *be* and a past participle.

Tense	Active	Passive
Past Simple	made	was/were made

We use the Passive Voice when

- we are more interested in the action or event.
  The museum is visited by many tourists every year.
  The pictures were painted by children.
- we don't know who does the action, or it is not important.
  That same music was played at my wedding.

We change an active sentence into a passive sentence in the following way:
The object of the verb in the active sentence becomes the subject of the verb in the passive sentence. The verb be is used in the same tense of the main verb in the active sentence, together with the past participle of the main verb in the active sentence.
*The children **sing** that song every week. That song **is sung** every week by the children.*
*My aunt **wrote** that book. That book **was written** by my aunt.*

Note: When it is important to mention the agent in a passive sentence, we use the word *by*.
*Picasso painted 'Guernica'. 'Guernica' was painted **by** Picasso.*

11.3 Narrative tenses

We use narrative tenses to help us recount events, anecdotes and stories.
We can use the Past Continuous for

- describing the setting or giving us background information.
  *It **was snowing** when the children **were playing** football.*
- describing an action that was interrupted by another action.
  *We **were watching** a film when the lights **went** out.*

We can use the Past Simple for

- actions that happened at specific times in the past.
  ***Last Monday** I went on the stage for the first time.*
- actions that happened in a sequence.
  ***First** we went on a boat trip to the island, and **then** we walked along the beach. **Eventually**, we found the cave.*

Note: Words like *while, first, then, after that, as soon as, at first, until, eventually, in the end,* are often used with narrative tenses.

Unit 12

12.1 Present Continuous: future plans & arrangements

We form the Present Continuous with *is / are* + verb + *-ing*.

We can use the Present Continuous for

- talking about plans and arrangements in the future.
  *We **are catching** the 10 o`clock ferry to France.*
- asking questions about future plans and arrangements.
  *When **are you coming** back from holiday?*

Note: When use the Present Continuous for the future we often use specific dates, days and time. We also use time expressions like *this weekend / week, next summer, in the summer, tomorrow,* etc.

12.2 *Be Going To*

Affirmative	
I **am ('m) going** to visit. He/she/it **is ('s) going to** visit. We/you/they **are ('re) going to** visit.	
Negative	
I **am ('m) not going to** visit. He/she/it **is not (isn't) going to** visit. We/you/they **are not (aren't) going to** visit.	
Questions	
Am I **going to** visit? **Is** he/she/it **going to** visit? **Are** we/you/they **going to** visit?	
Short Answers	
Yes, I **am**. **Yes**, we/you/they **are**. **Yes**, he/she/it **is**.	No, I'm not. No, we/you/they aren't. No, he/she/it isn't.

We use *be going to* for

- future plans and intentions.
  *We**'re going to visit** some friends in Greece next year.*
- plans we decided before the moment of speaking.
  *I**'m going to make** a sandwich. I'm hungry.*
- a future event based on evidence or what we know.
  *Nina likes sightseeing so she**'s going to love*** Italy!

Note: Time expressions indicating the future are also used with *be going to*: *this week/month/summer, tonight, this evening, tomorrow, tomorrow morning/afternoon/night, next week/month/year, at the weekend, in January, on Thursday, on Wednesday morning*, etc.

Writing Reference

Personal description

When writing a personal description,

- make it clear you are describing yourself.
- use informal language.
- don't make your sentences too long.

Plan

Paragraph 1
Introduce yourself. Say your name and how old you are.
Talk about your family and where you live.
Hi, my name is …
I'm …
I live …
I have got …

Paragraph 2
Write a description of your appearance and your character.
I'm tall /short.
I have got … eyes / hair.
I am sporty / shy / sociable …

Paragraph 3
Talk about your favourite things and what you like to do in your free time, for example, hobbies and sport.
My favourite … is …
I like / love …
In my free time I …

Personal description checklist

- I introduced myself. ☐
- I used adjectives. ☐
- I checked spelling. ☐
- I checked for words that needed capitals and for punctuation mistakes. ☐
- I read my description again to check it makes sense. ☐

Formal email

When writing a formal email,

- make it clear why you are writing.
- use formal language and full forms.
- make sure you focus on the subject you're writing about.

Plan

Greeting
Dear Sir / Madam, Dear Mr ..., Dear Mrs ..., Dear Ms ...,

Paragraph 1
Explain why you're writing.
I'm writing to ask about ... / because I'm interested in ...

Paragraphs 2
Give more details about what you are writing about and ask questions for the information you'd like to know.
I'd like to know / find out more about ...
When do / Where / How much ...?

Signing off
Kind regards, / Best regards,
(sign your name)

Formal email checklist

- I followed the plan. ☐
- I used formal language and full forms with no contractions. ☐
- I used a formal greeting and signed off correctly. ☐
- I checked for spelling and punctuation mistakes. ☐
- I read through my email to check it makes sense. ☐

Email

When writing an email,

- make it clear why you are writing.
- be friendly and use informal language.
- remember you still need to use a greeting at the beginning and sign off at the end.

Plan

Greeting
Hi … ! Hi there! Hello … ! Dear…,

Paragraph 1
Begin with polite phrases. Thank the reader for his/her email or ask how they are and say why you are writing.
How are you?
Thanks for your email.
I'm writing to …

Paragraph 2
Give more details about why you are writing.
We're going to … / I'd like to … / Do you want to …?
I am thinking of …

Paragraph 3
Give more information or ask any extra questions if necessary.
Also … / Can you …? / Have you got …?

Signing off
See you soon! / Hope to see you soon. / Let's meet soon. / I look forward to seeing you.
Love, / Bye for now,
(sign your name)

Email checklist

- I followed the plan. ☐
- I used informal language and verb contractions. ☐
- I checked for spelling and punctuation mistakes. ☐
- I checked the verb forms. ☐
- I read through my email to check it makes sense. ☐

Instructions

When writing instructions,

- make it clear what the instructions are for.
- tell the reader what they need: ingredients, utensils, tools, etc.
- write a step-by-step guide.

Plan

You will need:
If you are writing instructions for a recipe, experiment or craft activity, write a list of the ingredients or materials and the quantities of each.
3 eggs
50g flour
A4 card
colouring pencils

Include a list of utensils or tools.
a large frying pan
a salad dish
2 dice
scissors

Method
Use sequencers or numbers to show the order of the instructions. You can address the reader as 'you' or use the imperative, 'cut', 'add', etc.
First, (you) …
Then, (you) …
Next, …
After that, …
Finally, …

Suggestions
Sometimes, there is a final suggestion.
Serve with rice / a salad / yoghurt / nachos …
Display your model for everyone to see.
The winner now plays the next player.

Instructions checklist

- I followed the plan. ☐
- I used the 'you' form / imperative form. ☐
- I used sequencers / numbers. ☐
- I checked for spelling and punctuation mistakes. ☐
- I checked that I didn't forget any information. ☐

A diary

When writing a diary,

- describe an experience, an event and your feelings.
- include details to make your description more interesting.
- give reasons why the experience / event was special.

Plan

Introduction
Some people like to address their diary,
Dear Diary,
Today I ….

If you are not actually writing in a diary but in a notebook, include the date.
Give a reason why you are writing about a particular experience / event. Use adjectives to describe how you felt.
Today I was excited/happy/sad because …
Today was perfect because …

Paragraph 2
Describe your experience / event in detail using the past tense. Use sequencers to show the order in which things happened.
As soon as I … / First I … / Then, … / Next, … / After that …

Paragraph 3
End your description with an opinion or an action plan.
It was the best day ever.
I'm definitely going to go there again!
I need to find out more about lighthouses!

Diary checklist

- I followed the plan. ☐
- I used the correct tenses. ☐
- I added detail. ☐
- I used adjectives to describe how I felt. ☐
- I used sequencers to show the order of events. ☐
- I read through my diary entry to make sure it makes sense. ☐

Fact file

When writing a fact file,

- use a title and headings to show what you are writing about.
- make sure your facts are correct.
- do not include opinions.
- write in note form without a subject or verb.

Plan

Title
Choose a short title so your reader knows what the fact file is about.

Headings
A fact file does not have a specific order for information. Choose headings for the most interesting pieces of information or the information you want your reader to know. Create a table for the information or use the headings and a colon (:).
Type of animal: mammal
Size: 1 metre long
Animal diet: insects and fruit

Ending
Include a sentence at the end with an interesting fact. You can introduce your fact with 'Did you know that … ?'
Give a reason why something is the way it is by using 'because'.
Did you know that fruit bats are also known as flying foxes? This is because they have a face like a fox.

Pictures
Include a photo or illustration to support the facts in your file.

Fact file checklist

- I followed the plan. ☐
- I included a title and headings. ☐
- I included pictures. ☐
- I checked the facts. ☐
- I read through my fact file to check spelling. ☐

Captions

When writing a caption,

- keep your sentences short.
- make sure your caption goes with the correct picture, cartoon or selfie.
- make sure the caption helps us understand what we are looking at.

Plan

Look at the picture or photo.

- Write a sentence that helps your reader understand what they are looking at. A caption can make your reader look at the picture in more closely.
- A caption can be funny and make your reader smile. *That's not a nest on my head, that's my hair!*
- Sometimes, captions are factual and can be included in a report or fact file. *Female elephants are very caring with their babies.*

Caption checklist

- I looked at the photo before I wrote the caption. ☐
- I wrote a short sentence. ☐
- I made sure my caption was clear. ☐
- I checked the facts. ☐
- I checked the verb forms and spelling. ☐

Blog

When writing a blog,

- write about what's important to you and show your personality.
- keep your paragraphs short and use headings and subheadings.
- use a chatty, informal style.
- include a picture and links to websites.
- be prepared to write back to your readers' comments and opinions.
- call your readers to take action.

Plan

Heading
Write a heading so that your readers know what the topic of your blog is.
Now I know what 'extreme' really means!

Paragraph 1
Write a short introduction. Add a photo if possible.
I love flying. I've flown to lots of different countries. But jumping out of a plane is a totally different experience!

Paragraph 2 & 3 & 4
Keep paragraphs short and add more details and subheadings.
Add a link to a website.
Sky Fall Co. has great instructors. Check out a demonstration class on YouTube: www.youtube/firstimeskyfallers.com

Call to action
Persuade and encourage your readers to join a club, try something new, or talk to others about your topic.
If you love flying or bungee jumping, you'll love skydiving! Try it and see!

Blog checklist

- I followed the plan. ☐
- I wrote short paragraphs with headings. ☐
- I added a photo. ☐
- I added a link to a website. ☐
- I called on my readers to take action. ☐
- I read through my blog to make sure it makes sense. ☐

An invitation

When writing an invitation,

- use the Present Continuous for plans and arrangements.
- include information about who, what, when and where.
- ask people to respond to you.

Plan

Paragraph 1
Tell people what the special event is.
I'm having a party for my 18th birthday.
Come to our Halloween party!

Paragraph 2
Persuade people to come.
It's going to be fun!
We've got some great party games!

Paragraph 3
Give details about the date, time and place. Give an address.
It's on 31st May, at 7 p.m.
My address is 42 Trafalgar Road (near Green park Station).

Paragraph 4
Add an email address or phone number so people can reply to you.
Please reply to …
Let me know if you can make it.
My email address / phone number is …
Call me on …

Invitation checklist

- I followed the plan.
- I included information about who, what, when and where.
- I included my contact details.
- I persuaded people to come.
- I checked for grammar, spelling and punctuation mistakes.

Reply to an invitation

When writing a reply to an invitation,

- read the invitation carefully and decide if you will accept or refuse.
- reply with polite phrases.
- if you refuse the invitation, give a reason why.

Plan

Paragraph 1
Say thank you for the invitation. Choose formal or informal language, depending on the situation, the place or the person.
Hi Georgia, thanks for inviting me to your birthday barbecue. /
Thank you very much for inviting me to an interview.

Paragraph 2
Decide if you will accept or refuse the invitation.
If you accept, ask a question or offer to do or take something.
I'd love to come! Can I bring some snacks? / Shall I come early and help you prepare? / I would be very happy to attend… .

If you refuse, explain why.
I'm sorry, I'm afraid I can't make it on Friday night. I've got football training. /
I apologise but, unfortunately, I will be away on that day.

Paragraph 3
Talk about the future to finish.
Can't wait to see you there! / Really looking forward to your barbecue, hope there's good music! / Sorry I can't come but hopefully the next time! /
I look forward to meeting you another time. / I look forward to hearing from you / meeting you in the near future.

Reply to an invitation checklist

- I followed the plan. ☐
- I used the correct expressions to accept or refuse the invitation. ☐
- I was polite. ☐
- If I refused the invitation, I gave a reason why. ☐
- If I responded to a friend, I offered to help or asked a question. ☐
- I reread my reply to check for spelling and punctuation mistakes. ☐

A short narrative

When writing a short narrative,

- use narrative tenses like the Past Simple and Past Continuous.
- divide your story into beginning, middle and end.
- describe a problem and how it is solved.
- use expressions (*suddenly, meanwhile, in the end*) to make your narrative more exciting.

Plan

Paragraph 1– beginning
This is the beginning of your story so set the scene by describing who is in your story, and when and where it took place.
Beth loved cats but her parents didn't. She didn't have a cat at home but she was always watching them in other people's gardens. One day, her neighbour's cat sat next to her and asked her a question!

Paragraph 2 – middle
Describe a problem.
Beth decided to ignore the cat and walked quickly back towards her house. Meanwhile the cat followed her everywhere she went and started to sing. Beth felt embarrassed.

Paragraph 3 – end
Describe a solution and a conclusion.
Beth told her parents about the cat when she got home. They laughed and told her that she fell asleep on the sofa watching a documentary about cats and how they could sing. In the end, her parents realized that Beth really wanted a cat and when a neighbour's cat had kittens, they gave one to Beth. Fortunately, it wasn't a singing cat!

Short narrative checklist

- I followed the formula. ☐
- I set the scene. ☐
- I described a problem. ☐
- I described a solution and conclusion. ☐
- I used the Past Simple and Past Continuous to describe events. ☐
- I used some expressions such as *suddenly, meanwhile, in the end, eventually.* ☐

Speaking Reference

Talking about yourself
I've got one brother/two sisters/a cat.
I haven't got any brothers/sisters/pets.
My brother's/sister's/pet's name is …
My favourite colour/food/animal/sport is …
In my free time I usually …
My hobby is swimming.
My hobbies are swimming and football.

Asking to hear something again
Sorry, can you repeat that?
Can you repeat the question, please?
Sorry, can you say that again?
I'm sorry, I don't understand.

Asking about travel
How often are the buses/trains/planes from X to X?
How long does it take?
How much does it/a ticket cost?
When does the train leave/arrive?

Answering about travel
There are a lot of buses/trains/planes between X and X.
The journey takes 2 hours.
A ticket costs $150.
The train station is on York Road.

Describing a celebration
It's very special. I like it because it's special.
I love the food, especially the cakes!
It's fun/exciting.

Giving dates
on the 14th of February
Talking about activities with to go
We went on a boat ride.
I went camping.
I went for a walk.
We went sightseeing.
I went skiing / swimming / skating / cycling / horse riding.
We went on a ride in an amusement park.

Showing interest
That sounds interesting! / great!
How fantastic!
Did you enjoy yourself?

Talking about pets
It's easy to look after
It doesn't need a lot of attention.
It needs exercise.
It's fun / soft / cute.
It's not dangerous.
It's good company.
It's a good pet because …
It's better than … because …

Giving directions
It's next to / opposite / between …
It's on the ground / first /second / third floor.
Go to X, then turn left /right.

Asking for information
Where is the exhibition?
What floor is it on?
Are the toilets on the ground floor?
How much does it cost?
How can I get there?
What date / time does it open / close?

Asking questions about games
What type of game is it?
How do you play it?
How many people can play?
Whose turn is it?
How old must you be to play?
How long does it take?
Do you need dice/counters to play?

Asking for details
I'd like some information about …
What's the address?
When do the classes start?
What time do the classes start?
How many students are there in a class?
How much does it cost?
Do I need to bring …?

Giving details
The address is …
The course starts on/at …
It costs …

Asking how someone is feeling
What's the matter?
What's wrong?
Are you feeling OK?

Talking about your health
I've got a temperature / a fever / a cold / toothache / a headache.
I feel sick / tired / thirsty / hungry.
My … hurts.
I fell down / over / off.
I cut / burnt / hurt myself.

Giving advice
You should …
You shouldn't …
If you feel sick, you should …
Eat / Drink / Go / Do …
Don't eat …
Why don't you …?

Responding to advice
Thanks. That's a good idea.
That's good advice. Thank you.

Asking about preferences
What / Which do you prefer?
Which one do you like better?
Do you prefer A or B?
Do you prefer reading the book or seeing the film?

Expressing & responding to preferences
I prefer to read the book.
I prefer reading the book.
I prefer detective novels.
I like fantasy novels better.
I like it too!
Me too!

Asking about holidays
What was the hotel / beach / weather like?
When did you go?
How long did you go for?
Who did you go with?
Did you have a good time?
Where are you going next summer?
What are you going to do there?
Where are you going to stay?
How long are you going for?

Speaking Information for Student A and B

Unit 3, page 39

Card 1

Prepare your **answers** about going to San Francisco **by train**.
Hotel receptionist

- Every two hours
- About nine hours
- $65
- Next 10.30 a.m.
- 7.50 p.m.

Card 2

Prepare your **questions** about going to San Francisco **by bus**.
Tourist
How many buses … ?
What time … next bus … ?
Where … leave … ?
How long … ?
How … cost?

Unit 6, page 77

1
Questions to ask Student A

- What pet have / got?
- What / its name?
- How big?
- Jump?
- Why / like it?

2
Questions to ask Student B

- What / name?
- Easy to look after?
- Where / sleep?
- What / eat?
- Why / like it?

Unit 7, page 91

Science Fair questions

- Where / Science Fair?
- When / start?
- What time / open?
- How much / cost?
- What floor / light show on?
- What / telephone number?

Science Museum questions

- Open every day?
- What time / open?
- How much / cost?
- What floor / IMAX theatre on?
- Where / museum?
- How can / get there?

Unit 8, page 103

1
Questions to ask Student A

- What kind / game?
- How many / play?
- How much?
- Dice?
- How old / must be?

2
Questions to ask Student B

- Where / play?
- How / play?
- How many / play?
- Boring?
- How long / take?

Speaking Information for Student A and B

Unit 9, page 117

Questions to ask Student A

- What extreme sport / teach?
- Have / beginner classes?
- What time / classes?
- How many students / class?
- How much / cost?
- What equipment / need?

Questions to ask Student B

- What sport / do?
- When / go?
- Where / go?
- Enjoy?
- Who / go with?
- What equipment / need?

Unit 12, page 155

Questions to ask Student A about camping holiday

- What / campsite / like?
- What / weather / like?
- What / beaches / like?
- What / people / like?
- What / food / like?

Questions to ask Student B about cruise holiday

- What / cruise ship / like?
- What / cabins / like?
- What / swimming pools / like?
- What / people / like?
- What / food / like?

Irregular Verbs

Infinitive	Past Simple	Past Participle
be	was/were	been
beat	beat	beaten
become	became	become
begin	began	begun
bite	bit	bitten
blow	blew	blown
break	broke	broken
bring	brought	brought
broadcast	broadcast	broadcast
build	built	built
burn	burnt	burnt
buy	bought	bought
can	could	–
catch	caught	caught
choose	chose	chosen
come	came	come
cost	cost	cost
cut	cut	cut
deal	dealt	dealt
do	did	done
draw	drew	drawn
dream	dreamt	dreamt
drink	drank	drunk
drive	drove	driven
eat	ate	eaten
fall	fell	fallen
feed	fed	fed
feel	felt	felt
fight	fought	fought
find	found	found
fly	flew	flown
forecast	forecast	forecast
forget	forgot	forgotten
get	got	got
give	gave	given
go	went	gone
grow	grew	grown
have	had	had
hear	heard	heard
hide	hid	hidden
hit	hit	hit
hold	held	held
hurt	hurt	hurt
keep	kept	kept
know	knew	known
lead	led	led
learn	learnt	learnt
leave	left	left
lend	lent	lent
let	let	let

Infinitive	Past Simple	Past Participle
lie	lay	lain
light	lit	lit
lose	lost	lost
mean	meant	meant
make	made	made
meet	met	met
pay	paid	paid
prove	proved	proven
put	put	put
read	read /red/	read /red/
ride	rode	ridden
ring	rang	rung
rise	rose	risen
run	ran	run
say	said	said
see	saw	seen
sell	sold	sold
send	sent	sent
set	set	set
shake	shook	shaken
shine	shone	shone
show	showed	shown
shoot	shot	shot
shut	shut	shut
sing	sang	sung
sink	sank	sunk
sit	sat	sat
sleep	slept	slept
slide	slid	slid
smell	smelt	smelt
speak	spoke	spoken
speed	sped	sped
spend	spent	spent
stand	stood	stood
steal	stole	stolen
stick	stuck	stuck
stink	stank	stunk
sweep	swept	swept
swim	swam	swum
take	took	taken
teach	taught	taught
tell	told	told
think	thought	thought
throw	threw	thrown
understand	understood	understood
wake	woke	woken
wear	wore	worn
win	won	won
write	wrote	written

NATIONAL GEOGRAPHIC LEARNING

National Geographic Learning,
a Cengage Company

***Close-up A1+ Student's Book* with Online Practice and Student's eBook**
Author: Montse Watkin

Editorial Manager: Claire Merchant
Commissioning Editor: Kayleigh Buller
Editor: Cathy Rogers
Head of Production: Celia Jones
Content Project Manager: Melissa Beavis
Manufacturing Manager: Eyvett Davis
Compositor: Wild Apple Design Ltd
Audio Producer: James Richardson
Recorded at: Soundhouse Studios

Student's Book with the Spark platform
ISBN: 978-0-357-96012-7

National Geographic Learning
Cheriton House, North Way, Andover, Hampshire,
SP10 5BE United Kingdom

Locate your local office at **international.cengage.com/region**

Visit National Geographic Learning online at **ELTNGL.com**
Visit our corporate website at **www.cengage.com**

Printed in Greece by Bakis SA
Print Number: 05 Print year: 2025

MIX
Paper | Supporting responsible forestry
FSC www.fsc.org FSC™ C169932

Cover Images: (front cover) ©Filip Fuxa/Shutterstock Inc, (back cover) ©aodaodaodaod/Shutterstock Inc

© Alamy:

6 Ian Lamond; **6** Studioshots; **7** Dbimages; **9** Richard Ellis; **9** Kakimage; **9** AF Archive; **14** Heatherwalker/RooM the Agency; **16** Disability Images; **18** Luciano Leon; **18** Chris Pancewicz; **18** Bob Daemmrich; **18** Blend Images; **18** Blend Images; **18** Tom Bourdon/ Images of global celebrations; **21** Murray Hayward; **24** MBI; **32** World History Archive; **32** 2ebill; **34** Image Source; **36** Ableimages; **38** Witold Skrypczak; **40** Ian Dagnall Commercial Collection; **46** Caia image; **51** Radius Images; **60** Stefano Politi Markovina; **65** Chris Whiteman; **70** National Geographic Creative; **90** Steve Marcus/Reuters; **96** Urban Zone; **96** Carolyn Jenkins; **96** Nicholas Burningham; **98** PhotoAlto; **98** MITO Images; **98** Hero Images Inc.; **98** Hero Images Inc.; **102** Jim West; **102** Keith morris; **104** Lisa F. Young; **110** ZUMA Press, Inc.; **111** Action Plus Sports Images; **112** Hero Images Inc.; **112** Stephen Frink Collection; **113** Ariadne Van Zandbergen; **116** ITAR-TASS Photo Agency; **116** Prisma by Dukas Presseagentur GmbH; **130** Richard Levine; **136** Paul Swinney; **136** Geraint Lewis; **136** Theatrepix; **138** CBW; **140** JHPhoto; **142** Grant Rooney; **148** Justin Kase z12z; **148** Grethe Ulgjell; **149** Sunpix Travel

© Getty Images:

7 Lew Robertson; **8** David Sacks; **12** Ethan Miller; **44** Anouchka/E+; **44** Roslan Rahman/AFP; **44** Natthawat/Moment open; **44** Stephen Lam/Dorling Kindersley; **44** Eugene Gologursky; **45** Nicky Loh/Bloomberg; **50** Mohammed Mahjoub/AFP; **51** Jade/Blend Images; **51** Subir Basak/ Moment; **63** Image Source; **64** Kali9; **69** Pete Oxford/Minden Pictures; **70** Joel Sartore/National Geographic; **90** Frederic J. Brown/AFP; **96** Noam Cohen/EyeEm; **103** Photofusion/UIG; **116** Bilgin S. Amaz/Anadolu Agency; **124** PhotoDisc; **126** Jeff J Mitchell/Staff; **132** John Cancalosi; **136** Jodi Cobb; **137** Winfield Parks/National Geographic; **157** Johner Images; **158** Flip Nicklin/Minden Pictures

© Image Source :

36 Image Source

© Imagestate:

110 John Foxx Images; **124** John Foxx Images

© iStockphoto:

124 Valentyn Volkov

© National Geographic Creative:

5 Jodi Cobb; **17** Design Pics Inc; **31** Norbert Rosing; **40** Tim Thompson; **43** Mike Theiss; **57** Bill Curtsinger; **71** Joel Sartore; **73** Joel Sartore; **75** Ralph Lee Hopkins; **76** Aaron Huey; **78** Christian Ziegler; **83** Jason Edwards; **95** Paul Chesley; **109** Robert Madden; **121** Design Pics Inc; **135** O. Louis Mazzatenta; **144** Barrett Hedges; **147** W.E. Garrett

© Robert Harding:

32 Jevgenija Pigozne; **58** Adam Burton; **58** Juice Images; **72** Konrad Wothe; **110** Himsl Leo; **110** Markus Keller; **122** Bruno Morandi; **142** Martin Siepmann; **151** Helmut Corneli; **155** Godong

© Shutterstock:

6 Megastocker; **6** Stefan Petru Andronache; **6** Paul Stringer; **6** Andrey Popov; **6** Elena Elisseeva; **6** Richard Frazier; **6** Petr Jilek; **6** Jinga; **6** VitaminCo; **6** Cynoclub; **6** Pilipphoto; **9** Ariusz Nawrocki; **9** Umberto Shtanzman; **9** Claire Norman; **9** NDT; **9** Khun Nay Zaw; **9** Photopackpl; **11** Ljupco Smokovski; **11** Gravicapa; **11** StockphotoVideo; **11** Suriya99; **11** Robynrg; **12** India Picture; **12** JanVlcek; **13** Helder Almeida; **13** Monkey Business Images; **14** Volodymyr Krasyuk; **15** Scanrail1; **16** Fedor Selivanov; **16** Jeroen van den Broek; **16** Sofya Apkalikova; **16** Pavlinas; **16** Africa Studio; **18** SantiPhotoSS; **18** Littlekidmoment; **20** Lakov Filimonov; **23** Monkey Business Images; **24** Nejron Photo; **24** DavidTB; **24** Fotoluminate LLC; **25** Berna Namoglu; **25** Anton Ivanov; **25** 2xSamara.com; **26** Wavebreakmedia; **27** Martynova Marina; **28** John Wollwerth; **28** Linda Hughes; **28** Anton Ivanov; **34** Rannev; **34** Marlee; **34** 1000 Words; **34** Dvoevnore; **34** Kukuruxa; **34** Oprea George; **34** Kondor83; **34** Don Pablo; **35** Carroteater; **36** Vvoe; **36** Preechaf; **36** Cebas; **36** TinnaPong; **36** Azovtsev Maksym; **36** Dusan Milenkovic; **37** Everett Art; **38** Philip Pilosian; **39** Benny Marty; **39** Parrot Ivan; **42** Kiran Photo; **42** PJ photography; **42** MyImages Micha; **42** Roger Clark ARPS; **44** Monkey Business Images; **46** NadyaEugene; **46** Videokvadrat; **46** Lilly Trott; **49** Kalapangha; **51** Luciano Mortula-LGM; **51** Ilike; **51** Lemon Tree Images; **52** Mikhail Zahranichny; **52** Helena Zolotuhina; **53** Bitt24; **53** El Nariz; **54** Naparat; **54** Radiokafka; **54** LMspencer; **54** Jasni; **54** Pavel Vakhrushev; **60** Racheal Grazias; **60** Chere; **60** Sirtravelalot; **61** RDaniel; **63** Klenger; **64** Syda Productions; **64** Monkey Business Images; **65** Photomario; **66** Remik44992; **66** Amfoto, **66** Andrey Popov; **67** Business Stock; **68** Monkey Business Images; **68** Rock and Wasp; **68** Jumpot Tharungsri; **70** Eric Isselee; **70** Fivespots; **70** Robert Eastman; **72** Edwin Butter; **72** Lotus Studio; **72** Arka38; **72** Lovely Bird; **74** Paula french; **77** Andrea Izzotti; **77** Edwin Butter; **77** DJ Srki; **77** MaxShutter; **77** AndraÅ_ Cerar; **77** Ewan Chesser; **77** Joshua Haviv; **77** Marek R. Swadzba, **79** VinceBradley; **80** Gudkov Andrey; **84** Skylines; **84** Teddy Leung; **84** Marko Poplasen; **84** Nednapa Sopasuntorn; **84** Billion Photos; **84** Viktor Kunz; **84** Africa Studio; **84** Sarawut panchawa; **86** MN Designs; **86** Chutima Chaochaiya; **86** Nito; **86** PK.Phuket Studio; **86** Ldprod; **86** Georgejmclittle; **85** Alexander Sviridov; **87** Mtr; **87** Simon Krzic; **87** Gino Santa Maria; **87** Ppart; **88** Charles taylor; **92** Anna Mari West; **92** Colin13362; **92** Eakkachai2520; **92** SisterF; **92** Chriss73; **94** Brendan Howard; **96** UfaBizPhoto; **96** Robert Kneschke; **96** Viachaslau Kraskouski; **96** Txking; **98** Dinga; **98** Suzanne Tucker; **98** Karla Caspari; **99** Mathias Richter; **102** Kievstock; **103** Svetoslav Radkov; **104** Angellodeco; **104** Kzenon; **104** Syda Productions; **105** Monkey Business Images; **106** Roongzaa; **106** Bogdan Ionescu; **106** Nito; **106** Andrey Osipets; **106** Andy Piatt; **110** Bluecrayola; **110** Krichie; **110** Juanamari Gonzalez; **110** Sinesp; **111** Protasov AN; **114** Vadim Petrakov; **115** Ivandan; **117** MarcelClemens; **118** Pio3; **118** DanyL; **120** Pinggr; **122** Kubais; **122** Ekaterina Pokrovsky; **124** O.Bellini; **124** Adriana Nikolova; **124** Eugenia Lucasenco; **124** Tim UR; **124** Lotus Studio; **124** Minicase; **124** Sarsmis; **125** BestPhotoStudio; **125** Eakachai Leesin; **125** Littlekidmoment; **125** Subbotina Anna; **125** BravissimoS; **128** Alena Brozova; **128** Zero99; **128** SpicyPXL; **128** Alhim; **128** Susan Law Cain; **129** PrinceOfLove; **129** Image Point Fr; **129** Kunlanan Yarist; Kunlanan Yarist;**129** ClaudioValdes; **129** puhhha; **132** Matee Nuserm; **132** Saltodemata; **132** BruceParrott; **132** RAJU SONI; **136** Stefan Holm; **136** Meunierd; **138** Ververidis Vasilis; **138** Ferenc Szelepcsenyi; **139** Ondrej Prosicky; **142** Christian Bertrand; **142** Tang Yan Song; **143** Stephen Rudolph; **143** Rubtsov; **143** Clivewa; **144** Mcky Stocker; **146** Anton Petrus; **146** Simple Photo Shot; **146** Abramova Elena; **148** Andrew Babble; **148** NAPI WAN ALI; **148** Monkey Business Images; **148** Netfalls Remy Musser; **148** Ruth Peterkin; **152** Mapics; **152** S-F; **154** Leoks; **155** Alliance; **156** Embrace of Beauty; **158** Cedric Weber; **Multiple pages (Exam Close-up Icon)** Nikkytok; **Multiple pages (Ideas Focus)** Kaesler Media; **Multiple pages (Ideas Focus)** Kostudio; **Multiple pages (Review Pages)** Pikselstock; **Multiple pages (Review Pages)** Odua Images